Relationship Truths

"Straight With No Chaser"

Jonathan Devon Bryant Sr.

Contents

Chapter 1

A Laboratory for Relationships

In the vast laboratory of life, relationships are the fascinating experiments that shape our very existence. At the heart of human existence, God made the foundational relationship of husband and wife within the garden of Eden.

There are many other relationships that will be important throughout your life, such as that with your children. However, nothing is quite as important as that special bond between husband and wife. This significant placement highlights the primary role of the marital bond in shaping the human experience.

We Crave True Connection

Our existence is meant to be shared, and our lives are shaped to be connected with each other. This innate need for relationships is inherent in every individual, irrespective of whether they are married or not. We crave human connection, and we all want to have love in our lives in some capacity—it fills a void.

We are made for meaningful connections with others, where our lives intertwine, and our hearts find solace in the embrace of genuine love and understanding. This longing for connection and love is an integral part of our human nature. This is at the heart of who we are, and they make up what we crave to thrive in our lives.

This Union Is So Important

Relationship, like the process of gem formation, involves the fusion of two individuals into one united entity. It signifies the joining together of two lives, with their unique qualities and characteristics, to create something beautiful and valuable.

Just as gems are treasured for their rarity and brilliance, marriage is a precious and highly valued union. It is what we may crave and search for throughout our lives, and it makes us feel whole when we find it.

There Are So Many Ups and Downs

Love and relationships are the stages where joy and pain intertwine. Among them, marriage takes the lead, providing the backdrop for this captivating drama.

Yet, doubts loom over its future, questioning its significance as the foundation of our social fabric. Though we may wish to achieve that ultimate relationship goal of marriage, it may not always come easily. It may have its ups and downs, but it remains the ultimate goal for so many of us.

A Culture That Just Quits Doesn't Work

In today's society, relationships are often treated like clothes that can be easily discarded and replaced. People approach relationships with a "Try it on, see if it fits, or either change it." Of course, if it doesn't meet their expectations, they move on to the next option.

Anytime you go outside the will of God to get something, you're going to have to stay outside the will of God to keep it. When marriage may get challenging, this is when so many people want to leave the situation. Certainly not how it was intended to be!

You Can't Quit When Things Get Tough

A wise person can comprehend, sense, and notice that this route is dangerous and will not end well. There is some pain that can be avoided, though there may be some hard work associated with this path as well. When people continue to go the wrong route in relationships, pain, heartbreak, disappointment, and distractions, and those who settle for less than God's best, it's imminent.

All of us will experience a level of pain in relationships, but according to Scripture, some pain can be avoided. It's time for you to stop falling for somebody who is not trying to catch you. "A sensible man watches for problems ahead and prepares to meet them. The simpleton never looks and suffers the consequences". (Proverbs 27:12, Today Living Bible)

It's Worth Fighting For

Once they find something that suits them for a while, they may eventually discard it when it loses its appeal or becomes outdated. Our world has become disposable, lacking a sense of lasting commitment.

It is when the hard work kicks in that so many people want to just quit. Rather than work at things and try to make them better, people are so ready to just quit and this has created a culture of failed marriages and discarded relationships.

It is a society driven by expiration dates, limited durability, and planned obsolescence. Absolute truths are subjective, and morality is shaped by fleeting preferences. In such a cultural context, it is no wonder that people yearn for something enduring, something they can truly rely on.

It Can Work If It's Right

That relationship can be achievable when it is with the right person. That relationship can last and stand the test of time if you put in the work. It is not always easy, but it's worth it when you find the right person to move throughout life with.

God put the man to sleep and, from his side, took a rib and formed the woman. Not stopping there, God took the woman by the hand and led her to Adam. Therefore, marriage is a unique relationship, having its root in divinity (Genesis: 2:22)

Nobody Wants to Be Alone

A relationship is a union intricately entwined with God's plan for humanity in the biblical framework. It is written in the Word of God that He purposely created relationships. God created humanity in His own image and declared, *"It is not good for the man to be alone"* (Genesis 2:18).

In the early chapters of Genesis, we find a concise account that highlights key aspects of God's teaching to the first couple. It is evident that God imparted His Way to them, a path that leads to peace, supreme happiness, abundance, prosperity, and all the good things in life. God, in His infinite purpose, created Adam and Eve as free moral agents, granting them the "Power of Choice" or "Free Agency." He did not impose His way upon them but instead provided instructions, leaving the decision in their hands.

The account in Genesis 3 depicts the cunning subtlety of Satan as he tempted Eve and sought to discredit God while appealing to their vanity. Two significant trees were present in the garden: the "Tree of Life," representing God's Way, from which Adam and Eve were permitted to eat freely, and the "Tree of the knowledge of good and evil."

The couple received a clear command not to eat from the fruit of this forbidden tree, as God warned them that it would lead to their certain death. God alone has the authority to define sin. The man was not granted the power to determine what constitutes sin but instead to choose whether or not to engage in it.

You Always Get a Choice

The Bible emphasizes that individuals possess the ability to make choices between good and evil, and it urges believers to prioritize righteousness and love in their relationships. You always get the choice to make it work rather than just quit.

Passages such as Galatians 5:22-23 highlight the fruits of the Holy Spirit, including love, joy, peace, patience, kindness, goodness, faithfulness, gentleness, and self-control. These virtues serve as guiding principles for nurturing wholesome and flourishing relationships. By aligning their actions with these qualities, individuals can cultivate and sustain healthy connections with others.

Applying This to Your Situation

What does this mean to you in your relationship and your everyday life? It means that we were intended to be together for the entirety of our lives. It means that the connection that you have searched for your entire life can be yours for the rest of your life.

It means that the marriage that you always wanted can be for a lifetime. It means that you must put in the work, persevere through the ups and downs, and therefore maintain that connection no matter what life may throw at you. It's worth it in the end, and that will show itself in the way that you move forward together. It's worth the work!

The Path to Happiness Can Be Yours

This profound choice of humans has resulted in a lack of understanding regarding the true purpose of dating and having a good relationship. Instead, people have chosen a path that combines elements of good and evil, leading to mixed outcomes in marriages.

Just as you put in the work when you are in the marriage, you must put in the work to find the right match for you. This isn't about just getting married, but rather finding the partner that can be by your side for the rest of your life.

Some relationships may function to some extent, while others experience constant ups and downs, and many marriages simply do not work at all. As a result, the supreme happiness and joy that God intended for every marriage are elusive for all but a few select couples. The mixture of good and evil is inherently destructive. Just as adding a small amount of arsenic or cyanide to a cake would result in fatal consequences.

Relationships hold the highest priority for God, yet they remain a weak point for mankind. Relationships have an eternal nature, but in our world, we frequently witness the devastating effects of broken relationships.

Far Too Many Marriages Don't Make It

An example of all of this is if you consider the breakdown of marriages and families. It's astounding when you stop to consider how many marriages don't make it. You will find it sad when you see the statistics about how few relationships can really stand the test of time.

According to the divorce rate statistics, divorce rates are high, with 2.3 per 1,000 people. Based on the most recent divorce data, one out of every three marriages ends in divorce. As a result, many children grow up in broken homes, lacking the stability and love they need. This not only affects the individuals directly involved but also has a ripple effect on society as a whole.

Broken families can lead to emotional distress, financial hardships, and a cycle of dysfunction that perpetuates through generations. It's a sad cycle that nobody wants to see continue, and yet it happens more than you realize. It's heart wrenching for everyone involved.

There are individuals who, even when being with someone or getting married, continue to prioritize their own interests above everything else. They will often disregard the needs of their partner and family, placing emphasis only on the things that matter to them personally. This self-centered attitude, often characterized by the "Me, Myself, and I" mindset, has caused significant damage to numerous households.

We All Have the Tendency to Be Selfish

The bigger problem is being selfish is human nature. We naturally think about our interests, our pain, how we look, and how we feel. Even culture tells us: "Do what you think is best for you." We are conditioned to believe that our needs and our desires are the only thing that matters when we are looking out for ourselves.

The bigger problem is that this is in stark contrast to what the Bible tells us. When you look closely, the Bible says, ***"Look out for one another's interests, not just for your own"*** (Philippians 2:4 GNT). This is a contradictory fundamental belief within the Bible and its teachings, and it is to say that we must put other people's needs before our own.

I believe that there are two possible "Heart Sins" — selfishness and pride that can wreak havoc in a relationship. I believe that selfishness is perhaps the most destructive force that works against us. Selfishness is the cancer that eats away and ultimately destroys relationships. When we are focused on ourselves and our own needs and wants (selfishness), and then we don't get those things, we get angry.

We are told and led to believe that we deserve these things and that wanting them is looking out for our own best interests. When we don't receive those very things that we want, we believe that we have a right to be angry. Why is this happening to me? Why can't I get what I want? Yet maybe what we are desiring is the problem in and of itself.

We Believe We Deserve Everything We Want

We justify that our anger or resentment is something we are entitled to. We dwell within a culture that places great importance on our ability to get what we want. If we work hard enough or we want something badly enough, then it will be ours. Then when it doesn't happen, we are wronged! This is flawed thinking and yet it is what we have engrained into our heads every day.

Think of this in a Biblical sense. Let's look at how this works, for example what James says: "Where do you think all these appalling wars and quarrels come from? Do you think they just happen? Think again. They come about because you want your own way and fight for it deep inside yourselves. You lust for what you don't have and are willing to kill to get it. You want what isn't yours and will risk violence to get your hands on it." (James 4:1-2 The Message Bible)

Let's refer back to Hebrews 13:5, which advises us to *"Keep your life free from the love of money and be content with what you have."* The love of money is a sinful desire that displeases God, as stated in 1 Timothy 6:10, which says, *"For the love of money is a root of all kinds of evils."* However, the remedy for this sinful love and its negative consequences is found in contentment—being satisfied with what we have.

Compare and Contrast in Real Life

You have likely been taught to look out for yourself to get what you want and deserve out of life. You may have also likely learned from the teachings of the Bible. The problem is that they often contrast sharply, particularly when it comes to selfishness in general.

In modern times, one of the most common ways the love of money manifests in relationships is through materialism. The relentless pursuit of wealth and material possessions can create a superficial and transactional dynamic, where individuals prioritize their financial status over the emotional well-being of their partner.

This can lead to a sense of emptiness and dissatisfaction as genuine love and emotional connection take a backseat to the pursuit of material wealth. It can become the pursuit of how many material items one can get rather than fostering that emotional connection that really matters. This may lead to competition with others and even with one another within the relationship.

One partner may sometimes feel controlled or marginalized if their financial contributions or aspirations are not valued or respected. Such conflicts can erode trust and breed resentment, causing the relationship to suffer. This is a very unhealthy dynamic!

Remember What Is Truly Important

The book of Hebrews provides a foundation for contentment by reminding us of God's promise: *"For God has said, 'I will never fail you nor forsake you.'"* This promise is derived from Deuteronomy 31:6, which reassures us to be strong, courageous, and unafraid, for the Lord our God will go with us and never abandon us.

True relationships/marriages thrive on selflessness and consideration instead of self-centeredness. In fact, from the moment you say "I do," it is important to let go of yourself and embrace a mindset that accommodates your partner's needs and happiness. Though your needs matter, you are now part of a true partnership. You want to be sure to consider both of your needs and not just take a selfish point of view.

The reality is that it is through selflessness that true fulfillment in marriage is achieved. You don't want to be selfless to the point of unhappiness in your life. However, it can be beneficial to be more selfless than selfish, and to find that right balance. The Bible emphasizes selfless love and sacrificial service in relationships.

"Do nothing from selfish ambition or conceit, but in humility count others more significant than yourselves. Let each of you look not only to his own interests but also to the interests of others."

(Philippians 2:3-4)

Think of This in Your Own Life

It is truly beneficial for believers to deeply internalize and meditate on the passage of Scripture mentioned. Allowing these words to permeate their minds and hearts can have a transformative impact on their lives. If believers were to sincerely walk in the light of these verses, many of their problems would find a resolution.

Consider how you could transform the dynamic of your relationship if you were to focus on what it would take to make both of you happy. Think of how you could cater to your partner's needs, all while working to find your happiness along the way. This can be achieved, but it takes thoughtfulness and careful determination to make it all work.

Another example of this in the Bible is to take in the powerful message in 1 Corinthians 13:4, "Love endures long and is patient and kind." Often, people may endure challenging circumstances, but they fail to display patience and kindness while enduring. Their endurance may stem from obligation rather than a genuine heart of love.

There will always be challenges in life and in our relationships. It is how we rise to meet those challenges that matter greatly. It is how we learn to put our partners needs in a place of importance as we care for our own. It is how we find that true balance and prioritization of the happiness of our marriage that matters.

How Does This All Work?

Let's think about how this may work in real life and in your relationship. It may be that a husband may tolerate difficulties in his marriage for the sake of his wife, but he may not consistently demonstrate kindness in the process. Similarly, a wife may endure certain aspects of her husband's behavior but make it known that she is suffering. Tolerating but being miserable is of course not good for anyone.

However, the love that aligns with God's nature endures long, remains patient, and shows kindness even in the midst of challenges. This kind of love does not weaken, fade away, or come to an end. It is unwavering and never fails. So, while it may be challenging to work through the differences and the low points together, we do this in the unity of marriage.

You want to find that happy balance of making each other happy and ensuring your own needs are met. You want to find a way to tolerate and even embrace each other's differences, while at the same time being an individual who focuses on what really matters in your life and your relationship. It's all about balance and harmony!

There Is a Human Factor in This

When Adam and Eve disobeyed God's command in the Garden of Eden, sin entered the world, causing profound consequences that extend to all aspects of human life, including relationships. Sin, manifested through selfishness, pride, dishonesty, lack of forgiveness, and other negative qualities, has the potential to inflict harm upon relationships, leading to damage or even their destruction.

But you no longer need to be ignorant of the fact that God created men and women to have the capacity to love and be loved, desiring them to experience true love in their lives. Finding genuine love in a relationship is possible, but it requires a clear understanding of what love truly entails. It goes beyond mere infatuation and superficial attractions.

True love is a deep and meaningful connection that is built on mutual respect, selflessness, and genuine care for one another. To embark on a journey of true love, it is essential to grasp the essence and significance of love itself. You have to start by loving yourself first and foremost. Then you can open yourself up to being loved by somebody else, and experiencing it in the most profound and meaningful way possible. This connection helps you to stay together and move through the good times and the bad as one.

Times Have Changed

Society has developed significantly over the past century, in some good ways and some bad ways. The landscape of the dating scene and dating practices have undergone significant transformations in recent times. In the past, there were traditional norms, morals, and rules when it came to dating.

Things were done in a certain way, and that's just the way that it was. It was normal for a young man to ask a young woman's father for approval before asking to court her if he was interested in dating her. There was a widespread attitude at the time that "sex is shameful," which decreased immorality and its detrimental impacts.

Significant Changes Have Come Over Time

Due to the complexity of the human heart and the impossibility of knowing what another person is thinking, relationships have become incredibly exciting and difficult at the same time. Many individuals have endured the plight of misinterpreted connections, while others have shed tears over heartbreaks when they find there isn't any genuine heart-to-heart inclusion or ineffective communication.

The destructive force of broken relationships spreads like a contagious illness, corroding the fabric of society and leaving a trail of devastation. It's akin to malignant cancer, tempting others to follow the path of devastation and later opting for an easy gateway.

There Is Still Hope

The state of affairs and where we have arrived can be truly heartbreaking. It is so much easier to just break things off when they aren't working. It's easy to dispose of a relationship when you feel like you're not in sync anymore. It's easy to walk away or start over because you feel like the two of you will never find your way back to each other. Yet there is hope!

Yet, there is hope. God, in His wisdom, will intervene in the affairs of mankind, stepping in to halt this downward spiral. He will not allow such extinction to prevail. The impending intervention will save us from the brink and preserve the sanctity of marriage and the timeless concept of families. He is the ultimate authority in this world who facilitates a meaningful connection between you and your partner. He is capable of orchestrating circumstances and situations that work in your favor. He understands how to garner support from your parents and those around you to align with His divine plan for your life.

You have to have this knowledge and hold it close to you. It's imperative that you open your heart to God and allow Him to come into your marriage and your life. You must find a way to maintain the connection and happiness, all while welcoming God into your relationship. When you can get to that point, then longevity will be yours.

Changing Your Mindset

Personally, I held the belief for a very long time that relationships could only be comprehended through firsthand experience and learning from mistakes. They didn't seem to be things you could research. It turns out I was entirely misinformed. Being a supportive partner and a reliable friend is not an innate trait but, instead, a skill that can be learned or acquired over time with trails and error.

You may be blessed with the gift of giving or listening, or being supportive. Learning how to be present for a partner and put in the work that it takes to keep a relationship going however—that takes work. You can be the most supportive person in the world, but you have to learn how to navigate life and make this all work for your partner. You show up for them, and they show up for you!

There was a beautiful story where a conscientious female employee became infatuated with her manager. The manager continually offers constructive feedback, compliments the employee on a job well done, and offers words of support when required. An environment of friendliness and respect is fostered between them by this strong rapport. However, the employee misinterprets the manager's encouraging demeanor and friendly actions as indications of personal/love interest.

She begins feeling romantic sentiments for her manager, thinking that their relationship is more than just work-related. When the employee finally finds the strength to express her feelings for him, she becomes heartbroken when he eventually clarifies that he's married and his intentions were supportive and professional.

Take A Step Back

When you feel or think that someone is growing emotionally attached or developing fondness towards you, it is wise to kindly seek clarification on the nature of your relationship. It prevents confusion and misunderstandings, and seeking clarity from God is paramount. Sometimes things are misinterpreted, and you must take a step back to state your situation. You don't want to go down a path towards temptation or anything that could take you away from your loved one and relationship.

Until both aspects are clarified, the relationship should be considered platonic, as stated in Song of Solomon 8:4. *"With the guidance of God, you can trust that you will not miss out on what is meant for you, in the name of Jesus!"*

Finding oneself and immediately convinced that they have met the right person upon locking eyes is a stroke of luck (unless it becomes a recurring pattern, indicating self-deception). The crucial aspect is to refrain from committing until certainty is achieved.

Maintain Clarity

Many individuals have expressed doubts even on their wedding day, saying, "I wondered if I was doing the right thing." If such doubts persist on such a significant day, it would be unwise to enter into such commitments before having a sense of clarification. You want to be sure that the feelings are real, that they are reciprocated, and that you are engaging in a true relationship that you both want.

Feeling uncertain at the beginning of a relationship is normal and understandable. It can take time, whether weeks, months or even years, to gain clarity, especially for those prone to doubt. Until you are genuinely sure, it is advisable not to make a permanent commitment to marriage. Know that for some people this is perfectly normal, and it's okay to take your time to navigate through everything.

It is possible that your partner may reach a point of certainty before you do. We all have different timelines. However, it is important not to succumb to pressure and make a decision before you are truly ready. While it is natural for them to desire your commitment, however, prioritize making the right decision for both parties involved. The right person will understand that you need time and to gain clarity. Never rush yourself or try to work off of somebody else's timeline.

Marriage is big. What you're considering or preparing for here is no trifle. Don't think you can just add marriage as another layer to an already busy life. Shucks, marriage is for a purpose. Why are you getting married? If you marry because of Instagram pictures and matching outfits, and the likes, you have lost the plot. Know this, marriage is a full-time job, with no off days please rethink your normal and check your priorities.

Take Your Time and Be Sure

This is the ultimate commitment and it's something that you want to be really sure of. You need to know that this is the right person to spend your life with. Remember this is not a commitment that you should take lightly, and therefore you need to take your time and gain clarity. You will know when it's right and it will all just click and come together.

If this person is truly meant to be your lifelong partner, you won't find yourself thinking, "I'm not sure. Is this right for me?" Instead, you will be filled with enthusiasm and a resounding "Yes!" if you are not experiencing that level of certainty, it indicates that you are not yet prepared to make a commitment. Though the timelines may differ, the end result should ultimately be the same—you should know without a doubt you are right for each other.

The Connection Should Be Real

When two individuals are genuinely drawn to each other and decide to pursue a romantic connection, they hold hopes of the relationship evolving into something meaningful, leading to marriage and finding a lifelong soulmate. Initially, things may seem promising, but sometimes after a period of time, things turn out to be very different and go in a completely different direction. This will of course result in heartache, disappointment, and a sense of loneliness. Regrettably, this pattern often repeats itself in subsequent relationships.

That is why some people believe that refraining from dating may be beneficial for a minority of teenagers who are susceptible to negative outcomes in romantic relationships, being manipulated, or evading personal growth. However, for the majority of young individuals, dating serves as a valuable avenue for personal development and learning to navigate the complexities of romantic connections. Engaging in dating experiences allows them to confront various challenges, fostering maturity and emotional growth. The intention behind not dating is to provide those who require it with a chance to cultivate their personal growth and self-awareness.

Basic Relationship Fundamentals

Freedom and responsibility are fundamental to the success of all types of relationships, extending beyond dating to include marriage, friendship, parenting, and business connections. These two elements play a pivotal role in nurturing strong attachments and fostering growth within these relational dynamics. As stated in 1 John 4:18, *"Perfect love eliminates fear, emphasizing that love should not restrict or hinder personal freedom."* Instead, it should create an environment where individuals feel safe, valued, and empowered to express themselves authentically.

God's role in the process of selecting a life partner is to offer guidance and direction, helping individuals in applying scriptural principles and discerning through the Holy Spirit's guidance. God respects our freedom of choice and does not impose or coerce anyone upon us.

It is our responsibility to accept or reject the guidance that God provides, and we bear full accountability for our decisions. We must open ourselves to finding the right person, and then trust God to foster it and make it work. We also must put in the hard work and willingness to stay together through the ups and downs of marriage. It is a process and a journey, and one that can be really great with the right person.

Turning to God for Guidance

Building good and meaningful connections with others is indeed a lifelong journey, and it can be greatly enhanced when guided by principles and values that are important to us. For many people, their faith in God provides a powerful source of guidance and transformational power in their relationships.

When we approach relationships with the belief that every individual is created in the image of God and deserves love, respect, and compassion, it can shape the way we interact with others. The teachings and principles found in various religious traditions often emphasize the importance of virtues such as patience, kindness, forgiveness, and empathy, which can greatly contribute to the strength and depth of our connections with others.

In a world unaware of the keys to true fulfillment, happiness eludes the masses. We all yearn for joy, assuming that conforming to societal norms will lead us there. Yet, many find themselves trapped in misery, clueless about the cause. This rings particularly true in the realm of modern dating, where confusion reigns supreme. It's time to break free from ignorance and discover the right values that unlock the desired results. Happiness awaits those who dare to venture beyond the established norms.

Chapter 2

All Couples Face Difficulties, and All Couples Have Differences

In the realm of love, relationships, and marriage, many captivating narratives have been unfolded, adorned with romanticism and idealization, weaving a tapestry of enchanting expectations. Hollywood, fairy tales, and fantasy novels enchant us with idyllic portrayals of harmonious relationships, conveniently sidestepping the complexities of disagreements, conflicts, and confrontations. Of course, this is not the truth or reality!

There Is a Reality to Things

Real life happens, and we must remember that where our relationships are concerned. Once the newness of any relationship wears off, we are faced with reality. It is learning how to navigate that reality together as a couple that really matters here. It is not always about happily ever after, and if it is then you have to work for it. Before you ever get to know anything else about relationships and marriage, all you should know is that all couples face difficulties and all couples have differences. I believe that our minds shouldn't be clouded with the idea of finding perfectionism.

Perfect Doesn't Exist

These days, it seems like everyone is looking for perfectionists who often have an all-or-nothing mindset, seeking flawless performance and outcomes in every aspect of their lives. The Bible emphasizes the importance of extending grace and acceptance toward ourselves and others. Romans 15:7 states, "Accept one another, then, just as Christ accepted you."

This encourages an attitude of love, understanding, forgiveness, patience, and realistic expectations instead of demanding perfection from others. Nobody is perfect, and neither are you. So why would you expect that from your life partner? We need realistic expectations, and we also need to put into it what we want to get out of it.

Through my research, I have discovered that people consider multiple dimensions when choosing a life partner. These dimensions include physical attraction, intellectual compatibility, and spiritual connection. When individuals sense a bond in any of these realms, they often assume that the person would be a suitable companion.

While this perspective is not entirely incorrect, it is important to recognize that choosing a life partner should not solely depend on one dimension. What seems to be perfect today might not be tomorrow. Things change, and people certainly change, so we need to keep that at the forefront of our minds always.

You Want to Think About Forever

So why not hold onto something (a partner) that will endure forever and learn to embrace qualities and flaws? When it comes to relationships, remember: "Opposites Attract and Sparks Ignite!" The most important consideration in choosing a life partner is accepting the way he/she is. You want to be sure that those opposites aren't fundamental to the way you live your life. However, the right mix can mean that you complete each other and really harmonize well together.

I would say everyone is born different, and no one is in a position to change or transform into the person that you desire. Many relationships break up today because they have not come to terms with this truth. It's okay to have differences, so long as you embrace them. It's okay if you are opposites on some issues, so long as they don't cause you to be somebody that you really aren't in the end.

Relationships exist in all their beautifully imperfect glory. But love does not necessarily mean being adorned with perpetual sunshine and rainbows. You will have good days and bad days, and sometimes you will argue or disagree. A bunch of stumbling blocks in the way of your relationship is no exception. That doesn't mean that you just give up, but rather you put in the work. It's worth it when you are truly with the right person!

You Will Have Highs and Lows

Every relationship embarks on a unique journey characterized by highs and lows, presenting challenges as diverse as the individuals involved. Although we typically associate love and relationships with teddy bears and boxes of chocolate, the concept of a true relationship is full of many ups and downs and in-betweens. The reality is that disagreements, arguments, and disputes emerge as natural elements of this intricate link, testing the strength of our bonds.

Yet, amidst the ebbs and flows, there exists a magical interplay of profound love and happiness. These moments envelop us, evoking a sense of eternal bliss as we cherish the depth of our relationship. We will be tested all throughout our relationship, but it is how we respond to that which matters most. We will have times where we feel challenged, but it is rising to that and working through the difficulties that truly matters.

You may struggle, you may have days where you aren't exactly fond of one another. You may feel tested, tempted to quit, and may even feel that this is too much. It is out of the darkest hours like this that we show our true commitment to the relationship. We show that we are meant to be together and that this can challenge us, but it will not break our bond with one another.

A Time for Everything

Think of this-- have you ever found yourself captivated by the mesmerizing transitions of the seasons? The thawing of winter's cold giving way to the delicate blossoms of spring. The vibrant transformation of summer's leaves transitioning into the kaleidoscope of colors that adorn the fall. Seasons, in essence, are divisions of the year, distinguished by shifting weather patterns and variations in daylight hours. Interestingly, just as there are four distinct seasons in a year – spring, summer, fall, and winter – our relationships too can be likened to these four seasons. Each season, both in nature and in our relationships, brings forth its unique focus and purpose.

We will have seasons of bliss and utter happiness where we know that we are with the right person. We will have seasons of profound sadness where we feel challenged, and where arguments and disagreements will happen frequently. We will even have seasons of feeling content, where we just go about our lives and stay with this person in more of a routine or everyday life sort of way.

In the book of Ecclesiastes, we are reminded of the profound truth that there is a time for everything and a season for every activity under the heavens. It is through this divine order that we witness the awe-inspiring beauty of God's creativity, wisdom, and majesty, even within the realm of our relationships.

Shucks, Preach on Pastor Bryant!

"There is a time for everything and a season for every activity under the heavens."

(Ecclesiastes 3:1)

You Have to Experience Each Season

Sometimes, individuals journey through the four seasons of a relationship without comprehending their significance. They usually navigate the elements of these seasons unprepared, very often unintentionally forfeiting invaluable opportunities for personal growth, maturity, and deepened intimacy. Without recognizing and embracing the seasons, we miss out on the profound lessons they hold.

The idea that relationships go through cycles, similar to the seasons, is regarded as a metaphorical concept often used to describe the various stages and phases that couples may experience. While it can provide a general framework for understanding the dynamics of a relationship, it's important to understand that every relationship is unique, and not all relationships will follow the same pattern.

Every single season in a relationship happens for a reason, just as it is in life. Everything happens to strengthen your bond and to solidify your commitment to one another. You must experience all of these things to enjoy the love and lasting commitment.

Winter: Dormancy

During the winter season of a relationship, one may not be ready to fully embrace new love due to the process of healing from past relationships. This season serves as a time for individuals to recover from the wounds caused by loss, rejection, and abuse experienced in previous romantic relationships. The sacrificial commitment during this time involves avoiding the numbing effects of substances, addictive behaviors, and hasty rebound relationships. It is a period of letting go of past lovers and allowing oneself to feel the pain associated with those experiences. There is BREAKTHROUGH after the breakup!

Personal disclosure becomes essential in the winter season as individuals reflect on both the positive and negative aspects of their previous relationships. Self-reflection is a lacking trait in relationships. It is a time of introspection and learning from past mistakes. When it comes to romantic affection, the warmth and support of friends, family, and the community of faith can provide solace.

Similar to the weather outside, when winter arrives, everything becomes cold and dreary. The landscape gets covered in snow, the trees appear lifeless, and the absence of birds adds to the desolation. In marriage, the winter season reflects a similar sense of desolation. It's when the emotional relationship in your marriage is cold and distant. This is not a phase that many of us want to experience and we try to avoid it at all costs. However, this is an essential part of building a bond that will stand the test of time. You must go deep into the valley and experience the challenges in order to enjoy what lies ahead. This is the negative and undesirable phase in a relationship, but you will look back on it and realize that it happened for a reason.

The icicles of indifference are beginning to form because your marriage lacks the warmth of a cozy fire that once burned bright. Couples going through this phase may no longer feel the warmth of love and instead experience resentment towards each other.

Unresolved conflicts become prominent, and their needs go unmet, leading to unhappiness. I don't know any couples who enjoy winter marriages. This is not an ideal period of time, but it is often necessary.

Winter marriages are characterized by coldness, harshness, bitterness, hurt, anger, disappointment, loneliness, rejection, and sometimes hopelessness are the emotions that couples experience when their marriage is in the winter season. What brings a couple to such an ice age? Rigidity - the unwillingness to consider the other person's perspective and to work toward a meaningful solution. The dreams of spring are covered with layers of ice, and the forecast calls for freezing rain.

It is during this time that we can be easily swayed by negative thoughts and draw false conclusions, questioning the validity of our relationship and marriage and thus feeling trapped in unhappiness. Sometimes, you can really miss your spouse — even when you are sleeping in the same bed or working in the same office. You can feel the emotional distance despite the physical proximity during this season of our marriage.

When one or both marriage partners insist on "my way or not at all," they are moving their marriage toward an ice age and begin to demonstrate the negative attitudes of a winter marriage. In such an ice age, the problems seem too big to tackle. Positions appear frozen in place because disagreements have gone on for so long. The tendency is to blame the other spouse for the decline in the relationship. Marriage is like two people living in separate igloos.

Every couple goes through the phase of dormancy during the course of their relationship. The winter season of marriage may last a month, or it may last 30 years. It may begin three months after the wedding or hit in the mid-life years. If your marriage is in winter, it may appear beyond hope. But don't give up. Just as most people wouldn't lie down in the snow and wait to die, there's no reason to passively accept the coldness of a winter marriage. There is a way out, and it begins with a change of attitude within yourself first, not your partner. (Shucks, Pastor Bryant)!

You can and will work through this. You have to have a willingness to do so, but beyond that it will get better. It will change to a more meaningful way of life and ensure that you come together. You will see the reason that you are in this Winter phase eventually, and that's when you start the work needed to get out of it.

Changing your own behavior may trigger your spouse to want to be more intentional about thawing the marriage out. Our capacity to change others is entirely based on our willingness to change ourselves. If you create a change in your own attitude and behavior, your spouse and the marriage itself will automatically be forced to change. Start by digging deep and doing some soul-searching here, for that is what is essential for moving forward and getting out of this chilly phase.

Typically, we want to focus our attention on our partner's behavior and what they are or aren't doing. Instead, I want to encourage you to focus on what you have control of — you! You can change many things, including your behavior, your views, your attitudes, and your perspectives. These will all have an impact on your marital system, and who knows the positive effect it may have on your spouse! Is there a behavior you desire to see in your spouse? Model it! It's catchy! Be the change that you want to see, and there will be no stopping you in life.

It sounds so simple — but we can influence our partner's behavior to a certain degree by modeling what we desire to see. If you want your partner to speak kindly to you, speak kind words to them. If you want your partner to compliment you, speak affirming words to them. If you want your partner to praise you, speak words of gratitude to your partner. You will never know the impact unless you try it consistently and not on and off again when you get to the spring season!

The coldness of winter often stimulates a desire for healing and health. A winter marriage often makes couples desperate enough to break out of their silent suffering and seek the help of a counselor, pastor, or trusted accountability partner. You have to go to this "rock bottom" phase of marriage in order to get to the good stuff. You have to feel the challenge of wanting to give up before you can start to make amends. You have to feel the frustration and desire to quit in order to realize that you want to work through this, and that the marriage is worth saving.

Thawing the ice of a winter relationship requires work. The

focus should be placed on resolving disagreements, meeting one another's needs, enhancing communication, and spending quality time together. Your relationship demands a lot of work and attention during the winter time. Now is the moment to get in and put in the required time and effort to grow it.

Spring: Dating Light

Spring is the season of new life and rejuvenation. The earth is waking up from its slumber, plants are growing, and beautiful flowers are in their bloom. Spring also signifies new beginnings. The beginning of a marriage is often compared to the arrival of spring, a season known for its joy and harmony. This initial stage of marriage ushers in a romantic journey, emphasizing self-discovery and getting to know our partners. The spirit of spring infuses couples with energy, resilience, and the desire to cultivate a deep and meaningful connection.

There is so much to find and appreciate in the spring season. This often signifies the beginning of a relationship or marriage, but it can go beyond just that. Spring in this context may also mean beginning again or breathing new life into an existing relationship. It may signify that things are getting back on track, or even that you have a newfound love and appreciation for each other.

The purpose of the spring season in a relationship is to enjoy oneself, assess potential partners, and determine their compatibility and lovable qualities. Marriages often find their beginnings in the enchanting season of spring, where the air is filled with the promise of new life and the courage to embark on a shared journey.

It is during this time that men and women are inspired to make a covenant commitment to build a life together, embracing the vows of love, support, and devotion through all seasons of life. "To love and to cherish, in sickness and in health, in poverty and in wealth, so long as we both shall live." These words resonate with the vibrancy and hopefulness of spring. They capture the essence of joining two lives as couples embark on a shared path to fulfill their individual purposes and support each other's dreams.

The excitement and anticipation that spring brings mirror the exhilaration of uniting in marriage. It is a time when the possibilities seem endless, and the shared vision of building a life together propels couples forward. The season symbolizes growth, new beginnings, and the blooming of love, making it an ideal backdrop for the start of lifelong partnerships.

There is much excitement and anticipation in this spring season, both in everyday life and in relationships. It's all new and therefore you can't wait to see what you will uncover. Each day brings about excitement on some level, and you are constantly learning and growing with one another. There is great fondness for these days in a relationship, and some may look back upon it as their favorite.

In regards to personal disclosure, the focus should be on

presenting oneself in the best possible way and showcasing who each person is at present. This includes sharing information about friends, family, feelings, beliefs, habits, personal history, and future plans that the other person would likely find enjoyable. This is where you really start to learn about one another. You gain an appreciation for who this individual is and what they are all about.

Romantic affection during the spring season should be light and gentle, expressing warmth through quick hugs and kisses, typically at the end of a date. The emphasis is on creating a comfortable and enjoyable atmosphere as the relationship continues to develop. You can always build up, but this is the season of newness and the affection is a reflection of that. As you grow as a couple, so too will your connection on every level.

So, as you go off on this amazing journey with each other, let the excitement and optimism of spring flood your hearts. Take advantage of the season's attitude of expansion, rebirth, and limitless opportunity. May the strong roots of love, comfort, and the lovely blossoms of ambition be the foundation of your marriage for all time. Welcome to the blossoming season of your marriage, where romance blossoms and fresh chapters start—this is the good stuff!

Summer: Steady Dating

This phase is often referred to as the "Honeymoon Period" of a marriage. It is a time when partners essentially have no boundaries and overlook red flags. Summer shows up as a time of great connection, fulfillment, joy, and contentment in the marriage journey. It radiates beauty and life, much like brilliant flowers, but they need constant attention and maintenance. If you thought that spring was great, then summer is going to be amazing!

Couples who enjoy a long summer season have perfected the skill of protecting and keeping what they have cultivated. They are aware that the summer did not just happen; it was the result of careful preparation, seeding, and maintenance of their marriage. Many couples in this phase have gone through the courtship, really worked at growing and strengthening their bond, and now they get to enjoy the fruits of their labor.

During this sacrificial phase of marriage in summer, the aim is to strengthen the bond while developing an in-depth understanding of each other (constructive behavior). Giving each other the freedom to be unique is a second crucial step in maintaining a good marriage. Although differences are unavoidable, they can also be quite polarizing. You tend to celebrate differences here.

Couples who want their relationship to last through the summer will actively allow each other the space to feel, think, and act in various ways. It's a balance between identifying and celebrating each other's differences, and working to further strengthen the bond that you have created. You know that you have a good thing here, and you really want to keep that going.

Just as the summer months require nurturing and attention to thrive, these couples are willing to invest the necessary work and dedication to maintain the splendor they have achieved. They recognize that complacency and stagnation can hinder the vitality of their union, so they remain proactive in their pursuit of mutual growth and shared experiences. In their pursuit of sustaining the radiance of their marriage, these couples understand the importance of ongoing communication, vulnerability, and shared goals.

They cherish the happiness and fulfillment they have found and are committed to protecting and nourishing it. Like skilled gardeners, they water the seeds of love, kindness, and understanding, ensuring that their relationship continues to flourish in the abundant season of summer. There is work required here, but things are still new and fresh. You want to hold onto the positive momentum that you have enjoyed, even if that means putting in some work to perfect things.

In this stage, personal disclosure involves delving more profound into each other's past and discussing more intimate and perhaps delicate aspects of each other. This can include talking about diseases, mental health issues, genetics, and fertility. Both individuals start to acknowledge their mistakes and character flaws, demonstrating a genuine effort to address and improve upon them. We are all aware that our thoughts determine how we develop. Because of this, the Bible cautions that you should guard your heart with all diligence because matters of life arise from it (Proverbs 4:23).

This is where you both must have open and honest communication, and it must come from both sides. You need to put it out there to share the good and the bad about yourself, and you should receive the same from your partner. You may have to dig deep to uncover some truths that you may have been initially unsure about sharing, but it is only when you do that the bond strengthens and the relationship grows.

It goes without saying that you can't have a great relationship with somebody if you only pay attention to their positive qualities; you also need to embrace their flaws and limitations. This is the definition of true love!!! It is best to keep any romantic feelings at this point in check. This might entail light petting without probing over erogenous regions.

We all have things that we like and dislike about ourselves. We all have aspects of our being, our lives, and our relationships that we have learned from and some which we wish went differently. There are so many positive and negative things that make us both who we are today. It is only when you are truthful in sharing the good, the bad, and the ugly that your relationship will be able to move forward fully.

This is where the buildup of excitement occurs, and you really feel as if you are connecting on another level. You can see what this person is all about, and you feel stronger than ever. You want to keep things going and you start to think about what the future could hold. There is so much promise in this season, though you do want to take your time and be mindful as you move through it into the next season.

Summer may easily turn into a fall in any marriage, perhaps even before the couple is aware of it. Winter is less frightening than fall, but summer is still much more pleasant. There are so many positive and wonderful feelings here, and you do want to take the time to enjoy them. You will likely look back on this period of time and feel fondness for it.

Fall: Harvesting (Engagement to Marry)

Fall is a season of change: leaves turn to brilliant colors; days grow shorter; nights cooler. As a result, we may become unsettled as we expect the harsh Winter to come. So, it is not hard for us to become uncertain, negligent, and apprehensive. This is a season of preparation, but we may not know exactly what we are preparing for in the winter months. We may feel some anxiety as we transition into a completely different season and time of our life. This is common as so many of us wonder the fate of our relationship. This is a time where it is common to have doubts to a certain degree.

The gentle descent of leaves in autumn serves as a profound analogy for the delicate transitions experienced within the fall season of marriage. At first glance, the external façade of marriage in early autumn may appear intact, evoking admiration from onlookers who perceive a seemingly happy or perfect couple.

However, behind closed doors, a subtle transformation unfolds, and as the chilling winds of change grow stronger, the gradual deterioration of the marriage becomes unmistakably apparent to all. Thus, autumn is the time to watch out for marital conflicts. It is normal for conflict to exist, but it may still come as a surprise to those of us caught off guard with it.

In the early stages of autumn, couples become aware of the subtle changes in their marriage, and there could be a feeling of discomfort. It usually happens slowly and gradually the changes and shifts become apparent to both people in the relationship. They soon become intensely aware of the necessity of attending to underlying problems and tending to their relationship's emotional terrain. It is a period of thought during which open discussion and sincere reflection serve as the cornerstones of understanding and growth.

However, as the season progresses, couples may find themselves confronted with cooling winds that threaten the warmth they once shared. The changing dynamics require intentional efforts to rekindle the flame of love and to reestablish a sense of connection. It is essential for couples to embrace vulnerability and show one another empathy during this transforming season. They must understand that the difficulties they encounter are not insurmountable but rather present chances for development in both their personal and interpersonal relationships.

There is opportunity within this uncertainty. If you keep the lines of communication open, that will help dramatically. If you are open to the changes and embrace them as opportunities to come together that will strengthen your relationship. If you can stick with it even with the anticipation of difficult times and uncertainty, it will ultimately help you in the long run.

In some cases, couples may find it necessary to establish boundaries regarding financial matters, conversations, or knowing each other's whereabouts as a means to foster trust and security. This is where you learn about each other's hot buttons, and you find a way to avoid them. This is the time when you begin to really look at what makes the other person happy—but also what really upsets them so that you can avoid unnecessary conflict.

A key objective during this phase is to let go of past romantic attachments and minimize influences that may be detrimental to the marriage. Personal disclosure in this stage involves envisioning and discussing the future, both individually and as a couple. You both have things in your past, but that is where they remain. This is where you look towards the future and build it together. You must let go of the past, live in the present, and plan for the future. That is the recipe for a loving and lasting relationship moving forward.

It is important to explore the desired growth and development as individuals, as well as jointly setting goals and establishing priorities for the future. In situations where doubts or uncertainties arise, seeking a premarital evaluation from a qualified professional such as a psychologist, marriage counselor, or pastor can be a beneficial step. This evaluation can provide insights and guidance in navigating the complexities of entering into a marital commitment. All of this can help to protect your relationship and ensure that it can stand the test of time. You will face trials and tribulations in your marriage, and any work that you can put in ahead of time will benefit you greatly.

It's ideal to wait until the personal union of marriage to have a physical union during intercourse in order to maintain everything in balance.

"For this is the will of God, your sanctification: that you abstain from sexual immorality; that each one of you knows how to control his own body in holiness and honor, not in the passion of lust like the Gentiles who do not know God."

(1 Thessalonians 4:3-5)

The Bible encourages believers to maintain sexual purity and avoid sexual immorality in their relationships before marriage. Individuals may interpret and apply biblical teachings on this subject in line with their own faith and personal convictions. Another relevant passage is found in Hebrews 13:4, which states, *"Let marriage be held in honor among all, and let the marriage bed be undefiled, for God will judge the sexually immoral and adulterous."* This verse highlights the sacredness of the marital union and the need to honor the marriage relationship by keeping sexual activity within the boundaries of marriage.

Not all relationships have the privilege of experiencing a fall season characterized by a sense of harmony and stability. Some relationships may encounter challenges and conflicts during the power struggle of the Summer Season. If you and your partner have managed to navigate through the difficulties and reach the Fall Season, I congratulate you on your perseverance and growth together. It is a testament to your dedication and resilience as a couple.

Every couple will face adversity of some type, as that is part of life. When you face the conflict or when the dynamic shifts may vary greatly. Going into a relationship and a marriage with your eyes wide open to this is instrumental to your success. Being realistic and being open to working through the conflicts will help you to stay connected, even through the toughest times.

As the latter stage of fall unfolds, the once vibrant leaves vanish, leaving behind a poignant emptiness that unveils the true state of the marriage. This is where things get real. This is where you see the person and the relationship for what it is. This is where you must take the good and the bad, as they are readily presented to you. This is where you invest into the relationship if it is truly right for you.

It is within this emotional void that concern, uncertainty, and fear take root, casting shadows of doubt on the once-flourishing connection. During this pivotal phase, fall has the potential to pave the way for a renewed spring or a return to the warmth of summer. The trajectory of the relationship is determined by the choices and actions of the couple. The predominant mindset of a marriage in the fall is one of intense worry about the state of the union and anxiety about the future. Most people are worried because they do not want to be in the fall season of marriage. Couples can escape the grip of fall's gloom and recapture the liveliness that previously characterized their relationship by tackling the issues head-on.

You must do some soul-searching as an individual and as a couple. If your relationship is worth fighting for, which hopefully it is, then you are honest about the hard parts. You recognize that there may be things that aren't ideal, but you are happy to work through them as a united front. Couples are often urged by the season to reexamine their deepest motivations, find common ground, and lay the new emotional and trusting groundwork. Couples set a new course that could result in a spring that blooms or a summer that is revived by making conscious efforts and a commitment to growth. Every relationship will take a different path, and many will have very different ways to get to the end goal.

Marriage relationships are in a perpetual state of flux, undergoing constant transformation. These transformations manifest in distinct seasons that recur throughout the journey of marriage. Winters, summers, springs, and falls, each with their own unique attributes, will be encountered by every couple at various points in their marital life.

Recognizing and understanding the current season of your marriage holds great significance as it brings awareness to the present state of your relationship and enables you to identify the prevailing attitudes, emotions, and actions that shape your bond.

You want to be with the right person, and you want that wonderful happiness that you have always dreamed of. You deserve that—but it also means that you need to put in the work. Nobody is perfect and the only way that this will work is if we are honest with ourselves and our partners. You don't have to like everything about your partner, but you do have to embrace even the differences. Then you can grow through each season and ensure that the dynamic between the two of you is a positive one.

Why Are Four Seasons in A Relationship Important?

Relationships tend to experience various transitions and transformations akin to the ever-changing seasons. These distinct phases have their own rhythm, encompassing both moments of harmony and discord. In the tapestry of every relationship, the seasons reveal themselves in unique ways. Some seasons may grace us with delightful warmth, while others present more arduous trials.

In any relationship, it is important to acknowledge and embrace the fact that differences and difficulties are inevitable. No two individuals are exactly alike, and conflicts or challenges are bound to arise. The true measure of a successful relationship lies in how couples handle and deal with these situations together.

Each couple is unique, with their own set of personalities, backgrounds, and perspectives. A relationship is not just a stage in life. But I believe that it is a part of your life where you prepare yourself before tying the knot. You wouldn't want to be with somebody who was exactly the same as you on everything. The differences are what make us unique. We create something special based out of the way in which we come together in the good times and the bad as well.

Be watchful and conscious while choosing a partner prior to making a lifelong commitment to marriage. This is why you want to take your time and allow your relationship to go through the various seasons.

Be in tune with who this person is and see how they are, and ensure that you can build a life with them. Look at what they are showing you and see if this is in line with the types of things that you want.

It is essential to cultivate an environment of acceptance and understanding where both partners observe differences as opportunities for growth instead of sources of conflict. It involves valuing and respecting each other's viewpoints and finding common ground through communication.

Real growth and connection occur when just one partner embraces oneself but also their beloved companions in all their complexities and evolutions. This is truly a two-way street and it is up to you to create something special and meaningful together. It takes time, patience, and dedication to the relationship before you.

As we navigate the seasons of change, we discover the beauty of mutual understanding, acceptance, and growth. The flames of passion and romance may flicker and wane, but with nurturing and intention, they can be reignited, blossoming anew.

It's essential to note that agreement does not mean there will never be disagreements or differences of opinion. When couples fail to negotiate and do not settle their issues, more challenges surface between them. Disagreements are a natural part of any relationship. The key is how couples handle those differences and work towards a resolution with respect and love for one another.

When you hear a couple say that they never disagree, this is actually concerning. You are meant to disagree on certain matters, and sometimes you just may not see eye to eye. You are going to have times when you feel frustrated, but it is your willingness and ability to work through it that really matters in the end.

In a relationship, for two individuals to walk together in harmony and unity, there needs to be agreement and mutual understanding.

"Can two walk together, except they are agreed?"

(Amos 3:3)

This verse holds a significant meaning in the context of couples and relationships. It emphasizes the importance of shared values, goals, and beliefs as the foundation for a strong and successful partnership.

Disagreements Are Normal Sometimes

I firmly believe that when couples are aligned in their perspectives, desires, and principles, they can journey together on a path that leads to fulfillment and mutual support. These are all tests and trials to see how committed you are to one another. These are all things that you must work through in order to remain committed to one another. It's a normal and healthy part of life to disagree at times.

Someone rightly said a relationship is often described as a school where we learn and put into practice the lessons we have acquired. Instead of being trapped in the dark cloud of despair and confusion in regard to your partner, a better approach is to pray for them, as mentioned in James 5:16.

"Therefore, confess your sins to each other and pray for each other so that you may be healed. The prayer of a righteous person is powerful and effective."

Entrust your fears and concerns to God and seek His guidance in helping your partner to steer any behaviors that you perceive as potentially harmful to your relationship. Remember, you are united in this journey, and the well-being of one person directly impacts both of you.

You Are More United as A Team

Together, you can support and uplift each other, seeking growth and healing as a team. Divine wisdom shall illuminate the grey areas, bringing clarity and guidance to your relationship. With God's presence, your home shall be a sanctuary, an earthly manifestation of heaven itself. Failure and hardship shall not be written in the pages of your story, for God's hand shall protect and guide you through every challenge.

In times of need and despair, divine intervention shall be your refuge. God's unwavering support shall be a steadfast pillar, providing comfort, strength, and assistance whenever you call upon His name. Trust in His divine plan, for He shall grant you the blueprint to create a marriage that shines brightly, surpassing all expectations.

With God as your guide, your union shall radiate with love, peace, and harmony. Embrace His divine presence, and witness the transformation of your relationship into a testament of His grace and blessings. With God all things are possible, and that will really show itself when it comes to your relationship and its long term success.

Chapter 3

I Fell in Love with Spiderman, but I Got Clark Kent

"All that glitters are not gold!" Yes, that's absolutely true. Everyone likes to have a beautiful or handsome partner, but that can't be the end all be all. I'm simply stating the truth as it is; long gone are the days when people used to consider relationships or marriage as a lifelong matter. But as of now, prudent choices appear to be the top priority of relationships.

Just a basic reminder for you: Beast needed Belle to see him for who he truly is and to love him for that. We have become so enamored by our own reflections and the allure of flawless features that we forget the true essence of our worth. How comical it is that we measure our value by external appearances, as if a perfect nose, figure, or radiant complexion were the pinnacle of our existence.

Appearance and chemistry matter, there is no doubt about that. It will matter greatly that you are attracted to your partner, but this also comes through in much more than looks. You must also remember that looks fade and you want to think about what you are left with when that happens.

Looks Only Matter So Much

So, what's the purpose of having a dashing companion? Will looks in a relationship make any bigger difference? This is the ugly reality of humankind that makes them puzzled and confused often. Do looks matter that much? Sure you need that attraction because it does matter where chemistry is concerned. However, you have to ask yourself if you look beyond just the physical appearance, aren't there other things that matter more?

When love is said to be blind, then why do people go for looks and appearances? In today's modern image-centric world, the allure of looks holds a captivating sway. Society buzzed us with curated ideals of beauty standards for both men and women, shaping our perceptions and fueling the desire to conform.

We are constantly shown what beauty is, and these images invade us on a daily basis. We are told that to be worthy we have to be good looking, which is grossly unfair. So while looks matter to a certain extent, just how important are they?

Have you ever shown a picture of someone you thought was attractive to your friends, but they only thought they were average-looking? You begin to defend yourself by saying that "pictures don't do him justice" and "he looks better in person." All this means is that physical attraction matters.

Weighing Out Looks in The Big Picture

Anybody who doesn't meet the "beauty standards" automatically isn't a good match as a mate. This is what we're told and why we seem to place so much of an emphasis on looks in the first place. But are looks everything? It seems great and exciting in the beginning, but I bet if you give it time, it will not last a lifetime; then what's the point of indulging in the desire to get a perfect partner?

The fact is the influence of media, the pressures of comparison, and the innate human inclination to seek attractiveness all contribute to the emphasis placed on appearance. We are practically conditioned to believe that looks matter to such a great extent. We are instantly put off if there isn't that magnetic attraction at first that comes about solely because of good looks.

People always say, "Looks do Matter!" I would say Yes and No because it's both really. Despite the wisdom imparted by age-old sayings like "Beauty is only skin deep," "Beauty is in the eye of the beholder," and "Don't judge a book by its cover," it seems that we often fail to internalize their lessons. We may understand the logical reasoning behind these notions, yet we become naïve to accept them. We have to believe them and live them in order to embrace them at their core.

Society Dictates Much of What We Believe

Actually, we are helpless in this situation because humans are naturally drawn to attractive people. In the beginning, you will find yourself drawn to a person. The first thing you notice about someone is how they appear, dress, speak, etc. They don't merely reveal their personality to you at first glance. And if someone flirts back, we get a rush, and it's incredibly difficult to resist, and as long as no one is getting hurt, why would we? Everyone around someone with extraordinary looks gets smitten, as we all know. There is no use denying that. And who knows, that early flutter could turn into really real and intense love.

While looks may not always be a top priority for everyone, the reality is that not everyone in the world can be perfectly fit or breathtakingly beautiful. The majority of individuals fall into the average category. With this being said, I meant to say that everyone in some aspect is good-looking. Your partner is human, and it is impossible for them to fulfill all of your expectations.

What you must also realize is that what you find attractive may vary significantly from what others find attractive. Therefore, the idea of good looks is an individual thing, and we need to remember that. You will also find your partner even better looking if they have other wonderful traits to offer as well.

Getting Beyond the Fairy Tales

The expression "love at first sight" refers to the idea of being able to tell someone you love them the moment you set eyes on them. This, perhaps, is better understood as an intensified level of physical attraction, which people subsequently mistake for love. I vehemently agree that there is a chance for physical attraction to be mistaken for true love. While physical attraction matters, it's not the only thing!

But as you gradually become acquainted with their personality, qualities, and attractiveness, trust me when I tell you that the mantra of good looks will automatically diminish. The point here is that this thing can be overlooked. An enduring romantic relationship cannot be based only on physical attraction, even though it is true that love can sometimes be ignited by it in the beginning. Beyond physical attraction, love comprises deeper emotional ties, compatible values, and compatibility.

The idea of a perfect partner may be elusive, an ideal partner can be discovered in someone who has cultivated personal growth beyond superficial attributes such as looks, charm, and success. While each individual seeks qualities that hold personal significance, there are certain psychological characteristics that both you and your partner can aspire to, which greatly enhance the likelihood of a successful and lasting relationship.

Consider What Really Matters to You

So, let me ask you, are you in search of finding the "right" person? How would you do that? And how are you so sure that it will make your relationship successful? What does "the right person" mean to you? What sort of traits are the most important?

In a world obsessed with comparisons and idealized images, it's easy to overlook the beauty of individuality. We find ourselves chasing after fictional characters, hoping to find someone who perfectly embodies our sought-after qualities. But what if we let go of those expectations? What if we started appreciating people for who they truly are without constantly measuring them against an unrealistic standard?

Imagine a world where we understand and accept others in their unique entirety. A world where we no longer rely on fictional comparisons or idealized images to define our relationships. Instead, we dive deep into the depths of genuine connections, embracing the complexities and quirks that make each person truly special. Accepting and appreciating people for who they truly are instead of comparing them with Hollywood actors and actresses. They appear in some of our favorite movies and TV shows. They appear on talk shows and in advertisements. We see them on red carpets and on their Instagram, p

Be Sure You Are Looking at Reality

You are, indeed, not finding common ground between reality

and falsehood if you are considering your partner to have the same charm and personality as a famous celebrity. You are looking at an illusion and not a clear depiction of what a normal person is like in everyday life. The celebrities you see before you have teams of people to make them look a certain way. This is what their reputation and their living is based around. It's not the norm at all!

Rather than fixating on the disparities between your idealized vision and the actuality of your partner, consider shifting your perspective. Your partner may not possess superhuman abilities like Clark Kent; they likely possess their own set of admirable qualities and strengths that make them a remarkable partner in their own distinctive way. Consider what makes them special, unique, and attractive beyond just their looks.

Let's clarify something upfront. I'm not saying that you should refrain from having a good and positive partner. This goes beyond looks and really considers the personality and positive impact that your partner can and should have on your life. Sure, you can have that, but let the other person be herself/himself. Be sure that what you are seeing from your partner is truly and authentically who they are. Be sure that they have a positive impact upon your life because that matters tremendously.

Look at What Really Matters

If you find yourself emotionally affected by past relationships, it is essential to take the time to heal before seeking a new partner. Prioritize being your true self wholeheartedly, focus on your new partner, and try not to preoccupy your thoughts with personal issues of the past. Spend time with your friends and family while you heal before having someone new in your life. You must give yourself time to heal, and when you do then you can start to really focus on what matters to you in a partner. This will undoubtedly go well beyond looks.

When you embark on the journey of finding love again, consider choosing someone whose emotional wounds have also been given time to heal. This healing and readiness to move forward with your life must come from both of you. That is when you will be ready for a relationship, and when you will begin to look at what really matters to you in a partner. This approach works both ways, and both individuals can see each other authentically and in a long-term trajectory.

Philippians 4:11-12 serves as a gentle reminder for believers to cultivate contentment in every situation they encounter. While it is natural to have personal desires and preferences, it is equally crucial to foster a sense of gratitude for the blessings present in one's life, including the person with whom they share a relationship.

You Will Know and Recognize What You Really Want

Shift your focus towards developing a loving and fulfilling connection with your partner; we can nurture a deeper appreciation for the joys and blessings that accompany their presence in our lives. When you have done the soul searching and put in the time to what really truly matters to you, then you will have a much easier time finding that sort of partner.

You have a clear head and a clear heart when you go through this process properly. You have a better idea of who you are and what you want when you look inside first. You begin to really understand and appreciate what a loving relationship can be. You know without a doubt what you want out of a partner, and you won't stop until you get there.

I'm quite certain that on the day of your wedding, if you find yourself second-guessing your choice, it is a clear clue that you might be doing something wrong or made some mistake. Even when you are confident that you have found the ideal companion, marriage and the prospect of beginning a family are already difficult. Without a genuine sense of assurance, it would be foolish to make such promises. You don't want to go down the wrong path with the wrong person. When you are mindful of what you want and who you are searching for, then it makes obtaining that much more tangible.

Listen to Your Heart

Indeed, it is an undeniable truth that our hearts can deceive us because it is desperately wicked, as stated in Jeremiah 17:9. The Scripture reveals that the human heart is desperately wicked and can lead us astray. It is only God who possesses full knowledge of the intricate depths of our hearts, including the hidden corners of our own. If God were to unveil the true contents of our hearts, it is highly likely that we would deny ownership, for the darkness within would be exposed.

If you desire a spiritually inclined partner, seek them wherever the Spirit of God is present. According to God's divine plan, we often discover what we need and desire when we are not actively pursuing it but rather directing our focus toward the Lord and His Kingdom. When our gaze is firmly fixed upon God, He orchestrates the convergence of everything else into our lives.

Jesus articulated this concept in the following manner: So, do not worry, saying, "What shall we eat?" or "What shall we drink?" or "What shall we wear?" For the pagans run after all these things, and your heavenly Father knows that you need them. But seek His kingdom first, and His righteousness and all these things will be given to you. Therefore, do not worry about tomorrow, for tomorrow will worry about itself. Each day has enough trouble of its own (Matt. 6:31-34).

Trust That the Right Person Will Come to You

In his teachings, Jesus advised us not to be anxious about our daily needs, such as food, drink, and clothing. I firmly believe that this principle extends to all areas of our lives, including our relationships and the quest to find that "special someone." As believers, our primary focus should be on seeking the Kingdom of God and living in accordance with His righteousness.

By prioritizing our devotion to God and aligning ourselves with His will and Word, we can trust Him to take care of all the other aspects of our lives. The key lies in directing our attention and trust towards God's will, His Word, and His glory, allowing Him to guide and provide for us in all things. He will bring us the right person and we will know it when they are ours.

Why is it so tough to find true love? There are so many moving components in relationships that even the finest and happiest ones take a great deal of time and effort. Love is a verb; it demands constant work. With time, love also changes, moving from being intense and passionate to being companionable, intimate, and dedicated. I'm not sure if this is totally true, to be perfectly honest. Some relationships have a true shift, while others maintain that spark all through the years. Love is very different for everyone, and so too is the relationship you share with somebody.

The Way It All Works Will Vary

Some people can tell right away that their future spouse is the one they have been searching for their entire lives. But not everyone experiences it in the same way. The actual rule is to not bet on something if you're unsure of whether it's the right choice. Just as attraction is different for everyone, so too is the way in which you find love. It will look different and feel different for every single person.

You never want to compare and you certainly never want to put unrealistic expectations on yourself either.

Give yourself grace to find the right person in the right way and in the right time. Though this may take longer than you might like, it will be well worth it in the end. Even if it takes some time, you will be able to tell if they are the perfect choice. In other words, if it's the right decision, you will know for sure—either right away or a little later.

"Charm is deceitful, and beauty is vain, but a woman who fears the Lord is to be praised."

(Proverbs 31:30)

For a relationship to flourish, inner qualities and character over external attractiveness are foremost. It encourages valuing a person's reverence for God and their moral character rather than being solely swayed by physical appearance.

"But the Lord said to Samuel, "Do not look on his appearance or on the height of his stature, because I have rejected him. For the Lord sees not as man sees: man looks on the outward appearance, but the Lord looks on the heart."

(1 Samuel 16:7)

Look Deeper to Uncover True Love

God values the heart and character of an individual rather than their outward appearance. In many aspects of contemporary society, there is a blurring and distortion of the distinctions between men and women. The authentic and inherent image of God, as intended, is being eroded. Somebody may look attractive on the outside, but be very ugly inside as they are not a good person. Sometimes you don't know that right away, but that's why you want to go beyond just outward physical appearance.

Think about a job interview. A candidate's outstanding appearance, assured demeanor, and polished resume may at first dazzle a hiring manager. As the interview goes on, they realize that the applicant is unqualified for the position due to a lack of knowledge, honesty, or experience. The person's qualities or character were not appropriately reflected by their external look in this scenario.

This Concept Applies to So Much in Life

Just take a quick glance at your surroundings. What do you see? Broken families, miserable marriages, single-parent households, unbelievable ignorance, and anguish are all over the place. Do you ever ponder why? WHY has humanity never been able to find a solution to these and other major issues? Why do they seem to worsen as time goes on? The answer lies in the fact that humanity, with its billions of inhabitants, frequently disregards the laws and principles set forth by God.

Life happens, and sometimes things are beyond our control. Some of the things that happen in our lives is very difficult to deal with. However, there may be times where we have to reassess, truly look at our priorities, and determine what really matters to us in the long run. We all have an innate longing for joy, love, and a sense of purpose as humans.

We yearn for something incredible to fill our hearts.

Simple pleasures like relishing the first taste of a slightly overcooked brownie, feeling the thrill of a playoff triumph in overtime, or splurging on a new outfit or pair of shoes can briefly bring happiness into our lives. These happy times, however, just serve to remind us that there is something more fundamental and larger that we are created for.

We Must Value Marriage for What It Is

There is a pervasive belief in modern society that marriages no longer hold a sacred place. Instead, marriage is often perceived as simply a legal contract or social experiment in which individuals mainly put their own personal interests first. A no-fault divorce is frequently an option for unhappy marriages, and this is frequently followed by fresh attempts at marriage. The cycle repeats over and over again in various ways, but the mindset and way in which it is treated remains the same.

The prevalence of materialism in our era has stripped life of its moral and spiritual significance. It obstructs our ability to perceive the world with a sense of awe and wonder, and it obscures our true purpose. Consumerism, which has infected our souls and spirits, has eroded our conscience to the point where distinguishing between good and evil becomes increasingly challenging.

Simply put, we as a society care about the wrong things. We are so focused on what is new and shiny that we don't take notice of what profoundly matters. Nevertheless, within each of us, there remains an inherent longing for goodness, a profound and fundamental need that persists.

We Must Really Focus On What Matters

It is quite improbable that two people would have the same types of interests. It is impractical to expect a couple to constantly desire to do the same things at the same time, in the same style, or for the same reasons, given the wide range of interests and the dynamic nature of human preferences. The secret is to evaluate a possible partner's interest compatibility, paying particular attention to how well those interests line up.

If there aren't at least a few common interests, problems could develop, and the couple might end up living in separate universes despite having the same last name. You want to have some sort of common ground and some things in common that matter. You want to be certain that you share similarities with your philosophies and morals for certain. Even seemingly insignificant differences, like one person wanting pets while the other detests animals, can indicate compatibility and possibly contribute to incompatibility.

In a true marriage, both partners actively strive for each other's fulfillment. Through their qualities, the union between a husband and wife is strengthened. Their love for one another, their unwavering commitment, and their ability to bear fruit together reflect a mysterious and beautiful reflection of God's image.

The Two Truly Become One

When two individuals come together as one flesh, they cease to exist as separate entities and instead form a profound unity. The relationship or marriage goes beyond mere companionship or partnership; it represents the deepest form of intimacy. This is how it is intended to be. This is what marriage is meant to be like, and what you can hopefully model your own after. As Friedrich Nietzsche eloquently expresses, *"The resolve of two to create a unity which is more than those who created it. It is reverence for one another and for the fulfillment of such a resolve."*

Our love becomes distorted when we idolize our spouse or kids to an extreme point. It is tough for us to publicly admit either our own or our family's flaws. This cycle gradually alienates us from both God and one another. It invites negative influences, particularly those related to sexuality, and results in loneliness and emptiness on the inside. Because of their broken union with God, Adam and Eve experienced the loss of innocence. The void that followed led to a blame game, with men trying to dominate women and women holding grudges against men and blaming Satan. As a result, their harmonious union was shattered, and they became adversaries (Genesis 3:7–19)

Have You Seen Changes?

Has your partner changed significantly since you first got together? Has your partner undergone any unpleasant changes recently? It's likely that while you were dating, you saw your partner through an idealistic lens; that lens has since been removed. When things are new and we are lovestruck, everything looks and feels different. Don't be too hard on yourself if you fell prey to seeing this person or this relationship for more or less than it is in reality.

There's another thing to keep in mind on the other side of this. It's quite possible that you aren't what your spouse had in mind when you two were first together. Before getting married, differences between spouses frequently seem attractive, desirable, and exciting. However, what was alluring in the semi-fantasy world of courting may suddenly seem far from perfect after a few months or years of marriage. Fantasy morphs into reality, and before you know it things may have changed dramatically.

Through my studies, I have come to understand that people choose life partners based on multiple dimensions: physical, intellectual, and spiritual. When a bond is sensed in any of these realms, individuals often perceive that person as a potential companion. It's hard to see all of these in their truest form at the beginning of a relationship.

Think of The Big Picture

Admiring and appreciating physical attractiveness, appearance, eloquence, or academic accomplishments is common and it's something that we all do. However, relying only on these qualities for a relationship or marriage can ultimately result in disaster. But let me remind you about the reality of life that these qualities cannot make a stable and happy bond. Tastes and preferences change with time, and beauty fades. What can be ideal and alluring today could simply become unimportant and dated tomorrow.

When the looks fade and you are left with the personality and other traits, you want to be sure that's enough. Will you both be able to provide each other with a good life? Will you both be able to be happy in this relationship years from now when it's not just about the attraction? You want to consider this before you move forward.

It is better to give priority to something that will stand the test of time and need a lifetime of dedication. Then, verse 8: *"Above all, keep loving one another earnestly, since love covers a multitude of sins."* Love is essential, and it will be needed as much as anything else. Why? Because the challenges, pressures, and trials of the difficult days will place significant strain on our relationships.

You Need Somebody There for You in Good and Bad

However, during these times, we will need one another, and the world will observe whether our love is genuine. We need to know that our partner will always be there for us and take care of us. We want to be the first line of support for one another, and therefore ensure that we maintain that bond. As it is written, "By this, all people will know that you are my disciples, if you have a love for one another" (John 13:35). Will we choose to protect, support, and endure each other's flaws and weaknesses, or will anger govern our hearts? Though attraction may be important in the short term, the reality is that it is about much more moving forward. In the long term, you want somebody supportive, kind, dedicated, and who will see you through thick and thin.

The late actor Mickey Rooney once compared marriage to

batting in baseball, emphasizing the importance of not letting the right opportunity pass by. Mickey himself was married eight times, indicating that he encountered numerous potential partners throughout his life. This is an interesting situation to look at as it is extreme in the number of marriages that he was in.

Happiness Is About So Much

One could argue that Mickey held a belief similar to finding a "needle in a haystack" when it comes to choosing a spouse. According to this perspective, there is only one person with whom you can truly be happy, and it becomes necessary to search for that person, even if it means ending a marriage that no longer feels suitable.

The Bible does not provide a "wrong needle" clause that allows for an easy way out if one concludes that their spouse is not the right fit for them. Marriage is a commitment that requires dedication, understanding, and effort to navigate challenges and differences. Instead of seeking an escape route based on personal feelings of compatibility, it is valuable to focus on fostering love, forgiveness, and growth within the marriage relationship.

Marriage should not be solely focused on finding the perfect spouse but instead on becoming the right person. If both partners entered into marriage with the expectation that it would bring happiness and fulfillment to their lives as individuals, they might have found themselves deeply disappointed as their contentment levels decreased even further. This is about taking a short and long term view of what you want and what the relationship should be.

What Type of Mine Will You Find?

However, if they already had a sense of meaning and purpose in their individual lives and desired to share that with a lifelong companion, they likely experienced an increase in contentment. This perspective can be referred to as the "Mine Theory of Mate Selection." In marriage, you either discover a "land mine" that brings destruction or a "Gold Mine" that brings prosperity and fulfillment. The harsh reality is that this statement may be true. Not everyone in the world is going to be 100% physically fit or drop-dead gorgeous.

The majority of the world is average, and we may look at someone and think they have good looks, but as we get to know their personality and their characteristics as a person, it may boost up their looks tremendously. It has to be about both, not just a short sighted view of what is attractive right now.

What is considered to be moderately attractive varies from person to person. Not everyone has the same taste as significant others. That is what makes us all unique and different. So while you do want the chemistry and attraction, you need to be sure that there is more to it than that.

Consider The Source

Beware of false influences that could lead us astray when assessing the character of the unconverted. Satan may attract attention to desirable traits, making them seem alluring and desirable. He can slyly say, "She is so sweet and accommodating," in an effort to sway our opinion. But since Satan is the father of falsehoods, we shouldn't pay attention to these lies. We must keep in mind how Satan tricked our ancestors by tempting them with something that, on the surface, seemed nice and lovely (Genesis 3:6).

In order to truly grow spiritually and connect with godly ideals in our relationships, we must see past outward appearances. Look into the eyes of the person that you are with and past their looks. What type of a person are they? Can you see yourself with them long term?

God, in His wisdom, does not make the choice of a life partner for you. Instead, He guides you through the process by helping you apply Scriptural principles and providing direction through the Holy Spirit. It is important to understand that God does not impose or force anyone upon you in marriage. When He offers guidance, the decision ultimately rests with you, and you bear full responsibility for the choices you make.

You Get to Choose So Make It Count

As God respects your freedom of choice, it is equally important for others, including pastors, priests, or parents, to respect your autonomy. They should not impose or pressure you into accepting a specific person as your partner. It is crucial to prayerfully seek God's guidance, rely on His principles, and make decisions that align with His will for your life.

Yet, amidst this quest for physical perfection, let us remember that true beauty transcends the superficial. It resides in the depths of character, the authenticity of the soul, and the warmth of genuine connections. Embrace the power of inner radiance and celebrate the beauty that emanates from within, for that is where true allure truly resides.

While looks matter, they are most certainly not the only thing. There is much more to finding the perfect partner for you, and it must encompass what is important with you. Though they look good now, will they be there for you in the future? Consider everything and then you can make the right decisions for yourself accordingly.

Chapter 4

When We Deny Intimacy, We Are Cheating on the Marriage

God, the source of genuine love, is the Creator of intimacy in a marriage. As the ultimate authority, only He can truly define love and provide guidance on how intimacy and marriage can bring about our highest fulfillment. God's original intent is for sex to be a discovery, not an exhibit.

The instinct of intimacy is considered one of the most powerful among other instincts. It carries immense potential for blessings as a remarkable gift from God, yet the wrong use of intimacy has caused great havoc to humanity in modern times. Both men and women possess intimate or sexual instincts and desires to varying degrees. Sexual desire is a natural and normal instinct comparable to the desire for thirst and hunger.

In accordance with the Christian perspective, the body holds equal significance as the spirit and soul within God's creation. Consequently, the body has a specific purpose within God's divine plan.

Consider What This Means in Your Life

The teachings of the Bible emphasize that Christians should honor and bring glory to God through their bodies, recognizing them as the dwelling place of the Holy Spirit (1 Corinthians 6:13-20). As an act of worship, believers are encouraged to offer their bodies as living sacrifices to God (Romans 12:1).

You want intimacy, but your partner doesn't — and hasn't wanted it in a while. So, now what? When we deny intimacy, we are cheating on the marriage. In a marriage, when we withhold or deny intimacy, we are effectively breaking the vows we made to our spouse. This should be something that binds us, brings us closer together, and therefore ensures that we are connected on every level.

The Bible teaches that in the context of marriage, spouses have a duty to meet each other's needs, especially those related to intimacy. In 1 Corinthians 7:3-5, the apostle Paul addresses this and says,

"The husband should fulfill his marital duty to his wife, and likewise the wife to her husband. The wife does not have authority over her own body but yields it to her husband. In the same way, the husband does not have authority over his own body but yields it to his wife. Do not deprive each other except perhaps by mutual consent and for a time so that you may devote yourselves to prayer. Then come together again so that Satan will not tempt you because of your lack of self-control."

Paul asserts that a wife's body belongs to both herself and her husband and that a husband's body similarly belongs to both his wife and himself. We want to think about what this means to our relationship and to our life overall. The teachings of the Bible have a very important place here, as this is a fundamental aspect of marriage.

The Four Principles of Intimacy Between Couples

It's important to recognize and understand these four principles, as they hold a true place of importance in every marriage. You want to know what they are, and then ensure that your marriage embodies them. Intimacy is a part of any successful marriage.

Here's a brief list of four principles that can facilitate meaningful discussions between couples regarding the important topic of God-honoring sexual intimacy:

- Sexual intimacy in marriage is meant to glorify God.
- Sexual intimacy in marriage fosters unity between couples.
- Sexual intimacy in marriage should be regular and consistent.
- Sexual intimacy in marriage should prioritize the needs and desires of both partners.

Does It Matter That Much?

When couples are asked about the purpose of sexual intimacy according to God's plan, they usually respond by saying for pleasure, procreation, or love. While these responses are valid, it is essential to understand the overarching vision that guides and directs sexual intimacy within the context of marriage.

This perspective lifts sexual relations within marriage out of the negative influences of culture. If we acknowledge that humanity's ultimate purpose is to bring glory to God in all aspects of life, including sex, it becomes evident that this also applies to marital intimacy. In the beginning, God created Adam and Eve in His own image, placing them in the garden and instructing them to be fruitful and multiply, bringing glory to God through everything they did.

God intentionally made Adam and Eve in His image as gendered, sexual beings. Their gender identities are not mistakes but part of God's deliberate plan. The goodness of God's creation is evident in the way He intricately formed and designed men and women. Adam and Eve were purposefully created to bring glory to their Creator in every aspect of their lives.

Consider What These Teachings Mean

There was no division between the sacred and the secular and no separation between the soul and the body. Their entire existence was meant to honor and glorify God. The apostle Paul emphasizes this concept in his letter to the Corinthians.

In 1 Corinthians 10:31, Paul instructs the Corinthians that even the most ordinary activities, such as eating and drinking, should be done with the intention of glorifying God. If God has a plan for something as mundane as eating and drinking to be done in a way that brings Him glory, it should not be surprising that He has also provided a way for sexual intimacy to be good and worthy of glorification. This understanding underscores the importance of sexual intimacy within the context of God's purpose and design for humanity.

One partner (husband or wife) who wants a more intimate relationship will lack closeness if the other partner doesn't want to get intimate. It may weaken the emotional ties that bind partners together and contribute to a breakdown in trust and communication. You need to both be on the same page with this, though it is common to go through phases where you aren't. Be certain that you understand this, but that you also make it a priority.

It Is a Key to Thriving

There is no denying that sometimes marriages do survive in the absence of a sexual connection, but they will NOT thrive. The reasons for that could be varied. A couple could lose interest in sex after having children, or as they age, they might get busy with their careers and be okay with the intense and passionate routine taking a backseat. In such circumstances, the effects of lack of sex in marriage are not felt as acutely by either partner. However, when the man is interested in sex and his wife is not, the sexless marriage effect on a husband could be disastrous.

When couples do not maintain consistency in their sexual relationship, it opens the door to various temptations from Satan. These temptations can extend beyond sexual sins like lust, pornography, and adultery, to name a few of them. In fact, many will dibble in pornography as a "fair exchange justification" for abstinence...when it's really doing more harm than good. They can also manifest as feelings of being unloved, undesired, depressed, or insecure, which is particularly common for wives, especially after having children.

We All Need to Feel Loved and Needed

When the sexual union lacks consistency, wives may be prone to feeling unattractive and unloved, creating an opportunity for Satan to undermine their sense of self-worth within the marriage. Similarly, husbands, who often interact with members of the opposite sex outside the home, may be more susceptible to sexual temptations when the sexual union with their wives is inconsistent. *"Avoid sexual looseness like the plague! Every other sin that a man commits is done outside his own body, but this is an offense against his own body. Have you forgotten that your body is the temple of the Holy Spirit who lives in you and is God's gift to you, and that you are not the owner of your own body? You have been bought, and at what a price! Therefore, bring glory to God in your body"*

(1 Corinthians 6:18-20).

According to Ephesians 5:22, wives are encouraged to willingly submit to their husbands as they would submit to the Lord. This submission is not only a necessary requirement for a harmonious marriage but also a command from God. While the concept of submission may seem foolish to the world, believers understand it as wisdom. Many women have seen the positive effects of submission, leading their husbands to the Lord and preserving the unity of their homes.

Submission entails willingly placing oneself under the authority of another. In Ephesians 5:21-24, the apostle Paul conveys God's perspective on submission. He emphasizes the mutual submission of believers in fear of God and instructs wives to submit to their husbands as the head of the family, just as the church submits to Christ. This submission is to be practiced in all aspects of married life.

The Unifying Power of Sexual Intimacy: Strengthening the Bond in marriage

Sexual intimacy in marriage serves as a unifying force for couples. It is not only intended to bring glory to God but also to establish a deep bond between husband and wife, uniting them as one. We can find insight in the words of Genesis 2:22–25: "Then the LORD God made a woman from the rib he had taken out of the man, and he brought her to the man. The man said, 'This is now bone of my bones and flesh of my flesh; she shall be called 'woman,' for she was taken out of man.'" This profound intimacy between a man and a woman was always intended to occur within a specific context. It was not meant to be shared with just anyone but was designed to take place within the committed covenantal relationship of marriage, guided by God's presence and blessing. In the Bible, the act of sexual union between a man and a woman is described as "Knowing" one another. It is an intimate connection that goes beyond the physical realm and creates a mysterious bond between the two individuals involved. This union is not easily forgotten or disregarded. It has the power to unite the couple in a profound way, intertwining their lives on multiple levels.

In Genesis 2:24, it is written, "For this reason, a man shall leave his father and his mother and be joined to his wife, and they shall become one flesh." This verse highlights the profound oneness and unity that marriage brings, and one of the most profound expressions of this unity is found in the physical act of sexual intimacy. Through the sacred bond of marriage, a man and a woman are intimately connected in a way unlike any other experience they share together. In the act of sexual intercourse, they not only witness each other's vulnerability and nakedness, but they also embrace one another and become physically united, mirroring the spiritual oneness they share. It is fitting, therefore, that one of the initial acts after the wedding ceremony is the consummation of their union through the special and unifying act of sexual intercourse.

Regrettably, the potent force of sexual intimacy within marriage sometimes becomes a negative influence. Issues related to sex often play a significant role in marital breakdowns. When a couple allows their sex life to operate on autopilot, they run the risk of transforming the power of sex into a detrimental factor in their relationship. Of course, there are periods in every marriage where sexual intimacy may take a backseat. It would be unreasonable to expect a couple with three young children or a woman undergoing cancer treatment to prioritize sex above other pressing concerns. Many couples who neglect sexual intimacy do so out of mundane busyness, failing to make it a significant priority in their relationship.

It is not uncommon to hear individuals who are considering separation or divorce justify their actions by saying, "I'm not happy, and I know God wants me to be happy and fulfilled." It is true that God desires our happiness and fulfillment (John 10:10). We are created with a natural longing for satisfaction and contentment, and this longing is not inherently wrong. In fact, God has placed this desire within us. His primary desire is for us to find happiness and fulfillment in Him first and foremost before seeking it in other areas of our lives, including our marriages. True and lasting happiness can be found through a deep relationship with God, which then has a positive impact on our marriages and all other aspects of our lives.

We must constantly be reminded that marriage is a lovely representation of the bond between Christ and the church. The deep love between Christ and His followers is reflected and expressed in the emotional, intellectual, experiential, and sexual intimacy experienced by husband and wife. The church is lovingly nurtured and cherished by Christ, men are commanded to love their wives as they love their own bodies, and the marriage of husband and wife creates a profound oneness, according to Ephesians 5:28–31. Discovering satisfaction in God's presence ultimately leads to finding satisfaction in one another, including the realm of sexual intimacy.

It is important to recognize that engaging in premarital sex can have certain consequences and covenants that may hinder the possibility of marriage. By abstaining from sexual intercourse, these individuals could have fostered relationships that would have led to marriage. Once they allowed sexual intimacy to enter their relationships, the prospects of marriage often diminished.

When one engages in sexual activity with another person outside of marriage, it can have detrimental effects on their clarity of vision, weaken their connection with the Divine, and lead to various forms of bondage. I sincerely share this truth from my heart that negligence would be a disservice to God. Many of us had relationships that were a lesson and not a blessing. God's original intent was for us to become one flesh with one person, not many people. When someone has sex outside of marriage, they will enter into marriage with a sexual resume and begin comparing a sinful act to a holy covenant in their thoughts, and it may manifest in their action once in the bedroom. Many currently married people, if they could do it all over again, would have saved their sexual encounter for marriage. Your testimony should be that I don't want to compare nobody to my husband or wife when we consummate our marriage. Sex is a gift from God for married people.

I agree with the fact that, at some point, young people encounter temptations of unclean sexual thoughts. Men, in particular, may face a stronger and more aggressive sexual urge compared to women, leading to a greater struggle in this intimacy. In Mark 7:21, Jesus identifies evil thoughts as one of the primary issues that originate from the human heart. All unconverted individuals, as the condition of the heart, are universally fallen. Unclean thoughts can trouble the mind of a morally upright person just as much as they can affect someone engaged in immoral behavior. It's important to understand the distinction between temptation and sin. Even Jesus faced temptation in every aspect of His humanity but never yielded to it, remaining sinless. Similarly, we will face temptations throughout our lives, but we have the power to resist and refrain from sinning. Sin occurs when we accept lustful thoughts, allowing them to take root in our minds.

Indulging in lustful thinking can lead a person into deeper bondage, making it increasingly challenging to find deliverance. Seeking deliverance as early as possible makes the process easier. Job, despite being a married man with a family, understood the importance of exercising control over his eyes to safeguard himself from lustful thinking. He made a deliberate commitment, stating, "I made a covenant with my eyes not to look with lust upon a girl" (Job 31:1). If we are not cautious and allow impure thoughts or images to enter our minds through what we see, it becomes exceedingly challenging to remove them once they have taken root.

The Bible teaches that marriage is an honorable institution, and the sexual relationship within marriage is to be kept pure and sacred. Hebrews 13:4 emphasizes the importance of maintaining a pure and faithful bed while warning against the consequences of engaging in sexual immorality. Sexual intimacy is intended to be a seal of the marriage covenant, and any sexual activity outside of marriage is considered a violation of that covenant.

It is crucial to understand that within the context of marriage, sexual intercourse is a natural and God-given expression of love and procreation. God created human beings with reproductive organs to fulfill His command to be fruitful and multiply. In the fallen world, however, the misuse and perversion of sex have led to its degradation and distortion from its original purpose.

Christian marriages face opposition and are subject to attack, primarily from the enemy, Satan, who opposes God's plans. "Satan doesn't create anything, so he distorts everything." God always has our best interests at heart, and when our marriages thrive, Satan seeks to undermine and harm them. In 1 Peter 5:8, we are warned to be watchful and vigilant because our adversary, the devil, roams like a roaring lion, seeking someone to devour.

Satan is clearly aware that young people can quickly get caught in traps related to sex that can have a disastrous impact on their lives. God's Word contains instructions that are meant to protect us from the tricks that the enemy has laid for us. Particularly in the book of Proverbs, we find a lot of warnings, sage advice, and suggestions.

How to Make the Intimacy Work?

In a marriage, sexual well-being must be actively maintained. It might be tempting to overlook the vital component of sexual intimacy in the midst of life's hustle and stresses. Neglecting it, though, can make the relationship worse. It takes conscious nurturing to have a successful and mutually satisfying sexual relationship. Here's a list of a few important aspects to take into account when developing a healthy, intimate life.

Be Patient and Kind

At times, giving your spouse thoughtful presents or kind words can tremendously strengthen your bond and make it even more priceless. Have you heard of Elkanah and Hannah's? Let me tell you,

Elkanah had perfected the art of catering to his wife's emotional well-being because he was sensitive to her needs. "Am I not better to thee than ten sons," he was able to reassure Hannah. (8:1 Samuel).

Likewise, you should be aware that your wife may occasionally feel physically unwell, and the same goes for the husband. Love, care, and understanding have a healing impact on relationships. You can make the other feel better just by being a little more loving and caring toward them. An encouraging word from you, an expectation text message, a well-cooked meal with candles and some Teddy Pendergrass and Luther Vandross playing in the background, a relaxing tender touch, a kiss on the lips or side of the neck, a soothing voice. Laying with your life partner in your comfort zone. Feeling fingers running through your hair, a good scalp massage or a thoughtful gift can do wonders. These all regulate the nervous system. Schedule time to just be with your spouse. Your nervous system will thank you. Honesty is the highest form of intimacy. Safety is romantic. Having someone hold your hand and say let's talk about this. I've made the time in my day. We can work through this together. Do you want to share first, and I will just listen? Or should I go first?

Erase "I, Me, And Myself"

Several families and marriages have fallen apart as a result of the devastating power of selfishness, which frequently appears in the form of "Me, myself, and I." Contrarily, the foundation of marriage is respect for one another and selflessness. Jesus is the ideal model for us to follow since He willingly gave up His heavenly throne in order to spend thirty-three and a half years on Earth, displaying amazing selflessness.

We are reminded of the grace of our Lord Jesus Christ, who, despite being rich, willingly became poor for our sake. *"For ye know the grace of our Lord Jesus Christ, that, though he was rich, yet for your sakes, he became poor, that ye through his poverty might be rich."* (2 Corinthians 8:9).

Practice Obedience

Ephesians 5:22 clearly equates a wife's obedience to her husband with obedience to the Lord. The Living Bible translation emphasizes that a wife should submit to her husband "in the same way" she would revere God. This sheds light on Sarah's example of submitting to Abraham and even addressing him as lord. Those who desire to protect their souls from destruction should strive to obey this commandment. Keeping God's commandments safeguards one's soul, while despising them leads to negative consequences (Proverbs 19:16).

Effective Communication

Effective ongoing communication about intimacy is essential for couples, especially as various factors like children, work stress, financial pressures, illness, and aging can affect our sexual desires and needs. It's important to recognize that our sex drives may vary and change over time. Therefore, discussing sex should be an ongoing conversation that starts early in the relationship. This allows couples to address potential scenarios where one partner may be unable or unwilling to engage in sexual activity. If sexual intimacy is important to you and a significant aspect of your romantic relationship, the only way to ensure that both partners are on the same page is through open and honest communication.

Create a Balance

Achieving a sense of balance is crucial in marriage. While couples should have moments of genuine connection and attentive listening, they should also engage in shared activities that bring them joy, such as reading, exercising, watching movies, or traveling together. It's unfortunate that many couples enter marriage with the assumption that they have numerous shared interests, only to discover after the first year that their preferences diverge. During courtship, a woman may happily watch sports with her boyfriend simply because she cherishes his company. However, after marriage, she may decline to watch Sunday football games in favor of pursuing her own interests. Similarly, a man may accompany his girlfriend to the mall during courtship out of love for her presence, but in marriage, he may prefer staying home instead. It is not uncommon for initial passion to obscure the true essence of the person one is marrying, and couples should be mindful of this reality.

Couples should actively seek out activities they both enjoy, as this fosters and enhances intimacy. Christ, in His relationship with His disciples, exemplified the importance of sharing experiences and being together (cf. Matthew 17:1, John 15:15). To safeguard and nurture our marriages, it is wise to consider and plan for activities that can be enjoyed jointly, while also setting aside regular dates to engage in these shared endeavors. As Proverbs 21:5 states, "The plans of the diligent lead to profit as surely as haste leads to poverty."

Self- Awareness and Acceptance

A happy marriage requires both self-awareness and acceptance. Husband and wife have the chance to learn more about each other as well as themselves as a couple as they become more open with one another.

Both partners must feel comfortable asking genuine questions and seeking clarification when anything is unclear during the process of developing this understanding. It is essential to freely and honestly discuss any undesirable habits or patterns that one spouse observes in the other. Couples have the chance to collaborate on growth and improvement by talking about these challenges and bringing them to light.

How Far Should We Go?

The Scripture provides a nurturing environment for marital intimacy, but it is the gospel that serves as the essential foundation. It is through the gospel that our inherent selfishness, inability to forgive, and feelings of insecurity can be addressed. These deep-seated obstacles require the transformative power of the gospel to be fully overcome. However, the gospel directs our hearts towards Christ, who selflessly gave Himself up for our sake and bore the consequences of our sins. As we immerse ourselves in the good news of the gospel, we come to realize the immense love of God and the extent of our own shortcomings and sinfulness. By embracing the gospel, we are humbled by God's love and grace, which enables us to extend love, forgiveness, and security to our spouse. The gospel serves as a catalyst for personal transformation, leading to deeper intimacy in marriage as we reflect on the selflessness and sacrificial love of Christ.

Chapter 5

Expectations Unsaid Will Always Go Unmet

Our lives are shaped by our conscious or subconscious pursuit of fulfilling perceived needs, greatly influencing our decisions. This applies not only to various aspects of life but also to relationships. Whenever we sense a lack or incompleteness within ourselves, our existence in any relationship becomes an attempt, to varying degrees, to fill that void or achieve a sense of wholeness. When we feel inadequate, our entire relationship relies on that sentiment, leading us to depend on the other person to provide what we believe we lack.

Marriage is a remarkable relationship where two individuals express their desire for unconditional acceptance and lifelong love. However, being married doesn't automatically guarantee happiness, and the institution of marriage faces challenges.

Here's the Christian perspective on understanding the ideals of Christian marriage:

Jesus emphasized the sanctity of Christian marriage by referring to the creation account: 'Haven't you read that at the beginning the Creator 'made them male and female' and said, 'For this reason, a man will leave his father and mother and be united to his wife, and the two will become one flesh'? So, they are no longer two but one. Therefore, let no one separate what God has joined together.'

Consider a man who worked as a construction laborer, specifically in a company that specialized in building custom homes around a scenic lake. Among the various projects, one stood out as particularly intriguing and was appreciated by everyone. The homeowner had acquired a piece of land consisting of two sides of a ravine that extended down to the lake. To construct a house on this site, it was necessary to transport and deposit soil and rocks into the ravine until it reached its capacity. Subsequently, powerful machinery compressed the filled ravine, and pillars were then drilled into the ground until they reached the bedrock. This solid foundation supported the construction of a sizable dwelling in the long run.

Likewise, marriage, much like a house, is susceptible to erosion and collapse unless it rests upon sturdy pillars, requiring reinforcement for the relationship to stand strong.

The early stages of marriage are often filled with a sense of bliss, and the initial attraction and excitement during this phase can create a beautiful experience. It is a time when the couple is getting to know each other, and everything feels fresh and new. Their lives may revolve around each other at this stage. However, as time goes on, relationships naturally evolve, and accepting inevitability becomes crucial for the relationship to thrive. Love is responsive, not reactive. If your love is based on specific reasons, it becomes conditional since terms and conditions are subject to change. The physical appearance, weight, demeanor, and emotions of your spouse will inevitably change over time. However, when you love your spouse with agape love, the unconditional love of God, your love remains constant. While circumstances may fluctuate, true love remains steadfast and unchanging.

When you assign rigid roles within your marriage, you create expectations that often lead to unnecessary anger and frustration. This frustration can escalate into arguments, bitterness, and strife, ultimately straining the relationship and posing a risk to fellowship. True love expects nothing in return and operates without expectations.

It is common for couples to hold onto expectations they promise to meet at the beginning of their relationship. These expectations can become unrealistic as the marriage evolves over the years. Both partners become reluctant to embrace new changes and reasonable expectations that contribute to a satisfying and happy marriage.

Each individual has their own unique needs; there are certain reasonable expectations that can be considered fundamental in a marriage.

These expectations, often referred to as a "Bill of Marital Rights," focus on how each partner treats and respects the other. The significance placed on each expectation may vary between partners.

Jesus, as recounted in John 13:5, exemplified a servant's heart by humbly washing the feet of His disciples and drying them with a towel. His actions teach us the importance of seeking opportunities to serve rather than expecting to be served. Jesus didn't adhere to traditional roles or ask whose duty it was to wash feet; He simply responded to the need. Avoid placing the burden of all household tasks, such as cooking, washing, and cleaning, on one person. By not having such expectations, you prevent disappointment when those tasks aren't fulfilled. Moreover, when your spouse chooses to bless you unexpectedly by taking on a responsibility, you will be more inclined to express gratitude and appreciation.

Roles within a marriage should be temporary and based on the ability of the person who can respond to the particular need at that moment. Responsibility should be determined by both availability and capability. If you come across water on the floor, don't simply stand there, assuming it's your spouse's responsibility because they usually handle mopping. Instead, take the initiative and respond to the situation.

If you have the ability to address it, then it becomes your responsibility. In accordance with the words from 1 Corinthians 9:22, the principle of becoming "All Things" should guide your roles within your marriage. When worldly matters and desires take precedence over

God and your spouse, it inevitably leads to problems within your home.

The nature of sexual intimacy is temporary and subject to constant change. Therefore, relying solely on it as a foundation for your relationship is unwise, as it lacks trustworthiness. Commitment, not sex, is what truly sustains a marriage. Sexual intimacy is a result of the commitment found within a marital union. If your marriage relies solely on the sexual aspect, it cannot be solely broken by it either.

When communicating with your spouse, it is essential to recognize that their personal history may influence how they interpret your words, potentially leading to different meanings than what you intended.

To truly understand how to love your wives, men should study Christ's love for His church, as described in the Bible, which serves as the ultimate guidebook for love. God does not compare your marriage to those of others, including siblings, parents, or friends; instead, He compares it to the relationship between Christ and His church, setting the standard for marriage.

As husbands, the greatest testimony of Christ's love that you can offer is to love your wife as He loved the church. Our communities need men who embody the teachings of the Bible and understand the essence of true love.

Your wife longs to hear expressions of love and affirmation such as *"I love you," "You're beautiful,"* and *"You're precious to me.*" On the other hand, husbands often appreciate physical affection, such as a gentle touch on the head or neck while driving. Communication and physical affection are essential ways to connect with your spouse.

In 1 Corinthians 7:34, it is stated that married individuals are concerned with pleasing their spouse. Wives need not wait for their husbands to initiate sexual intimacy; they are encouraged to take the initiative themselves. Marriage does not require either partner to sacrifice their dreams and aspirations. Both individuals have their own needs and desires for personal fulfillment and success.

The person you married is not an exact replica of yourself. When unique or unusual qualities and differences between spouses come together, they create the precious gem that your marriage was meant to be. In Ephesians 5:25–27, husbands are instructed to love their wives just as Christ loved the church, sacrificially and with the intention of presenting them as a glorious and pure entity.

Your wedding ring serves as a symbol to the world that you are committed to another person and are not seeking anyone else, regardless of where you go. Always remember to wear it as a constant reminder of your commitment. Rather than competing with each other, the focus should be on complementing and supporting one another. Embrace the concept of completing each other, not competing.

As stated in 1 Peter 3:7, husbands are encouraged to be

considerate and respectful towards their wives, recognizing their inherent value and treating them as equal heirs of the gift of life. It is important to maintain a harmonious relationship with your spouse so that your prayers are not hindered.

Prioritize love, care, compassion, sensitivity, and attentiveness to your wife's needs. While God is paramount, He has connected the efficacy of your prayers to your relationship with your spouse. Therefore, loving your wife also safeguards your prayers.

The male figure plays a foundational role in the family. When a man neglects his responsibilities or leaves home, the family structure becomes unstable, akin to a house built on sand. The absence of a male presence leaves the household vulnerable to strain and instability during challenging times. Men should embrace their role as the foundation they were meant to be. By providing stability and support, you become someone your wife and children can rely on without fear of crumbling under pressure.

Our Expectations in marriage

In both religious and secular contexts, our society has established certain expectations for the institution of marriage. Let's explore some of these expectations:

Marriage Will Fulfill Our Needs

These needs include the desire for affection and sexual intimacy, the need for meaningful conversation, the longing for financial security, the aspiration to establish a separate home, the yearning for social acceptance, the wish for a family, and the need for companionship. These expectations often stem from valid and even God-given desires. However, problems arise when we pursue these desires with short-sighted strategies and motives.

Many individuals enter into marriage with the expectation that it will solve their existing problems. For instance, a daughter who is no longer able to endure her father's anger or the criticism from her stepmother may choose to get married simply as a means of escaping her current living situation. Likewise, a son who feels unappreciated by his parents may view marriage as an opportunity to find the personal affirmation he craves. Unfortunately, those who enter into marriage solely to solve their problems often find themselves facing the distress of a divorce, expressing statements such as, *"She [or he] is just not meeting my needs, your honor."*

There Will Be "No" Argument

One common complaint heard in relationships is, "We argue about the smallest things." These seemingly trivial conflicts often mask deeper underlying issues related to unmet expectations. It is not necessarily the small matters themselves that cause distress but rather the unfulfilled expectations that may accumulate over time. These unaddressed expectations can create a sense of frustration and resentment, gradually eroding the harmony within the relationship.

High Standards

Setting high standards for our partners can be a double-edged sword. While it is important to have certain expectations in relationships, excessively high or unrealistic expectations can place immense pressure on our partners. The constant need to meet these lofty standards can leave them feeling stressed, overwhelmed, and inadequate. This can create a toxic cycle where partners feel constantly judged and unable to live up to the expectations set for them.

Expecting your partner to never irritate or frustrate you is ridiculous. Since nobody is flawless, conflicts will inevitably arise in any relationship. Negative emotions should be handled with empathy and compassion rather than with wrath. Consider your partner's perspective for a time and look at the dispute as a chance for development and reconciliation. Remember that when handled correctly and constructively, conflict may actually deepen your relationship.

The biblical passage Proverbs 27:5–6 (NIV) provides enlightening advice on the significance of constructive criticism and honest communication in relationships. It implies that it is better to directly express true worries or problems rather than to keep them hidden, as doing so can result in unsolved difficulties and damage the connection. The passage also emphasizes the reliability of wounds or corrections from a good friend, showing that candid criticism, even when it is uncomfortable, may be beneficial for relationship and personal development.

People can develop healthier and more genuine relationships with their loved ones by embracing open communication and facing issues head-on.

Four Important Expectations in a marriage

The happiness we experience in our relationships can be greatly influenced by the expectations we hold. There are four key expectations that play a significant role in shaping our relationship dynamics:

1. **Connection:** This expectation revolves around the desire to feel emotionally connected and understood by our partner. We long for a deep bond where we can share our thoughts, feelings, and experiences, knowing that our partner will listen and empathize.

2. **Passion:** The expectation of passion involves the desire for mutual attraction, romance, and physical desire within the

relationship. We seek a spark that ignites passion and keeps the flame of intimacy alive.

3. **Destiny:** This expectation relates to our beliefs about the future of the relationship. We may hold the belief that the relationship is destined to succeed effortlessly or that it requires continuous effort and commitment to thrive. Our outlook on the long-term potential of the relationship influences our expectations and level of investment.

4. **Immediacy:** Immediacy expectations pertain to the pace at which love and connection should develop in a healthy relationship. Some may expect love to blossom quickly, while others prefer a gradual progression. These expectations can influence our perception/thinking of the relationship's progress and level of satisfaction.

The Expectations that God Holds for marriage

"But you say, "Why does he not?" Because the LORD was witness between you and the wife of your youth, to whom you have been faithless, though she is your companion and your wife by covenant."

– Malachi 2:14 (ESV).

The expectations God holds for marriage often differ significantly from our own. According to God's perspective, marriage is intended to be a union rooted in a mutual spirit of love. The Bible teaches that when a man and woman enter into marriage, they become one, with their oneness being sustained by their shared commitment to care for each other's well-being throughout their lives. This divine expectation of love requires us to prioritize bringing out the best in our spouses rather than focusing on their shortcomings. When we choose to serve and meet the needs of our partner, we are ultimately serving God. It is crucial to ensure that our commitment to marriage does not overshadow our commitment to the Lord and our dependence on Him.

God expects that marriage will transform us positively. Scripture does not instruct us to demand that our spouse love us, respect us, or fulfill all our emotional, financial, and physical needs. The Bible does not guarantee that God will mold our partners into the individuals we desire them to be. Instead, marriage, by its very nature, calls for our own spiritual growth. To experience genuine spiritual connection within marriage, we must continually strive for personal spiritual development. A marriage designed by God will foster qualities such as faithful love, honesty, moral courage, true humility, and extraordinary patience.

The third and paramount expectation that God has for marriage is that it reflects the relationship between Christ and the church. God desires that husbands and wives develop an enduring love by keeping their focus on the sacred union between Christ and His church. The apostle Paul, in his teachings, encourages both husbands and wives to understand their roles in light of this relationship. He writes, "For this reason, a man will leave his father and mother and be united to his wife, and the two will become one flesh." Paul explains that this union is a profound mystery that illustrates the unity between Christ and the church.

These divine expectations elevate us beyond ourselves and call for a love that originates from God. A fulfilling marriage is not simply a contractual agreement between a man and a woman; it is a sacred covenant involving three parties: the husband, the wife, and God. A biblical covenant is founded on the sovereignty of God. Therefore, when one or both partners fail to acknowledge God's authority in their marriage, it begins to drift away from His blessing. The Lord, in His wisdom, has brought each of us together with our respective spouses, and a marriage encompasses more than just the person we pledged to love, honor, and cherish. It also involves the vow we made before God on our wedding day.

Do Not Set Unrealistic Expectations

Unrealistic expectations often remain unspoken, lurking within our minds. These are the expectations where we anticipate our spouse to have the ability to read our thoughts, knowing exactly what we want and how we want things done. (For instance, knowing the precise way to fold towels – or maybe that's just specific to my marriage.) Our partners cannot read our minds as much as we may wish they could; unfortunately, it is simply not a realistic expectation.

Here are some instances of unrealistic expectations in a marriage:

- Expecting your spouse to be solely responsible for your happiness. You need to understand that individual happiness is a personal responsibility that cannot be placed entirely on your partner.

- Believing that your spouse will "complete" you. While a spouse can be a source of companionship and support, relying on them to fulfill all your needs and make you whole is unrealistic.

- Assuming that the person you married will never change. Change is a natural part of life, and both individuals in a marriage are likely to undergo personal growth and transformations.

- Believing that your spouse's life should revolve entirely around you. Each person in the relationship is an individual with their own interests, and a healthy marriage involves supporting each other's individuality.

- Thinking that all your time should be spent together. While spending quality time together is important, it's healthy for each partner to have their own interests and hobbies that they can pursue independently.

- Insisting that your way is always the right way. Let me tell you that successful marriages require compromise, understanding, and respect for each other's differing perspectives and backgrounds.

Having expectations in a marriage is natural, but it's crucial to approach them with open communication and a willingness to compromise and understand. If one of you struggles with unrealistic expectations or is unwilling to compromise, seeking the assistance of a marriage professional counselor who is invested in the success of your marriage can be beneficial in navigating challenges and finding solutions.

Here are four ways to resolve "Great Expectations"

Here are four approaches to addressing "great expectations" in a relationship:

Uphold your commitment to love and forgiveness made on your wedding day

Remain dedicated to your partner and prioritize love. Remember the biblical advice that "love covers a multitude of sins" (1 Peter 4:8), emphasizing the importance of forgiveness and understanding.

Foster Effective Communication and Mutual Understanding

Communication involves both speaking and actively listening. True understanding is achieved when you can accurately express your partner's needs and desires, and they agree with your understanding. Open and honest communication is essential for clarifying each other's needs. The Bible encourages husbands to "live with their wives in an understanding way" (1 Peter 3:7), which requires seeking to understand as men and assisting women in making themselves understood.

Cultivate a God-centered perspective of your spouse

Remember that your spouse was chosen for you by God. Accept this divine provision, recognizing that unmet expectations may be a part of God's larger plan for your life. Seek to align your perspective with God's perspective and purpose for your relationship.

Maintain hope and pursue shared dreams

Although some of the expectations you had for your marriage may not be fulfilled, it's important not to give up on your dreams. God may have new dreams and aspirations for you as a couple. Engage in conversations about your individual and shared dreams, and encourage each other to dream together, allowing for the possibility of a fulfilling future.

Sow the Seed of Blessings in Your marriage!

In the intricate spiral of marriage, unspoken expectations are the silent culprits that sow seeds of disappointment and unmet desires. Like a forgotten melody, they linger in the air, waiting to be acknowledged. However, expectations left unsaid will forever go unmet. To create a harmonious symphony of love, communication must reign supreme. Let your words be the bridge that connects hearts, your desires, and the lyrics that echo in unison.

For in the realm of marriage, where expectations are shared and understood, the melody of fulfillment will resound, and love will flourish in its sweetest harmony. When your focus is solely on pursuing the ideal person you desire, you risk losing sight of your own identity. Instead, God desires for you to be deeply devoted to His Kingdom and righteousness so that anyone you encounter becomes, above all, a fellow traveler on the same path. Furthermore, they should be at a similar point of progress and growth as you.

Unlocking the door to successful management of expectations in relationships lies in cultivating healthy relationship expectations and choosing not to be easily offended. However, the true catalyst for growth in this realm lies in prayer and spending meaningful time with God. By seeking guidance, wisdom, and strength from the Divine, we embark on a transformative journey toward understanding, empathy, and grace. Through this spiritual connection, we gain the perspective needed to navigate the complexities of expectations with humility, compassion, and love. As we align our hearts with God's guidance, our relationships thrive, and our souls find solace in the abounding peace that comes from surrendering our expectations to the hands of the Divine.

Chapter 6

The Season of Financial Stress

Love is in the air, but so are financial problems. It is indeed a common challenge for couples and can have a significant impact on their relationship. When couples face financial difficulties, it can create tension, arguments, and disagreements, which can strain the emotional connection between partners.

Financial stress and marriage can often bring forth disagreements, secrets, and conflicts that strain the relationship. When faced with financial stress, feelings of disappointment, frustration, and unexpected surprises can overwhelm your life. It is completely natural for couples to become frayed, and your perspective may feel chaotic.

A recent study conducted by Northwestern Mutual states that financial stress is the top cause of stress among adults in the United States. Unfortunately, this stress often spills over into our romantic relationships. The study revealed that 40% of respondents reported that money issues had impacted their relationships with their partners. Additionally, 1 in 5 respondents admitted to having financial disagreements with their significant others on a monthly basis.

"If therefore ye have not been faithful in the unrighteous mammon, who will commit to your trust the true riches?" (Luke 16:11). This verse highlights the importance of our faithfulness in handling earthly wealth or money. It suggests that if we are not responsible and faithful in managing material possessions, we cannot expect God to entrust us with the true riches of His kingdom.

The Bible contains over 2,000 verses related to money and possessions, underscoring the significance of this subject in the eyes of the Lord. How we handle money is intertwined with our spiritual lives. By aligning our financial practices with biblical principles of stewardship, we can grow closer to Christ. The parable of the Talents (Matthew 25:14-30) illustrates this connection.

In the parable, the master commends and rewards the servant who faithfully managed the money entrusted to him, saying, "Well done" and inviting him to share in his joy. Another servant, who hid his money and did not invest it wisely, does not receive the same commendation. The parable suggests that the way we handle money can serve as an indicator of our spiritual condition.

The Bible exhorts believers to be content and have faith in God's provision, even during hard times. This sentiment is expressed in Philippians 4:11–13 (NIV): "I have learned to be satisfied no matter the circumstances. I understand what it's like to have plenty of things and what it's like to be in need. I now know how to find contentment in every circumstance, whether one is well-fed or hungry when one is in abundance or want." The letter to the Philippians by the apostle Paul stresses the value of learning to be content in every circumstance, especially in difficult financial times. It emphasizes the idea that genuine satisfaction comes from a deep-seated trust in God's provision and a realization that true contentment is not found in worldly possessions or outside situations. Paul's words emphasize the importance of cultivating a mindset of gratitude, regardless of whether one is experiencing abundance or scarcity. The key lies in learning to rely on God's strength and finding contentment in His presence rather than being solely dependent on external circumstances for happiness.

Furthermore, husbands are called to display generosity and a spirit of giving. Ephesians 5:25-28 states, "Husbands, love your wives, as Christ loved the church and gave himself up for her… In the same way, husbands should love their wives as their own bodies." This love extends to financial matters as well; husbands are encouraged to sacrificially give to their families and provide not only for their basic needs but also for their well-being and happiness.

The Power Imbalance between Couples – Let's Talk About It!

Love often unites couples; financial matters can sometimes be the cause of their separation. Some couples don't necessarily care about financial inequality since they place more value on other parts of their relationship than money. They can see it as unimportant as long as one partner can make a sufficient contribution to household expenditures. However, it becomes essential for the other spouse to make obligations in various ways, such as by offering emotional support and actively helping with household chores and child care.

On the other hand, some people believe that financial imbalance in a relationship is substantial. Those who make more money than their spouses might wonder if it's a good idea to get married to someone who makes less income.

The majority of societies hold the view that a male should be the primary breadwinner. However, some also hold that both partners should make a contribution. One partner may become secretive if they feel it is unfair because they earn more money. And mostly, the conflict between couples that is exacerbated by financial disparity frequently results in divorce.

Several circumstances can give rise to power plays in relationships, including:

When one partner is employed and the other is not:

This situation can lead to imbalances in decision-making and financial control. The employed partner may feel a sense of power or authority, while the unemployed partner may feel dependent or lacking influence.

When both partners desire employment, but one is currently unemployed:

Similar to the first circumstance, the unemployed partner may feel a loss of power and control over their own financial situation. This can create frustration and potentially strain the relationship.

When there is a significant income disparity between the partners:

Income disparity can create a power dynamic where the partner with higher income may have more control over financial decisions and may inadvertently hold more influence in the relationship. This can lead to feelings of inequality and resentment.

When one partner hails from an affluent family while the other does not:

Financial disparities can exacerbate power dynamics and conflict within a partnership. A partner from a wealthy family can have different expectations or views toward money, which could cause conflicts and even power struggles.

Couples should be candid with one another about their financial hopes, objectives, and worries. Power disputes can be lessened by finding common ground, establishing joint financial objectives, and creating a sense of equality and cooperation in decision-making.

How Does Financial Stress Impact Intimacy in a Relationship?

Did you know that stress about money might impact your sex drive?

Having a secure financial future doesn't exactly have a seductive ring to it, but how you feel about money has a direct bearing on your sex life. Financial stress can have a pervasive impact on your moods, and yes, it can spill over into the bedroom when you're worried about putting food on the table, paying the rent tomorrow, or simply how to pay any bill.

Sad to say, but the link between stress and libido exists. Consider the exhilaration you experienced when receiving a coveted job offer or a well-deserved pay raise. These financial milestones not only enhanced your self-assurance but also boosted your overall sense of self-worth. Surprisingly, this newfound confidence can have a positive impact on your intimate moments. When we feel self-assured, we are more inclined to embrace our sexuality.

For instance, you might not believe that your choice of attire influences your sex life, but when you exude confidence and feel good about yourself, you are more likely to be open to sexual experiences. Confidence, undoubtedly, plays a significant role in fostering a satisfying and fulfilling intimate connection.

Contrarily, you may be suffering in bed if the repercussions of the economic world weigh heavily on you. Research conducted by the *American Psychological Association* revealed that financial worries were a significant source of stress in relationships, with 71% of adults indicating that money was a major cause of their stress (APA, 2020).

When one partner is struggling financially, they frequently end up working too much—putting in long hours, taking on more jobs, or being focused on financial planning. This might lead to a lack of quality time spent together because there is little time and energy left over for intimacy. Physical, mental, and emotional tiredness can result from financial stress. A partner's thoughts might be completely consumed by the concerns and obligations involved with handling financial challenges, leaving little time for intimacy or relaxation. Instead of participating in intimate activities, one should prioritize rest and refreshment during the given time.

In relationships, some individuals may resort to passive-aggressive behavior, such as withholding sex, as a means of expressing their anger or seeking retribution. However, there is a scientific explanation for the connection between increased stress and a decrease in sex drive. When we encounter stress, our body's nervous system triggers a fight-or-flight response, leading to the release of stress hormones like cortisol and epinephrine. However, when stress becomes chronic, and these harmful hormones persist in our system, it can have various negative effects on our overall physical health. Specifically, cortisol has the ability to suppress our sex hormones, ultimately diminishing our libido.

The Bitter Fact!

There's no denying the impact of stress on libido. Whether it's due to the immediate effects of elevated stress hormones like cortisol or the secondary effects such as fatigue and conflicts, stress can significantly dampen sexual desire and activity. This decrease in sexual intimacy can take a toll on the overall relationship.

But there's good news; a few steps can be taken to address this issue:

Learn how to handle stress and give self-care priority.

One of the finest methods to reduce stress is through exercise. The fastest method to "blow off steam" is to do this.

Be the first to resolve the issues.

Fortunately, there is Good News: attaining financial security can positively impact your sex life and help restore it to a desired state. The peace of mind that comes from being able to meet financial obligations, as well as the sense of achievement from financial successes, can have a compelling influence on our desires and serve as a significant catalyst for boosting libido.

Tolstoy's Anna Karenina famously states, *"All happy families are alike; each unhappy family is unhappy in its own way."*

In reality, money doesn't simply appear out of thin air. If you are already facing financial constraints and an unexpected bill arrives, there is no miraculous solution to instantly resolve the situation.

If not approached cautiously and with timely financial assistance, the consequences of money-related stress can extend beyond mere financial strain. It's important not to let money issues in marriage destroy your bond with your spouse.

Financial problems don't have to cast a constant shadow over a couple's life. By seeking financial planning specifically designed for couples and addressing the root causes contributing to financial issues in marriage, you can prevent financial dishonesty from taking hold and maintain financial harmony in your relationship.

So, How Should We Do It?

The following tips on managing money in a marriage can assist you in navigating and overcoming the stress caused by financial challenges, allowing you to build a solid and successful partnership.

Talk Openly, Communicate Effectively

Financial stress often gives rise to numerous unanswered questions and mounting pressures, leading to thoughts like, "What will our future hold?" or "How can we navigate this challenging situation?" During these times, it is crucial for married couples to come together and face the situation as a united front. Engage in honest and open conversations with one another. Transparency is key to overcoming financial stress in a marriage. Avoid keeping any secrets from your spouse, as open communication is vital in finding solutions and alleviating the strain.

Together, establish a shared direction that both of you can fully support. Once you have set your path, move forward with confidence in each other's abilities, knowing that you are working together to conquer the financial stress in your marriage. By fostering trust, communication, and mutual support, you can effectively navigate financial challenges and strengthen your bond as a couple.

Create a Contingency Plan – Don't Forget to Save

Making a contingency plan is a smart move for couples to be

ready for unforeseen circumstances. Setting aside money from your budget to create an emergency fund is crucial. The amount you save is up to you, but it's important to get into the habit of putting money aside for unforeseen expenses.

Think forward to any unforeseen events and make sure you have a strategy in place to handle them. Not simply severe catastrophes or job loss might take you by surprise. Daily occurrences like your washing machine, vacuum cleaner, and cooker all failing at once can also require financial care.

Establish Budget

Couples can efficiently manage their resources and align their priorities by creating a combined financial plan and budget. It allows partners to address potential differences in spending preferences and prevent ongoing disagreements, particularly in areas of discretionary expenses. By collaborating on budgeting decisions, couples can allocate a dedicated portion of funds for individual expenditures while also collectively determining shared financial goals.

This approach fosters transparency, provides a clear financial framework, and minimizes conflicts related to money matters.

Learn to Compromise

There will probably always be a spender and a saver in a marriage, which will always cause financial tension. Arguments and stubbornness on either side might make the marriage's financial difficulties worse. Philippians 4:11–13 highlights how crucial it is to find contentment in every situation, whether there is abundance or lack. It inspires believers to practice gratitude and to derive strength from Christ to overcome difficulties.

To deal with financial stress in a marriage, the couple needs to work together effectively, plan ahead, and be committed to finding a solution that has their shared consent.

Do Not Be Shy to Accept Help

Any marriage can be severely burdened by financial hardship, but many couples find it difficult to accept help.

Why? The short response is Pride.

Therefore, if you want to resolve this, put your ego in its place and don't feel shy about asking for help. Accept the generosity of a friend or family member if they can assist you in getting back on track. Don't let your intransigence spoil your relationship.

In some cases, financial bullying can occur within a marriage, which is a form of abuse. Financial bullying manifests as the withholding of funds, access restrictions, debt concealment, or the imposition of rigid spending and budgeting guidelines.

Avoid Debt

"The rich ruleth over the poor, and the borrower is servant to the lender."

(Proverbs 22:7)

Why is debt such a problem? Debt places the borrower in a position of dependency on someone else. It creates an obligation to repay the debt, which limits our freedom to allocate our financial resources as we wish. The greater our debt burden, the less freedom we have to make choices about how to use our money. The Bible urges us to live within our means and forewarns us about the potential dangers of debt. Couples should refrain from taking on extra debt and cooperate to pay off any already incurred debt as soon as possible. Be careful and try to handle your finances and marriage God's way.

Have Faith

Christian couples must remain composed under such circumstances and grow closer to God through prayer and faith. Psalm 46:1 states that "God is our refuge and strength, a very present help in trouble." God can weather the storm and guide them through the crisis safely with divine wisdom, grace, and favor. Let God guide you financially.

Count Your Blessings

Though troubles may abound and hardships may weigh you down, don't let your spirit drown in the sorrows that surround you. For amidst the darkness, blessings can still be found. Count your blessings, yes, count them one by one, in every situation, under the moon or shining sun. "The blessing of the Lord brings wealth, without painful toil for it." Proverbs 10:22 (NIV). Remember that blessings can be found in unexpected places, and maintaining a grateful perspective can bring positivity and resilience during tough times.

Stay in Control

You could feel like giving up and stating, "I don't care anymore." When financial pressures mount, it's easy to feel overwhelmed and lose control. But remember, you have the power to turn things around. Refuse to be driven to a breaking point; take control of the situation instead. Make wise decisions that align with your long-term goals. It's time to take charge and be proactive in managing your money.

Seek Help from a Financial Advisor

Consider seeking the guidance of a financial advisor as you navigate important aspects of financial planning, such as retirement and investments. Planning for retirement and making investment decisions can be complex and risky without proper knowledge and expertise.

When engaging in financial planning for married couples, it is beneficial to find a reputable, unbiased, and trustworthy financial advisor who can provide valuable support. A professional advisor can offer insights and expertise tailored to your specific needs, helping you make informed decisions and avoid costly mistakes.

If your budget doesn't currently allow for hiring a financial advisor, you can still take steps to educate yourself. Conduct research on retirement planning and investment opportunities, seeking reliable sources of information. However, when the opportunity arises, it is advisable to have your financial plans professionally reviewed to ensure you are on the right track and avoid any potential pitfalls.

Eight Lessons on Biblical Principles of Financial Handling

The God's Part

"Thine, O LORD, is the greatness, and the power, and the glory, and the victory, and the majesty: for all that is in the heaven and in the earth is thine; thine is the kingdom, O LORD, and thou art exalted as head above all. Both riches and honor come of thee, and thou reignest over all, and in thine, the hand is power and might; and in thine hand, it is to make great, and to give strength unto all."

(1 Chronicle 29:11-12)

The Lord is clearly identified as the Creator and rightful owner of everything in the Bible. We must understand that we don't actually "own" our possessions. God has given us the duty of taking care of His property as stewards. To fully enable Jesus Christ to rule over our lives and our belongings, we must come to grips with this reality.

Ownership belongs to God, and stewardship is our responsibility. A steward is someone who looks after or manages the property of another person. Faithfulness is the main criterion for a steward (1 Corinthians 4:2). In order to be a loyal steward, we must first relinquish our right to ownership.

Counsel

Unfortunately, pride and stubbornness can hinder us from seeking the guidance we need. Pride convinces us that seeking help is a sign of weakness, while stubbornness refuses to accept that we may need to make adjustments in our financial decisions. Proverbs 12:15 says, *"The way of a fool is right in his own eyes: but he that hearkeneth unto counsel is wise."*

One significant source of counsel is the Scripture itself. The Bible provides us with timeless wisdom and guidance regarding financial matters. When faced with a specific issue, the first step is to turn to the Word of God and seek what it says about the matter at hand.

Asking God directly through prayer, meditation, and listening for the *"Still, Small Voice"* of the Holy Spirit (Psalm 32:8) is the most crucial source of advice. Knowing God's will in a situation will reassure, inspire, and comfort us.

Honesty

Leviticus 19:11 states, *"You shall not steal, neither deal falsely, neither lies to one another."* The Bible contains numerous verses emphasizing the importance of honesty in our lives. In the Ten Commandments, we find clear admonitions against stealing and bearing false witness (Exodus 20:15-16). Honesty is not just a sporadic choice but a way of life that should permeate all our actions.

The Bible teaches us the principle of treating others as we would like to be treated, known as the golden rule (Luke 6:31). The Apostle Paul also reinforces this concept in Philippians 2:4. Honesty is a fundamental aspect of how we interact with others, demonstrating respect and integrity in our relationships.

The influence of our peers can be powerful, whether for good or bad. To maintain our commitment to honesty, it is wise to avoid close association with those who engage in dishonest behavior (1 Corinthians 15:33). While we may occasionally find ourselves in the company of dishonest individuals, we should carefully consider the character of our close friends and business associates, prioritizing honesty in those relationships.

Giving

Acts 20:35, *"I have shown you all things, how that so laboring ye ought to support the weak, and to remember the words of the Lord Jesus, how he said, it is more blessed to give than to receive."*

Our attitude plays a significant role in giving, as emphasized in Scripture. In 1 Samuel 16:7, God reminded Samuel that while humans focus on outward appearances, the Lord looks at the heart. Therefore, our giving doesn't impress God if it lacks a genuine attitude of love (1 Corinthians 13:3). The way we live matters more than the amount we give. Jesus exemplified this principle when He praised the widow who offered two small coins, which represented her entire livelihood (Mark 12:41-44).

Her sacrificial giving demonstrated a profound attitude of devotion. Likewise, our giving should stem from a willing heart, driven by love and not by a sense of obligation (2 Corinthians 9:7). When our giving reflects such an attitude; it becomes a heartfelt expression of faith, gratitude, and compassion.

Work

Colossians 3:23-24, *"And whatsoever ye do, do it heartily, as to the Lord, and not unto men; knowing that of the Lord ye shall receive the reward of the inheritance: for ye serve the Lord Christ."*

Right from creation, God assigned duties and responsibilities to Adam as the caretaker of Eden (Genesis 2:15). And when God instructed the Israelites to rest on the seventh day, He reminded them that they were to work on the other six days. In the New Testament, Paul gives this mandate to the Thessalonians: ". . . if any would not [is not willing to] work, neither should he eat" (2 Thessalonians 3:10).

Many passages in scripture promote diligence in work and condemn laziness (Prov. 18:9). Employment not only enables us to provide for our families, but it also develops conscientious work habits, which help build godly character.

Investment

Proverbs 21:5 states that diligent thoughts and actions lead to abundance, while haste and impatience often result in a lack or want. The Bible does not condemn money itself but warns against the love of money, as it can be the root of various evils (1 Timothy 6:10). Jesus taught this principle through the parable of the "rich fool," which focused solely on accumulating earthly treasures for himself without considering the needs of others (Luke 12:20-21, 34). His investment was imbalanced, lacking generosity and trust in God for security.

From these teachings, we learn that not all investment goals are commendable. Scripture encourages us to approach financial matters with wisdom, recognizing the importance of diligence, integrity, and a balanced perspective. It reminds us to prioritize generosity, be mindful of the needs of others, and cultivate a trusting relationship with God rather than relying solely on wealth and possessions for security.

Perspective

"Not that I speak in respect of want: for I have learned, in whatsoever state I am, therewith to be content. I know both how to be abased, and I know how to abound: everywhere and in all things, I am instructed both to be full and to be hungry, both to abound and to suffer need. I can do all things through Christ which strengtheneth me."

(Philippians 4:11-13)

God does not oppose us from enjoying a comfortable lifestyle. However, it emphasizes the importance of adhering to the principles found in His Word. These principles guide us to exercise wisdom and caution against excessive indulgence or materialism. Contentment in every circumstance, along with reliance on Christ's strength, allows us to navigate life's ups and downs with a balanced perspective and a focus on eternal values.

Eternity

"For what shall it profit a man if he shall gain the whole world and lose his own soul?"

(Mark 8:36)

The Apostle Paul addressed the Corinthians, cautioning them against the mindset of those who live solely for the pleasures of this world, disregarding the reality of eternity. In contrast, believers in Christ understand that our earthly existence is brief, while eternal life stretches beyond. Recognizing this truth, God has graciously given us time and opportunity to prepare for the eternal life that awaits us.

The concept of eternity serves as a valuable lens through which we can wisely manage our resources. Scripture reminds us that we are temporary residents in this world, journeying as strangers and pilgrims (Hebrews 13:14). As we navigate through life, we should be mindful that excessive accumulation of material possessions can hinder our journey and divert our focus. Instead, we should seek to possess only what is necessary for our well-being, to serve God, and to facilitate our journey toward our ultimate destination.

What's Next?

Money is constantly present in our lives, often portraying itself as a seemingly daunting problem. However, beneath the surface, it holds the power to unveil deeper aspects of our lives that may require transformation, growth, or a shift in perspective. It serves as a catalyst for personal development, urging us to examine our values, beliefs, and behaviors related to finances.

Initiating and nurturing a healthy relationship with money is a valuable endeavor that can be pursued at any stage of life. Getting started may seem daunting, but it is never too early or too late to embark on this journey. Once you have taken the first step, make a commitment to engage in ongoing discussions with your partner, even if they may feel uncomfortable or inconvenient at times.

Indeed, seeking God's wisdom and guidance is crucial for couples in managing financial obligations. Proverbs 3:5-6 provides a powerful reminder to trust in the Lord wholeheartedly and not rely solely on human understanding. Prayer serves as a means of seeking God's guidance and seeking His will in financial matters. Studying the Scriptures is another essential aspect of seeking God's wisdom. The Bible contains in-depth discussions and details about principles and teachings on money, stewardship, contentment, and effective financial management. Immerse yourself in God's Word and understand His principles to make informed decisions that honor God and benefit your families.

Chapter 7

How do you Love Again with the Same Heart that was Broken?

"A thousand half-loves must be forsaken to take one whole heart home."

~Rumi

There is no denying that we were born to love. The majority of us desire that loving sensation back in our lives, regardless of how many relationships we have had or how few.

Love is a pervasive force that manifests in various forms and arrives in our lives at the opportune moment. While circumstances may not unfold as expected, it does not signify a definitive conclusion or an insurmountable obstacle in your journey. Every marriage begins with an initial impression of grandeur and enthusiasm. But with time, things start to break down because one or both people have acquired set beliefs about the other person and think that certain things are not working or they might not work in the future.

What Does the Word of God Say About Divorce?

"To the married, I give this command (not I, but the Lord): A wife must not separate from her husband. But if she does, she must

remain unmarried or else be reconciled to her husband. And a husband must not divorce his wife."

1 Corinthians 7:10-11 (NIV)

The Apostle Paul addresses the issue of separation and divorce within the context of marriage. He advises couples to strive for reconciliation rather than pursuing a divorce. If separation does occur, he encourages them to either remain unmarried or seek reconciliation with their spouse. Another verse from Malachi 2:16 (NIV): "I hate divorce, says the Lord God of Israel." This verse expresses God's disapproval of divorce, indicating that it goes against His intended design for marriage. It reflects the importance of cultivating a strong and lasting marital relationship. Likewise, in a modern scenario, Malachi 2:16 can still be understood as reflecting God's disapproval of divorce and highlighting the importance of a strong and lasting marital relationship. The verse serves as a reminder that God desires couples to commit to their marriage vows and work towards maintaining a healthy and thriving relationship.

God designed marriage to be a relationship where two individuals can come together, support one another, and complement each other. It is a partnership that involves mutual accommodation and care.

It highlights the importance of valuing and preserving the sanctity of marriage. It encourages individuals to approach marriage with a commitment to uphold the bond, overcome challenges, and strive for harmony and unity.

"Is it lawful for a man to put away his wife for every cause? And he answered...Moses, because of the hardness of your hearts,

suffered you to put away your wives: but from the beginning, it was not so... What therefore God hath joined together, let not man put asunder."

(Matthew 19:3-8)

However, trying to manage marriage without God has resulted in unneeded confrontations in families. The mention of the word "Divorce" will be far from you when you accept God, give His word precedence, and let it direct you. Please be aware that God despises divorce if you are considering getting divorced but have not yet done so. Keep trying to save your marriage.

In a parable shared by Jesus, a householder sowed good seeds in his field but discovered that weeds had also grown alongside the good seeds. When questioned about this, the householder attributed it to the work of an enemy. Similarly, in a marriage, when couples are spiritually unaware or indifferent, the enemy can sow seeds of discord, disunity, hatred, and bitterness. These issues may start small but can escalate if left unaddressed.

Just as tall oak trees grow from tiny acorns, major problems in marriages often have humble beginnings. To resolve these problems, it is necessary to trace them back to their roots and identify where things went wrong. Taking responsibility for one's actions and reactions is essential, and honest confession before God in prayer is necessary. It is crucial not to shift blame, as doing so only seeks to absolve oneself and hinders the process of restoration.

Your spouse's actions, no matter how hurtful, can be forgiven through the grace of God. Even in moments of betrayal and disappointment, God's grace is available to help you move forward and leave the past behind. The Bible teaches us to have a tender heart and be ready to forgive, just as God has forgiven us (Ephesians 4:32). If you have truly forgiven, you can invoke the power of the blood of Jesus to cleanse your heart from bitterness, hatred, and other negative emotions. Whenever memories of past faults arise, plead the blood of Jesus to purify your mind and release any lingering resentment.

In today's world, divorce is often seen as a solution to marital problems or a way to escape a difficult situation. However, this verse reminds us that divorce should not be taken lightly and that it goes against the original intention of marriage. God's design for marriage involves a lifelong commitment, mutual love, respect, and support between spouses.

In the face of challenges and difficulties that may arise in a marriage, the verse encourages couples to seek reconciliation, forgiveness, and a willingness to work through their issues. Marriage is a wonderful institution! It should not be associated with shame or reproach. You don't have to settle for a mediocre or troubled marriage. Instead, you have the potential to make your marriage thrive and experience true fulfillment and God's blessings.

God desires for your marriage to be a source of joy, love, and harmony. You don't have to endure constant arguments and conflicts. With God's guidance, you can cultivate a marriage that is free from hurt and wounds, where both partners find fulfillment and experience His goodness.

Look at the family of Adam and Eve; even after they sinned and fell from grace, God's favor still remained upon their family. They realized their nakedness and tried to cover themselves with fig leaves. However, God, in His special favor towards families, overlooked their betrayal and provided them with clothing made from animal skins. This act of clothing them symbolically removed their shame.

Despite Eve's role in the deception and being the primary cause of the fall, God extended His favor to her as well. In Genesis 3:15, God made a promise to Eve, stating that there would be an ongoing conflict between her offspring and the serpent's offspring, but ultimately her descendant would triumph over the serpent.

God's plan for your marriage is extraordinary. He wants to bring you to a place where your family radiates His glory, where even others and the forces of darkness have no choice but to recognize the goodness and blessings in your marriage. This is the heritage and inheritance you have as a child of God.

Love is the Fruit of the Holy Spirit

Love is a remarkable attribute that can flourish and mature within us because it is a fruit of the Holy Spirit. When we talk about the fruit of the Spirit, we are not referring to the fruit that comes from receiving the Holy Spirit through baptism. Instead, love is specifically identified as the first fruit that emerges from our regenerated spirit when we experience a new birth.

In Galatians 5:22, the Bible mentions love as one of the fruits of the Spirit, along with joy, peace, patience, kindness, goodness, faithfulness, gentleness, and self-control. These qualities are not limited or restricted by any law or regulation.

Love is not a stagnant or fixed characteristic but rather a dynamic and growing aspect of our spiritual journey. Through the indwelling of the Holy Spirit, we have the potential to cultivate and exhibit love in our lives, allowing it to blossom and impact our relationships with others. Proverbs 24:3 says that a home is built upon understanding, which is crucial for effective communication. Understanding allows us to perceive beyond words, interpreting eye movements and voice tones, and it helps soften the impact of anger.

When you truly understand your spouse, their words may be few, but successful communication takes place because of that deep understanding. Abigail, known for her good understanding, effectively communicated with David, recognizing his thirst for vengeance against her ill-mannered husband (1 Samuel 25:23-25).

When there is an understanding between husband and wife, conflicts and breakups are reduced. With a good understanding of a partner, many homes can be saved from being torn apart due to misunderstandings, where the husband misinterprets his wife's actions, and the wife assigns meanings to simple statements from the husband. However, the Word reminds us that "Good understanding gives favor" (Proverbs 13:15).

Life is unexpected and rarely goes as planned, especially when it comes to our romantic relationships. Unexpected events, such as breaking a relationship, might occasionally rank among the most horrifying things you can go through.

Going through a breakup can be an incredibly painful experience.

Difficulties often arise in a marriage when one spouse has expectations for deep involvement in certain activities, such as hobbies, church activities, or raising children, that the other finds challenging or impossible to participate in. This mismatch in expectations can lead to the building of barriers fueled by hurt and misunderstandings. Over time, the once warm and positive feelings between the partners can transform into negative emotions, causing them to grow apart.

As the closeness diminishes, genuine sexual intimacy becomes increasingly difficult, and their physical relationship may deteriorate, becoming routine, obligatory, or even weaponized. Gradually, one or both partners begin to withdraw, and the relationship enters a state of decline. This process of decay can continue for years before the couple realizes the extent of the deterioration and eventually decides to seek a divorce.

Pure survival is the most fundamental need in every marriage. Both partners require clothing, food, and shelter. Couples rarely struggle to express this urge to one another because it is evident to both of them. (How they respond to it is a different story.)

We feel distressed when the most important person in our lives moves away, and this distress increases throughout the first few months after a relationship ends. This is so because when our spouse isn't emotionally or physically available to meet our expectations, our natural response is to "Up" the distress. There are two factors that contribute to this rise in anxiety.

First, we feel more exposed when our spouse isn't present to meet our needs.

Increasing our anxiety can signal to our spouse that we require their assistance.

This is why ending a marriage is so difficult: you lose the important person in your life who helps you deal with the good, the terrible, and the ugly. The depth of emotions experienced in such situations highlights the complexity of human connections and the profound impact they have on our lives.

The grieving process for the end of a long-term relationship involves not only mourning the loss of the person but also the loss of shared memories, dreams, and a sense of familiarity. It is normal for individuals to go through a period of adjustment and to experience conflicting emotions, such as longing for the past while acknowledging the reasons why the relationship was dissatisfying.

Three Phases of a Break-Up

When two people break up from marriage, they often go through three phases of loss.

In the first phase, there is a strong inclination to protest the breakup and try to reconcile with the partner. This stage is characterized by feelings of anger, distress, panic, and anxiety. These emotions, known as "separation protests," can drive individuals to make considerable efforts to get back together, even in toxic relationships. However, if the relationship has truly come to an end, engaging in such behavior only prolongs and intensifies the recovery process.

In the second phase, the person gradually realizes that reuniting is not feasible, leading to a predominant sense of sadness. Feelings of lethargy and hopelessness may also arise during this stage.

In the third phase, acceptance of the loss begins to take hold. The person comes to terms with the reality that the relationship has ended and redirects their time and energy toward other life tasks and goals. This may include seeking out new romantic opportunities.

The duration of these phases and the overall recovery process can vary significantly from person to person. The experience of relationship loss is highly individual, and there is no set timeline for how long it should take to heal.

However, despite the intense trauma it brings, divorce or the end of a relationship does not have to mark the end of a fulfilling and meaningful life. It only becomes an unmitigated tragedy if we allow it to define us and prevent our personal growth. While it may feel like your world is crumbling, it's essential to remember that you have the power to rise above the pain and transform it into an opportunity for self-discovery and renewal.

Instead of viewing the breakup as the end, see it as a chance for new beginnings. Take this time to heal, reflect, and reinvent yourself. Allow yourself to grieve, but also focus on rebuilding your life and pursuing your passions. Surround yourself with supportive loved ones who can help you navigate this challenging journey.

Break up or divorced? What's Next?

If you have already gone through a divorce, it's time to move on. Rise beyond your desperation and let go of your self-justification, resentment, and rage. Not all hope is lost. God is a God of opportunities. You can mend your shattered relationship according to His directions. Jesus has the power to resurrect your home, just as He raised Lazarus from the dead after four days. To attract the miraculous into your circumstance, have faith in the power of God. Even while it might seem impossible, keep in mind that Jesus has the power to give problems new life even when they seem to have died. Don't give up on your marriage and household because Jesus can still provide healing.

Rebuilding Your Love After Heartbreak

It probably won't happen immediately, but it is possible to move past a terrible relationship and start loving again. Even though everyone heals at their own rate, there are some things you can do to hasten the process and make the move from heartache to new love easier.

Accept the Reality

It may be difficult to accept, particularly when experiencing the aftermath of a painful breakup. It is crucial to extend compassion to yourself as you navigate through this significant transformation. Furthermore, the notion that time alone can heal emotional wounds is not entirely accurate. The duration since the breakup, whether it occurred recently or many years ago, is less significant compared to the emotions you are currently experiencing. If you fail to address and process your pain, it can continue to persist and affect you.

Guard Your Heart

"Above all else, guard your heart, for everything you do flows from it." This means that the condition of one's heart, including their emotions, thoughts, and attitudes, influences their actions and ultimately shapes their lives."

Proverbs 4:23 (NIV)

Just imagine a person who has recently experienced a painful breakup. His/her heart is filled with hurt, bitterness, and mistrust as a result of the breakup. And it's completely normal to feel awful in the aftermath of a broken relationship. If they don't guard their heart and address these emotions, it can have a significant impact on their subsequent actions and relationships.

Don't Victimize Yourself

Individuals can be categorized into three distinct levels:

- Victim
- Empowered
- Enlightened (each representing a different mindset and perspective).

At the bottom level is the victim, who tends to focus solely on the negative occurrences in their life. Frequently, they find themselves questioning why unfortunate events consistently happen to them. Moving up to the empowered level, individuals acknowledge the negative aspects but actively strive to reframe them into more positive experiences. They actively seek opportunities for personal growth and positive transformations in their lives.

Forgive Yourself and Others

Particularly when it comes to forgiving yourself, especially if you have been hurt or betrayed, forgiving yourself and your partner might take time and work. It is crucial to realize that forgiving someone does not include tolerating their cruel behavior.

Truthfully, forgiving frequently serves you more than it does the other person. You are given the choice to stop putting more time and effort into a relationship that is no longer healthy for you.

With this being said, there is another essential person you need to be ready to forgive in the process of recovering from a shattered heart and moving on: *Yourself.*

Although forgiving your ex might seem easier to handle, it is important to understand that it is the longest and most important relationship you will ever have.

Let Go of the Past

It can be tempting to hold onto the past for an extended period of time. You might still harbor anger towards your ex-partner or hold grudges against individuals from past relationships. Feelings of resentment and upset may linger due to the way your ex behaved during the relationship.

However, as long as you cling to these old resentments and grudges, it becomes difficult to move forward. When your mind is consumed with painful thoughts and memories, it becomes challenging to embrace new experiences. Holding onto what was and what could have been prevents you from fully living in the present moment. Philippians 3:13-14 (NIV): "But one thing I do: Forgetting what is behind and straining toward what is ahead, I press on toward the goal to win the prize for which God has called me heavenward in Christ Jesus." These lines stress the value of forgetting about the past and concentrating on the present. They exhort believers to advance with patience and an optimistic outlook. The longer you allow the past to hinder your progress, the longer it will take to truly move on and find love after heartbreak. Thoughts and emotions related to former partners can hinder your ability to engage in new relationships. Try to release these emotional attachments and open yourself up to new possibilities.

You Are Not Alone

No one is Perfect!!! We all have flaws. Each of us is "a work in progress." You must understand that every single person will carry baggage of some kind in any relationship. There's constantly room for development at every age. Each of us contributes a great deal of wonderful things to every connection.

Conquer Fear

Are you being hindered by fear? To conquer it, it's essential to acknowledge and embrace it. Take a moment to be truthful with yourself. What is the worst-case scenario if this fear were to materialize? How likely is it to actually happen? Reflect on past instances when you successfully confronted similar fears and overcame them. Envision the kind of love and relationship you could experience if you could set aside your fears and fully commit. Consider you have a fear of vulnerability in relationships, fearing that opening up may lead to rejection or hurt. By honestly examining the worst that could happen, you might realize that even if rejection occurs, it would not define your worth or diminish your capacity to find love. Reflecting on previous instances when you took emotional risks and were rewarded with deeper connections can give you the confidence to confront this fear. By embracing vulnerability, you can create the potential for a profoundly fulfilling and intimate relationship.

Release Yourself from Bitterness

To free yourself from bitterness towards others, shift your focus to positive qualities and experiences you shared with your partner. Remember that your ex-partner is not inherently evil; they simply weren't the ideal match for you. Rather than dwelling on their flaws and past mistakes, embrace the power of forgiveness to transcend the harm they may have caused. Reflect on the good they brought into your life, the ways in which they contributed to your personal growth and the joyful moments you shared together. By redirecting your thoughts toward the positive aspects of your past relationship, you can let go of bitterness and create space for healing and personal growth.

Heal Yourself Instead of Being in Rosy Retrospection

It is common for us to look back on our lives and previous relationships with nostalgia, highlighting the good parts while ignoring the issues that were present. This behavior, called "Rosy Retrospection," can make it difficult for us to comprehend the big picture and slow the healing process. Sometimes, both happy and unpleasant memories may play again in our brains, distressing us and slowing the process of healing. But it's important to keep things in perspective. There are ups and downs in every marriage. You may need to establish emotional and possibly even physical space if you find yourself romanticizing the past or elevating your ex-partner.

Do Things That Make You Feel Good

Engaging in activities that bring you joy is essential in the process of opening yourself up to love again. Finding happiness within yourself creates a foundation for accepting and experiencing the love you desire.

When you prioritize your own happiness and well-being, your defenses naturally come down. This allows you to be more receptive to love and form meaningful connections with others. Remember that self-love is a crucial component of being able to give and receive love in a healthy way. Consider the activities that bring you pleasure and fulfillment. Whether it's going to the movies, indulging in karaoke, dancing, attending wine tastings, or any other hobbies or interests, make time for them. By immersing yourself in activities you love, time will fly by, and you will make the most of every moment.

Try to Love Again. You Can Do It!

After a breakup, emotional anguish is not always a sign that something went wrong. In fact, it often means that you permitted yourself to be open to connection with another person and vulnerable. It demonstrates your capacity for meaningful connection and your knack for relationship involvement.

Many couples who experience unhappy marriages and failed

relationships give up on the idea of ever finding real love. However, once the dust has settled, the post-breakup period is a vital transitional stage that offers opportunities that can help you meet the appropriate person the next time around. They merely come to the conclusion that love doesn't exist. Try learning to deal with the losses and treasure the pleasant moments by reflecting carefully and being brutally honest with yourself. You'll quickly be able to move on, more trustworthy, and even more prepared for a healthier relationship when you learn from your mistakes.

You may actually take advantage of the hurt of a breakup as an opportunity for personal development and advancement by treating it with awareness and intention. It teaches you important skills that can guide your decision-making in romantic relationships moving forward and help you set healthier boundaries. It's crucial to understand that just because a relationship has some nice qualities doesn't mean that ending it was a mistake. Just as not being able to attend college doesn't mean that graduating was a failure.

A Word from Very Well!

Following a breakup, it can be incredibly challenging to maintain a cheerful demeanor and find motivation to focus on daily tasks. Life continues its course, necessitating the effort to rise from bed and fulfill work obligations, even when the desire to retreat to solitude is strong. The routine persists, including returning home and adhering to familiar patterns. Beyond dwelling on the past, there is a wealth of possibilities to anticipate in life, such as upcoming travels, professional achievements, and the pursuit of personal passions.

But,

There is always a light at the end of the tunnel. It can definitely succeed if two people are sincere in their efforts to mend their relationship. In that situation, communication is essential. Instead of pushing away the painful emotions, you should name them, such as dread, disappointment, and uncertainty, and discuss them with your partner.

"Confess your faults one to another…"

James 5:16

Maintaining healthy communication in a relationship involves being mindful of the words we use and the impact they can have on our partner. Guarding our tongue and choosing our words wisely can prevent unnecessary hurt and misunderstandings.

Acknowledging when we have offended our partner and sincerely apologizing demonstrates humility and a willingness to take responsibility for our actions. Saying "I am sorry" from the depth of our hearts shows genuine remorse and a desire to make amends. It is an essential part of fostering forgiveness and rebuilding trust in the relationship.

Furthermore, resentment should be dealt with as soon as it manifests since when we suppress our bad emotions, they grow and feed.

Where is your love, anyway? What about your heart? On things or on God? Your heart will be where your treasure is, not vice versa. People come in different sizes, and life has phases. The biggest error people can make is to think too highly of themselves. Everyone needs to understand that life has many stages. Yes, you can definitely love again if you have a strong faith in God and in yourself. Pray is the most powerful weapon that you can rely on for your next relationship or marriage.

While it is entirely understandable to feel sad or grieve occasionally, it's important to understand that your past relationships have the capacity to influence your entire future of love. Being steady after being injured is truly courageous because as long as you are a human, you are open to falling in love again with as many people as you can. Take a chance on genuine love when you think you've found it since, after all, falling in love is all about taking chances!!!

Chapter 8

Do You Meet the Requirements That You Require?

"But I would have you without carefulness. He that is unmarried careth for the things that belong to the Lord, how he may please the Lord."

-1 Corinthians 7:32-

Life is comprised of various phases, and one of these phases is singleness, which is inevitable for everyone, regardless of marital status, lifestyle choices, or career paths. Each stage or phase of life carries its own unique advantages and should be embraced and utilized. Singleness is no exception to this.

"Remember now thy Creator in the days of thy youth, while the evil days come not, nor the years draw nigh when thou shalt say; I have no pleasure in them."

(Ecclesiastes 12:1)

Being single is just a temporary phase of life, and if we do not make the most of it, it can slip away quickly and cannot be regained. This period of singleness is an opportunity to lay the foundation for the life we desire in the future. The present moment is the best time to start pursuing meaningful endeavors and making a difference in our lives.

Remember, we only have one life to live, and there are no second chances. We must handle our lives with care and avoid being careless, as being reckless can lead to our lives slipping away without achieving our goals.

Being single can be difficult, particularly in light of the widespread perception that one's life is incomplete without a loving partner. The idea that finding a significant partner is the ultimate aim is frequently implied in movies and television shows that suggest that a single life is a transient and unsatisfying condition. According to a 2008 study published in the European Journal of Social Psychology, this portrayal has contributed to the widespread belief that single people are sad.

Although I agree with the fact that relationships are mentally expensive and take up a lot of space in our heads, consciously or unconsciously.

But the Lord God said, "It is not good that man should be alone; I will make him a helper comparable to him."

(Genesis 2:18)

This verse lays the foundation for the institution of marriage, as God designed human beings to find companionship and support in one another. It highlights the significance of a deep and meaningful partnership between a man and a woman, which is further elaborated in the subsequent verses where God creates Eve as Adam's suitable helper and companion.

Similarly, Paul's words to the believers in Corinthians provide wise and practical counsel on the matter: "Now for the matters you wrote about: 'It is good for a man not to marry. But since there is so much immorality, each man should have his own wife and each woman her own husband. The husband should fulfill his marital duty to his wife and, likewise, the wife to her husband. The wife's body does not belong to her alone but also to her husband. In the same way, the husband's body does not belong to him alone but also to his wife.'"

Many of us are led to believe that each person is for us, like a "Prince Charming" for every woman or a "Sleeping Beauty" for every man, and only that particular person will suffice. Let's be honest; the notion of finding a single "Mr. Right" or "Miss Ideal" for every person is unrealistic. In reality, there are numerous individuals who could potentially be compatible with you due to shared personality, character, values, and interests. There might be thousands or even millions of potential mates who could be a great fit for you. Even if you do find someone you consider "perfect" and decide to marry them, you will likely encounter others along the way who would also have been a great match for you. Sometimes, these other individuals might even seem like a better fit than the person you ended up marrying. This has made relationships complicated and made people feel incapable of love.

Clearly, some individuals are single by choice, as they are not currently interested in pursuing a serious relationship. Others find themselves single due to various life circumstances. And let's face it; People set requirements that they feel are required while choosing their partner. Who doesn't want that?

What Causes People to be Single?

The idea that singles often have a long list of requirements for a life partner can be attributed to various factors:

Personal Standards:

Some individuals have clear criteria and specific qualities they seek in a partner. These standards could be shaped by their values, experiences, upbringing, and what they believe will lead to a successful and fulfilling relationship.

Here, you need to understand that your spouse is different from you in a few respects. However, the beautiful gem that your marriage was always meant to be will be formed when the differences between you and your spouse come together.

Past Experiences:

Previous relationships or interactions can influence what singles look for in a partner. Positive experiences may lead to wanting similar qualities in a future partner, while negative experiences can result in setting specific requirements to avoid similar issues. How do you know this? Live in the present. Your future is not determined by your past unless you dwell in it. Redirect your focus to the present moment and learn to value what you currently have. By doing so, you will experience a significant shift in your mindset. When you have entertained foolishness, a history of trauma can cause you to excuse and ignore mistreatment because you've survived the worst. Bare minimum feels like royal treatment when you are settling. Yes, they are "eye candy," but they are not "soul food." God doesn't give you a spouse for romance only, but for advancing His kingdom." It's about glorifying the Father, not about the self.

Societal Expectations:

Cultural norms, societal pressures, and media influence can create expectations about the "ideal" partner. People may feel compelled to seek certain qualities to fit in with or meet perceived societal standards. Well, God has a certain standard for your marriage that is different from that of your friends or families. Instead, He compares your union to the bond between Christ and His church, using that heavenly union as the ultimate standard.

Don't let societal pressures dictate your choices or settle for anything less than you truly deserve. Refrain from comparing yourself to others who are in relationships. Instead, cherish the freedom and meaningful connections you have in your life right now, valuing and savoring them to the fullest. When you allow culture to be your professor, it will cause you to only look for your preference but then overlook character. Hear me when I say that character is what you're gonna have to live with if you say I do. You might say I do to your preference, but you're going to experience their character eventually. Yes, the masks will eventually begin to slip off over time, and you will see their true character, not the fake one they presented on the dinner date. BE CAREFUL and BE WISE! "You cannot solve a problem with the same mindset you created it in." Holy Spirit, detox me from my preferences!

Fear of Settling:

Some singles may fear settling for a partner who doesn't meet their desired criteria. They want to avoid potential regrets or dissatisfaction in the long run. A bit of a stigmatized approach, right? Let me give you a hard truth: A self-centered individual seeks all the honor, all the praise, all the admiration, all the accolades, all the limelight, all the dominance, all the privileges, and all the rights. But a loving person wants to give what they have to others, and they don't fear settling with others.

If, like many others, you find yourself concerned about ending up alone or lacking a support system without a romantic partner, it can hinder your ability to discover genuine happiness.

Desire for Compatibility:

Compatibility is crucial for a successful relationship. Singles may believe that having specific requirements will increase the chances of finding someone with whom they can connect deeply. You may find yourself drawn to fair-complexioned individuals, while at other times, you might prefer someone with a chocolate or dark-complexioned appearance. Similarly, your admiration might shift from a short person to a tall one. These fluctuations can lead to a sense of confusion about your preferences.

Create a balance when seeking a life partner. While having standards and preferences is natural, being overly rigid can limit opportunities for meaningful connections. Being open-minded and flexible allows singles to explore relationships with a diverse range of individuals, increasing the likelihood of finding a compatible and fulfilling life partner.

Life Goals:

As people have specific life goals and aspirations, they may seek a partner who aligns with these objectives, hoping for mutual support and shared experiences. Don't ever become too preoccupied with the pursuit of life goals and ambitions. Who are you? You are the believer, and a believer has to learn ways of balancing everything. God desires you to be deeply devoted to His Kingdom and righteousness, to the point that anyone you encounter is firstly someone who shares your journey and, secondly, is at the same stage of the journey as you are. This alignment allows you to move forward, relate, and grow together, becoming complete individuals who develop and mature at the same pace.

What's Next?

The first question to ponder is, **how do I enter into marriage?** The answer lies in Proverbs 18:22: *"Whoso findeth a wife findeth a good thing, and obtaineth favor of the Lord."*

It is a conscious and deliberate act. Finding a spouse is not a passive experience that happens in dreams or while asleep. It demands an alert and engaged mindset, where you actively open your eyes and mind with whom you can share a lifetime of love and companionship.

Marriage is not a mythical or magical occurrence; it is a conscious and intentional relationship. You cannot wake up one day and expect to find your perfect partner beside you, as that unique event occurred only in the Garden of Eden and will not be replicated. Marriage is a beautiful institution established by God for the betterment of humanity. However, to fully enjoy its benefits, it must be approached in the manner that God intended. Building a solid foundation is essential for a successful marriage, as the Bible wisely states in Psalm 11:3: *"If the foundations be destroyed, what can the righteous do?"*

Ask Yourself: "Do I Want to Spend the Rest of My Life Alone?"

Once you transition from being single to committed through marriage, make a conscious effort to fully embrace your new role and responsibilities. Avoid behaving as if you are still single, and instead, wholeheartedly dedicate yourself to your marriage, giving it your utmost commitment and effort.

I have observed that sometimes couples forget that their marriage is a partnership despite having claimed to become one. Their actions often reveal a different story than their words. When listening to their conflicts, I attentively coach each individual through their challenges, but I always remind them that they are in this together.

Being in a marriage while feeling like you're single can be a difficult and, at times, perplexing situation. Although you are undoubtedly not single, you also don't feel entirely committed to your partner. You can feel estranged from your partner, unsatisfied with your relationship, or simply need extra space during this interim. Many worry that "I feel single in my relationship." But why does this unsettling and baffling sensation appear? Are you, your partner, or the relationship itself the problem?

Overcoming challenges in a marriage can be particularly difficult when both partners continue to maintain excessive independence and cling to their single-person mindset.

Here's an example of how someone may unknowingly act single while being married: Behaving as though you don't need your spouse. It's true that you are independent and can take care of yourself, and your spouse recognizes that too. However, your partner also wants to feel valued and needed in your life. They seek reassurance that they contribute to your happiness, provide support, and offer protection. Allowing your spouse to play a meaningful role in your life can strengthen the bond between you both.

A Quick Tip: Recognize that you have a partner in life and embrace the idea of depending on each other in certain ways. Let your spouse be there for you and show appreciation for their support and presence.

Marriage: Where Dedication Matters, No Room for a Horrible Work Ethic

Indeed, maintaining a marriage is a full-time task that calls for constant devotion, perseverance, and a strong work ethic. When two people make the decision to enter this sacred union, they start a journey that necessitates continuous effort to maintain a strong and happy partnership.

A poor work ethic can be detrimental to marriage since it impacts several facets of the relationship, including communication, responsibility sharing, and emotional support.

Purchasing a camera without proper training and ignoring the manual would be unwise, leading to frustration when unable to operate it effectively. Similarly, attempting to navigate a marriage without consulting its proper guide, the Bible is equally foolish. Marriage involves two distinct individuals, one male, and one female, coming together to form a covenant, exchanging vows, and committing to staying together until death.

When you assign specific roles within your marriage, you unknowingly set up expectations that can lead to unnecessary complications. These expectations often lead to frustration, arguments, and disappointment, straining the relationship and endangering the bond between partners. True love expects nothing in return!!!

"After that, [Jesus] poured water into a basin and began to wash the disciples' feet, and to wipe them with the towel with which He was girded"

(John 13:5).

In marriage, prioritize serving rather than being served, following the example of Jesus, who humbly washed the disciples' feet without questioning traditional roles. Avoid placing all household responsibilities on one person, such as cooking, washing, or cleaning, to prevent disappointment when expectations aren't met. Instead, view roles within marriage as temporary responsibilities based on each partner's ability to respond to the needs at hand.

When you see water on the floor, don't stand idly thinking it's solely your wife's responsibility to mop. Take the initiative to respond, regardless of traditional roles. If you have the ability to act, it becomes your responsibility to address the situation. "To the weak, I became as weak, that I might win the weak. I have become all things to all men, that I might, by all means, save some" (1 Corinthians 9:22). Becoming "all things" should be the principle that rules your roles in your marriage.

Prioritizing anything above God and your spouse will inevitably lead to problems within your home. Remember that sex is a temporary aspect of a relationship and is subject to constant change.

As a husband, your vision for your wife greatly influences the growth of your relationship. Instead of complaining about what you wish she could be, take an active role in nurturing her potential. If you want her to look nice, consider buying her clothes or supporting her trips to the beauty salon for a nice hairstyle. Encourage her health and well-being by joining her at the gym to stay in shape together. A true man prioritizes the needs of his wife and family above his own, selflessly serving and caring for them.

In the beautiful words of 1 Corinthians 11:7, *"The woman is the glory of the man."* This means that a husband's true fulfillment lies in the radiant expression of his wife's well-being and happiness. Just as the sun shines brightest at noon, a husband thrives when his wife is glowing and flourishing.

Men and women ought to value and cherish one another. When Jesus proclaimed that *"Love your neighbor as yourself"* is one of the greatest commandments (Matthew 19:19), He reaffirmed this idea. If we truly comprehend this reality. There's nothing more powerful than love. Be courageous enough to tear down the barriers separating you from your spouse in your heart.

I have heard people saying that a dog is a man's best friend. But is this true? How? I think it's misleading. A dog cannot tell your faults or guide you during difficult times. How cowardly is it to make your pet the object of your devotion instead of your partner? God created a woman and then drew her from a man so that he would have a partner in love.

Wives, and your abilities to think, strategize, and plan are meant to be valuable support for your husband. Reflect on how you utilize these abilities. If your intention is to prove yourself better than your husband, you are not fulfilling your role as his helper; instead, you become his competitor.

If your husband doesn't engage in prayer, avoid pressuring him by questioning why he doesn't pray. Instead, offer prayers on his behalf. Remember, your prayers can have a positive impact on him, as stated in 1 Corinthians 7:14. When your husband confides in you, be his encourager. As a wife, if your husband is unsure or struggling with something, your role is to provide assistance and support. Encourage him and help him find his path rather than taking over and diminishing his sense of responsibility. Never emasculate your partner. A good wife seeks to bring out the best in her husband and helps him reach his potential. Respect your husband's abilities and differences.

Just as Christ selflessly died for us while we were still sinners, true love is not merely spoken but actively demonstrated in our actions. Love is responsive, not reactive. Reacting impulsively can lead to hurtful words that wound the spirits of those we care for deeply. Instead, take a moment to breathe and gather your thoughts before responding, preventing unnecessary pain in your relationships.

If your love is based solely on specific reasons or conditions, the foundation of your relationship becomes precarious. Love should be unconditional, not subject to changing terms and conditions. Embrace a love that remains steadfast, unwavering, and devoted, just as Christ's love is for us.

God – Your BEST Match Maker!

Many young people find it extremely difficult to make the important choice of whom to marry at this key time. It is an undisputed fact. The Bible emphasizes how our hearts can deceive us because they are so profoundly wicked (Jeremiah 17:9). Only God has a complete understanding of the complexity and depth of the human heart, including your own. If you were to witness the true content of your heart through God's eyes, you might even deny that it belongs to you. Regrettably, numerous individuals have fallen victim to the deceit of their own hearts, experiencing. Regarding your life, the Word of God declares in Jeremiah 29:11 (TLB):

"For I know the plans I have for you," says the Lord. "They are plans for good and not for evil, to give you a future and hope."

Entrust God as your Match Maker. God has complete knowledge of who you are, understanding you fully, as well as having a comprehensive understanding of every individual in the world. He knows precisely who will comprehend you, compliment you, and wholeheartedly accept you for who you are. Above all, God knows the person who will play a significant role in helping you fulfill the purpose He has ordained for your life.

Choosing Who to Marry

There are a few things you should be aware of before choosing your spouse:

➢ God won't meddle with your free will until you consciously give Him permission to. God won't make your decision for you; He will only lead you through the process by requiring you to follow the guidance of the Holy Spirit and by forcing you to use Scriptural principles.

➢ He won't compel you to marry someone or impose someone on you. You must decide whether to follow His guidance when He gives it; you are entirely accountable for your decision.

I hope you get what I mean!

The Unequal Yoking – Listen to the God's Voice!

According to 2 Corinthians 6:14, marrying someone who is not born again is referred to as being unequally yoked. It is important to understand that regardless of a person's attractiveness, kindness, or care, if they are not born again, it is not advisable to pursue a relationship with them. The Bible encourages marrying someone who is unmarried, just like yourself. If the person interested in marrying you is already married, and their spouse is still alive, it is not permissible according to Romans 4:1-3.

Marrying such a person would be considered adultery.

The Bible says in Proverbs 11:14, *"Where there is no counsel, the people fall: but in the multitude of counselors, there is safety."* Proverbs 15:22 also says counselors, *"Without counsels, purposes are disappointed: but in the multitude of counselors, purposes are established."* Avoid rushing and hurrying through life. Haste and hurry are like twin sisters within the family of impatience.

Wear Your Wedding Ring – the Love's Gleaming Emblem!

Your wedding ring symbolizes your unwavering dedication and commitment to your partner, signifying that no matter where you are, you belong to one another and are not seeking anyone else. Always wear it as a reminder of your bond.

In a relationship, there will be unique abilities or qualities that your spouse possesses, which you may not, and vice versa. Instead of trying to outdo each other, embrace your differences and complement each other's strengths. Focus on completing one another rather than competing.

A Happy Marriage Is No Accident

A happy marriage is not a random accident. Just like any other aspect of life, achieving success in marriage requires intentional effort. The key to success in any endeavor lies in planning, and effective planning relies on having the right knowledge.

Love stories in movies often portray the magical moments of falling in love, the heart-pounding excitement, and the blissful journey of two souls uniting. While these moments are undoubtedly beautiful, they are just the beginning of what it takes to build a happy and lasting marriage. In reality, a happy marriage is not a mere stroke of luck or happenstance; it is the result of intentional and continuous effort from both partners. Like tending to a garden, a successful marriage requires care, nurturing, and hard work to flourish and grow.

The age-old saying holds much truth: when we share our sorrow, it becomes easier to bear, and when we share our joy, it multiplies. Having a soul mate to share difficult times with makes the burden lighter, while the presence of a close companion amplifies our joy and laughter.

Ultimately, a happy marriage is the result of consistent effort, compassion, and dedication. Couples who actively work on their relationship, show love through their actions, and prioritize each other's happiness are more likely to experience the fulfillment of lasting love. Indeed, a happy marriage is an ever-evolving tale of love, where the protagonists are two individuals willing to invest their hearts and efforts into a shared story of lifelong happiness.

Seek Divine Guidance: Praying for God's Blessing in marriage

Often, in the busyness of our lives, we tend to neglect prayer. We may only pray when we have urgent needs, failing to take the time to develop a closer relationship with God, understand Him better, and share our deepest desires with Him. By rushing through our prayers, we unintentionally close off the very channel through which God blesses us. Eventually, we may wake up one day with a sense of emptiness and insecurity, realizing that our foundation may be weakening and our protection becoming fragile. This was my personal experience.

Are you longing for marriage? Rest assured that God has not overlooked you. Trust that God is in control and will guide your life according to His perfect plan. Instead of desperately searching for a marriage partner at any cost, focus on making Jesus your Lord and surrendering to His guidance. Being deeply committed to Him forms an excellent foundation for your future. Alternatively, if you feel trapped by circumstances beyond your control, there is no need to worry or lose hope. Why, you may ask?

Marriage should not be pursued at any cost. It is important to remember that before Adam's wife was brought to him, he underwent a deep sleep (Genesis 2:21-22). Instead of fixating solely on marriage, it is crucial to pursue a relationship with God. By making God the center of your life, all other things, including a fulfilling marriage, will be added to you. Proverbs 18:21 states that finding a wife is a good thing and brings favor from the Lord. God is a just and fair God, and He does not show partiality to anyone. What He does for one person, He is equally willing, ready, and able to do for another. His righteousness and blessings are not reserved for a select few but are available to all who call upon His name, including you. God is fully aware of your circumstances in each season of your life, and He has not forgotten you. Do not allow yourself to live in doubt, questioning whether God has overlooked you or if you are under a curse. Rest assured that God is faithful, trustworthy, and more than sufficient. I can personally testify to His faithfulness and provision in my own life.

God's plans extend beyond your marital status and encompass your single days as well. God has good intentions for your life, whether you are currently single or married. Unfortunately, many individuals are unaware of God's purpose for them during the season of singleness and consequently fail to make the most of it. In Matthew 11:28, Jesus assures that those who come to Him will find rest. Allowing God to be your Match Maker brings clarity, eliminates confusion, and brings peace to your mind. As Psalm 125:1 state, placing trust in the Lord is like Mount Zion, steadfast and enduring forever.

One of the most crucial aspects to consider is that God is the ultimate designer of marriage, and His wisdom surpasses all. As believers, our foremost priority should be seeking and following God's will in every aspect of our lives. When a couple contemplates marriage, it is essential to dedicate ample time to pray together and seek God's guidance.

Merely both partners being believers does not automatically guarantee that they are suitable for marriage. Trust God's plan while honestly and humbly seeking His will and wisdom.

"Trust in the Lord with all your heart and lean not on your own understanding; in all your ways acknowledge Him, and He will make your paths straight."

(Proverbs 3:5-6)

If marriage is part of God's calling for your lives, He desires to connect you with someone who shares your vision, purpose, and commitment to building a strong, godly home filled with love and grace.

Chapter 9

Finding A Boyfriend After College

Do you feel as though you are starting your life over in a sense? Do you fear that finding a boyfriend is going to be hard after college life? Does it feel like far too many transitions all at once? If you find that you are having a hard time trying to figure out how to restart or jump start your love life after college, you are definitely not alone. When you go from a college environment where dating is easy to life afterwards, it can make for a huge transition. Though it may take more effort on your part, you truly can meet a great guy and turn it into a wonderful and lasting relationship with the right approach.

It's such a common scenario—when you're in college you feel like you're on top of the world! You are meeting new people all the time, you have plenty of social engagements, and you are grouped in with a bunch of people the same age and same stage of life as you. All of a sudden you graduate and enter the real world, and wow do things change!

There Is Hope

When it comes to finding a boyfriend after college, you just have to change your focus. The reason that you could find a boyfriend easily while you were in college is that you were in the right setting for it. You were constantly meeting new guys in class, in study groups, or when you went out on the town. There was a surplus of men that you could easily pick from, and this made things easier when it came to finding a good match. That changes when you graduate and go out into the real world—but that doesn't mean all hope is lost.

You are essentially a new person now, almost born again. You have a new job, you may be in a new town, and you are trying to navigate your way through this new life. That's exciting and perhaps a bit terrifying all at the same time. This can be a time to reinvent yourself, and to really focus in on what you want in your life. If you can try to shift your focus on the positive aspects of this, then it can lead to something really wonderful. Your dream guy is out there, but you just might have to work a little harder or search a bit more to find him!

He's Out There

Do you feel like something just isn't clicking? Are you wondering why your love life isn't working out the way that you wanted it to? Do you feel sometimes like you're running in place when it comes to your love life? If you feel that things just aren't the same as they used to be when it comes to your love life, then you are not alone! This is a whole new chapter in your life and that doesn't just pertain to your career but your love life as well. It's time to break free of the cycle and make effective changes that will stick with you over time!

You will find that your love life is the hardest thing to overcome and to adjust to when it comes to life after college. You may tend to follow the same patterns that you did in college, or you may have the same expectations about meeting the right type of person. Things are all new, you are likely in a new place, with all new people, and the reality is that you are going to have to adapt in some way to make this a successful experience. This is hard to swallow at first, particularly if you had absolutely no problem meeting men in college and now it's a hardship.

There are plenty of men that are searching for the same thing that you are. You just may not have the chance meetings that you once did in your college days. You don't have the parties or social events every single weekend, and you have to work at creating your own social life now. You may not have friends wanting to set you up all the time, and you may have to seek out a man and put in the work on the front end. This is a big adjustment if your dating life was blissful in college, but everything changes and this can be for the better.

You may find that you are actually more selective in finding a partner at this stage of your life too. Dating is practically a pastime in college and it's a big part of the social scene. You may have dated guys that you would never be interested in now that you are more mature. You may be more specific with what you want out of a man and in a relationship, and that's a good thing. As a matter of fact, as you focus on more meaningful relationships, this is a time where you can narrow down your list of most important characteristics that you want in a man. This is your time to get down to the things that matter the most, and then to go after them.

You want to be open minded, but it's okay to be a little picky too. This is particularly true if you dated a lot in college or if you are looking for something more long term and meaningful. Though you may not necessarily be ready to settle down, you do want to make your relationships count at this age and stage of your life. Every relationship teaches us a lesson, and hopefully by now you have learned what you want or don't want in the right relationship. You know what you want, what you need, and what you deserve—now it's time to put it all together and make it happen!

Learn from Past Mistakes

The thing about relationships is that you have to learn from past mistakes in order to move forward. With every relationship, you learned something. You had an experience that taught you something, and that's important to remember right now and always. This relationship was in your life for a reason, even if it's hard to see it at the time.

So think about what college dating life was like, and then focus on each relationship that you had. What did you take out of it? What did you do wrong that you would never do again? What would you do differently in a future relationship? If you could go back and give your college self some advice, what would it be? These are the things that you want to reflect upon so that you can learn the lesson that was intended for you.

We all make mistakes, and you are now at a point in your life where you can reflect upon that. The mistakes may not have even be your own, but rather the person that you dated. The mistakes may not have felt like that at the time, but there are lessons to be found. You are more mature now, you have insight about your past, present, and future, and you want to make effective changes. You can now determine where things went wrong and find a way to change that path.

Even if it was a relationship that was totally wrong for you, there is something to be learned here. Though you may wish that you hadn't dated certain people, figure out why that is and then make sure that you change that behavior or make different choices next time. Something made you find the people that you dated and something made you enter into a relationship with them. Then something made the relationship fall apart and caused you to go separate ways. Focus in on that and dwell in the mistakes so that a lesson can be found!

You are at a perfect phase of life for reflection and soul searching. You are trying to settle down and mature and grow into the person that you are going to be. We all go through a lot of different phases in college, and dating was a part of that. You were a different person than you are now and you have learned a lot, so put it to play now.

Out of the negative can come a positive, and as you embark on this next phase in your journey you want to make that transformation. Take the time to really think through the past relationships that you had and figure out what you would do differently—now you have the path towards finding a good partner and creating a meaningful relationship that will last. It's going to be a road full of great stuff ahead!

Do Some Soul Searching

This is not always very comfortable for us. Digging deep and really thinking about what we want is not always an easy thing. Dwelling in the space of thinking and feeling is not always something that we want to do. However, if you want to move forward and find that type of relationship that you have always wanted, then this is an essential part of the journey. This is how to move onto a better place.

Maybe dating in college wasn't a bad thing, but rather was just fun with no strings attached. Maybe you enjoyed meeting new people and the dating scene, but you just want something more meaningful. Maybe it's just time to figure out how to get things on track in a different direction. It may very well be that you have learned from previous relationships, you dated a lot and had fun, and now you are just ready for something more. Consider what your ideal man and ideal relationship looks like. Even taking the time to write down positive traits or ideal relationship types can help you. Once you have identified all of this then use this to help you to focus on these things. You deserve true happiness, and it comes with you identifying it first. Be certain that you take the time to focus on what it is that will make YOU happy and then go after it!

We are all coming from different points of view, and we all have different dating history. Therefore, we are all going to take different paths when it comes to finding somebody after college. This is where you have to do some thinking and really determine what you want. This is your time to be alone with yourself and really do the soul searching that you need. This can help you to find the right person, and to find a relationship that is truly right for you. Examine what went wrong and determine that it will never happen again: Chances are that you can identify when things went wrong in previous relationships. Either you were not asking for what you want, you were dating the wrong type of person, or the relationship was flawed from the beginning. It doesn't matter what the circumstances were, but rather that you learn from them and decide in this very moment that you will not allow that to happen again. This is empowering and it ensures that you won't fall prey to the same mistakes, the same patterns, or ultimately end up with the guys that don't make you happy as you deserve to be!

Focus On What You Want and Don't Accept Anything Less

When you take the time to really think through your dating past in college, then you can determine what you liked and didn't like. You can focus on what you learned from each experience. Best of all, you can focus on what you want moving forward. If something didn't work for you, then you know to avoid it. If something went well then take from that so that you can apply it to a future relationship. Decide here and now that you won't settle down and you WILL get what you want: This is absolutely vital for settling will never ever get you to where you want to be. Let go of this terrible and unpleasant pattern where you settle and convince yourself it will be okay. It never will! Be aware of what you want and don't stop until you get it. You will never find what you really want if you follow the same pattern of settling, so stop going down that path and you will undoubtedly find true happiness as you move into this new chapter of your life—the past mistakes can actually really help you greatly in the future!

You are in a big state of transition right now where you are making a new life for yourself. So you get to decide what will make you happy and what won't. You deserve everything that is going to make you happy. You know your own worth by now, and you don't want to waste time with anybody that doesn't see that. This is where you need to be confident in who you are and what you have to offer. The right person will see that and embrace it so that a good relationship can evolve. Get rid of the past negative feelings and turn that into positive energy moving forward: You have focused on the negative aspects of your relationships in the past. You have learned from your mistakes and you have learned to accept them too. Now let it go! You don't want to dwell on the past and you certainly don't want to let this ruin your chance at a happy future either.

Though you may very well have some negative aspects of your previous dating life, you learn from it and then you move forward. Turn those negatives into positives and allow this to propel you forward in a really great way. Learn from it, let it go, and then focus on the new you and what that means in your love life.

Whatever your dating past was like, you are ready to create a new chapter. You are in search of the right person for that right now and that means being very in tune with the things that will make you happy. You are going to date plenty of people before you settle down, and it starts now with focusing on the types of relationships that will bring you happiness. So, as you begin this next chapter of your life, be clear with the types of things you want in a partner and in a relationship—then you can focus on them to ensure that you have a good match to begin with. Never settle and always know your own worth! You probably don't realize it, but there is one aspect of your journey that matters more than anything else. You may not necessarily think that you have what it takes. You may not think of yourself as a positive or confident person. You might have convinced yourself that you aren't good enough or questioned or second guessed yourself every step of the way. That's all about to change—for when you discover just how important it is to be confident you will be more than happy to get in touch with this feeling deep within you!

There are things that you need to possess in order to find the right type of guy. If you're not confident or positive, then you are not going to have a good chance at finding Mr. Right. If you are only focused on getting into a relationship rather than seeing that you are worthy of having the RIGHT relationship, then you will constantly cut yourself short. Admittedly this is easier said than done and we all know that. This is, however, a truly important stage of the process. Until you reach the point where you value yourself, you feel good about yourself, and you move forward with a confident feeling within you, then you won't get what you really want.

When you're smiling and positive, it's almost contagious. Think of that on a broader level for when you feel confident about yourself then others can't help but take notice of this too. Here is why confidence will undoubtedly help you to get what you want in your love life.

Confidence ensures that you focus on what YOU really want: When you feel good about yourself then it allows you to have a clear head and a wonderful vision. When you know that you are worthy and valuable and wonderful, then this ensures that you focus on what YOU want and what makes YOU happy.

It isn't until you get to the point where you feel good about yourself that you can feel good about your future. This helps you to move forward with focus, with a positive mindset, with the right attitude, and with a determination that you will find the right person, and this will guide you along until you get to that point of true and lasting happiness.

Confidence just so happens to be the most attractive trait to possess: Others will notice your confidence and be attracted to you because of it. Though you may spend a lot of time on your appearance which does matter, it is your confidence that will draw the right person to you. When you feel good about who you are and you're self-assured, this draws people in—they are intrigued, and they want to get to know you better and see what makes you so special! Though it may seem like a lot to take in, you can take ultimate control over the process. This isn't just about what you want in a mate or in a relationship but also in what you want for yourself. Think of what will make you happy and visualize what that will look like. Compare this to other relationships where you weren't quite as happy as you could have or should have been. Think of what will contrast that and then consider how to make this happen in a really profound way.

Considering your own needs, your role, and what you bring to the relationship is a really powerful concept. It will help you to get what you want in love and also ensure that you enjoy long term happiness moving forward in the relationship of your dreams! Here's what it really means in the long run and why you must consider this in your reflection if you want to ultimately end up with the right man in a loving and nurturing relationship.

You get to be in the driver's seat, now consider what that means to you: What this all demonstrates is that this is all about YOU for a change. This can be exciting, cause you to feel nervous, and it may even be a little overwhelming. If you are used to just jumping into a relationship without thinking about it, then this is all new to you. If you never really stopped to consider what your feelings were or what you wanted or what type of energy you brought into the relationship, then now is your chance. You get to do it all over again and really focus on the things that make you happy.

You also get to dictate the type of role that you will play in future relationships. This can really be a lifesaving initiative where love is concerned for it can save you from past mistakes. If you find that you simply can't figure out what went wrong in the past, then it may very well have something to do with who you were in the relationship—and now you get to change that role and ensure that it's a much better fit for you to lead you to lasting and full happiness. Wow is that an amazing feeling!

It's time to consider what you bring to a relationship and what makes you a true catch: Think of what you are all about and what you can do to make others happy for this matters in the big picture too. Consider what you want to be in the relationship, whether that's more submissive or more in charge for there is truly no right or wrong. Think also of what makes you such a great catch in terms of your personality traits, your interests, your best attributes, and all of the things that make you intriguing overall.

If you can think through these things then you can embrace confidence, and you are also sure to capture this in the role that you play in a relationship. It really can be a wonderful thing for when you put this all to work and you enjoy what it feels to be loved and to give love. It really is a two-way street, and once you figure out what your role is then you get a better chance at enjoying long term happiness which is really what it's all about.

It's important to consider your role in order to find that lasting happiness that you are looking for: If you only consider what you want out of a mate then you are cutting yourself short. Think of what makes you happy, but also in a way of what you want to bring to the relationship. If you want to be more of the decision maker or if you simply want to be the one who gets to sit back and relax a bit, then you get to dictate all of this.

No right or wrong, just the point is that you put thought into this and use this to embrace some positive energy that you need to unlock what a relationship should really be all about. This is all a big part of the reflection process, and the more that you think about who you will be and what you want to portray in a relationship, the more that you will find happiness with the right guy who allows you to be yourself—you want somebody that will love you for everything and for all that you are so embrace this and let it shine to attract him once and for all! There are so many wonderful things to gain out of finding a boyfriend at this stage of your life. You just might find that you get to know yourself out of this journey above and beyond anything else. Be ready for some really effective changes and to go in with the right mindset and attitude, for when you do you find that happiness that you have always dreamed of. You will be much more likely to find happiness if you put in some work and effort, and if you think through what this happiness really means to you at this stage of life too. Wow there is so much to experience if you allow yourself to get there!

Though finding a boyfriend after college may not be as easy as it once was when you were in school, you may actually find a much better match for you in the end. You now have all of the tips and tricks to make your experience more enjoyable, to find the right type of guy, and to enjoy lasting happiness moving forward. That means that you can learn to focus on the things that really matter in a guy, and also that you can avoid making any further mistakes as you move forward. The relationships that you build from here on out will be wonderful ones and you are about to create a journey that you never dreamed possible—so embrace it and enjoy it for it will help you to find a great boyfriend!

Chapter 10

How to Get the Girl of Your Dreams?

If you really want the girl of your dreams, then it's time to focus on what really matters to get her. You need to stop playing games and using the same old boring pickup lines. You need to change the way you do things, or you will continue with the same ridiculous cycle. You don't like the way that your love life is going right now? Then maybe it's time to change up the way that you do things. You want to get a woman that is going to be a good match for you? Then start to think the way that she does. It may sound silly, but it's true and it will work!

The truth of the matter is that you have probably been approaching her all wrong. If you want to get to the heart of the issue, then you have to know how she ticks so to speak. It's important to understand a woman if you want to know how to best talk to her. Though not all women work the same way, their mindset is often similar enough that you can get to the heart of that. So if you have been struggling or finding it difficult to move forward with a relationship then it's time to change that around for good.

This isn't something that you will necessarily master overnight. It's not something that is taught and it's also not inherent to most men out there. This is very much about reflection, observation, and of course the need to get in tune with the signals that she's giving off. If you play this right, then you WILL be the guy who stands out and it won't even be that hard for you. If you think through what she wants and really get to understand her, then she will be yours—you have so much to gain but you first have to understand how she works once and for all!

So while you may think that you've got it all figured out when it comes to dating, ask yourself if things are working out as you want them to. Though you may certainly be dating, you may not be in the type of relationship that you really want. Your relationships may come together easily, but then may not necessarily last. You may find that you are having no problems in finding plenty of girls to date, but they are definitely not the right ones. This is where you need to take a step back and figure out how exactly you plan to get the girl of your dreams.

What is that going to take? What are you going to need to change up? How are you going to attract the type of girl that you actually want to be with in the long term? If you are asking yourself these questions, then there's a good chance that you are somewhat ready to settle down. You are looking for more meaning in a relationship, and you want something that will last. This shows that you are ready to take the steps needed to find that perfect girl of your dreams—so let's get this going!

You Need to Get into Her Mindset

This may sound like an impossible task, but it really isn't. It will require some work on your part, but you can definitely learn to think like she does. This is about being in tune to who she is and what she is really saying. You have to look beyond just the surface level commentary from her. You have to really learn to tune into her signs and nonverbal communication. You basically need to learn how to read a woman and to get into her mindset in an effective manner. It can be done, but just requires you to rework things a little.

Try to put yourself in her shoes and then consider if your approach is meeting her demands. Yes, this is about you but it's also about her, and that means that you are thoughtful and respectful of women in general. If you're not really considering what she wants, then you're missing the mark greatly. This will set you up for failure and ensure that you get a bad reputation too. Nobody wants that, especially if you're searching for the girl of your dreams!

Start to look at the world through her eyes and see things in the way that she would. This means that if your approach hasn't been working much beyond the initial stages of dating, you're going to need a do over. This means that you need to think about what she would want out of a guy and what makes you somebody that she would want to date. Consider what women want, how they act, what they are saying even with the nonverbal cues, and restructure your approach accordingly. Be compassionate, be kind, be cognizant of her feelings, be the kind of guy that a good girl is going to want to date. No more barbaric pickup lines or public displays of being the "typical guy"— your dream girl is not going to want that.

This is about getting to know your audience so do the things that they do and listen to your female friends talk. They will tell you what women want in a man, and this will make your job easier. Count on female friends and family members to tell you what you may be doing right or wrong. Ask for advice and really change your thinking in an impactful way. No woman wants to be aggressively sought after in a bar or club. She wants a good guy that is going to show that he has something to offer. It's not that hard to portray this either with the right amount of fine tuning.

Don't fake it either because she will know. Be your true authentic self and let that speak for itself. Work on the areas that may have kept you from getting your dream girl in the past, and above all try to think like she thinks. It's about the little things and when you start to notice them it will speak volumes. It will put her at ease, and you will find it much easier to connect with her. She will be much more interested if she sees that you are the type of guy who takes the time to notice things about her. This is a huge step towards getting the girl that you really want!

You Will Gain So Much If You Focus On What She Wants

This may sound like a lot of work, and it is. If you are at a point in your life where you want that dream girl, then you have to be willing to put in the work and change things up a little. Guess what happens when you take the time and effort to really focus on what a woman wants? It shines in you and it comes off as confidence, this will ultimately win her over. This shows that you really care, and that you are serious about finding a good long lasting relationship.

Women truly love a man that is compassionate and understanding of her needs. They adore a man who can be forthcoming with his emotions and who has an appreciation for HER. This can show through if you take the time to observe her and see what she's about. Show that compassion and understanding and she will be eating out of the palm of your hands. More so than that though, you will find somebody who is a match and do so in the right way.

Every relationship is worth working for, and therefore it's up to you to determine if you are willing to do this. There is so much to gain when you focus on the things that are important to her. You don't ever want to change who you are or compromise what you want, but if you can be more compassionate and caring for her needs it will give you what you want too. This is an effort worth taking!

You Need to Change Your Approach

If you haven't exactly been that happy with your love life lately, then you need to ask yourself why. Maybe you haven't been so lucky in love, or maybe you're having a hard time finding any girls that you're even that interested in. If you want more substance and a longer term relationship, then you have to start to think about what it's going to take to get there. You have to consider how you are going to find a girl that is your match and what it will take outside of your comfort zone and current approach.

If you have had no problems finding women in the past but the relationship never lasts, then you need to change your approach. If you are having a hard time getting past the talking phase, then it's time to change your approach. If you can keep the women interested but you find out very quickly that they are not a match for you, then you need to change your approach. If you just feel like your dating life and relationships are not working for you, then it's time to change things up. The things that may have worked in the past often don't work as you think about your future. Start to consider her feelings, focus on the type of woman that you want, be more mindful and compassionate in your approach—and you will quickly see how this works for you. In no time at all you will find a wonderful woman that is a great match for you, and you can learn what it takes to make each other happy moving forward.

Chapter 11

How to Use the Law of Attraction to Meet and Keep Your Soulmate?

You may feel as if you simply can't try anything else when it comes to finding the great love of your life. You may even feel as though you have tried everything to this point, only to come up feeling disappointed and frustrated. This is a common occurrence when it comes to love and romance, and so many of us have a tendency to give up when things get tough. The reality is that this is right at the point in your love journey when you need to change your mindset and adapt to a whole new way of thinking and living.

Maybe you feel like you need to shake things up so that you don't end up with the same exact outcome. You know that there is great power in the way that you think and feel, so maybe it's time to start focusing on that rather than just going through the motions. Perhaps you've heard of the Law of Attraction, or maybe this is entirely new to you. If you find yourself at a crossroads in love and romance, then this is most definitely where you want to shift your focus.

The Law of Attraction is really quite simple when you think about it. What you put out to the Universe is what you will get in return. So if you put negative thoughts, feel defeated, give up, or concede that you will NEVER meet the right person, then you will get exactly that. Guess what happens if you reframe your thinking though? If you put the thought out there that you are ready for your next great love, that you believe you will find them, that they are meant for you, and that you are ready for something wonderful—then you will get that too!

So why wouldn't you shift your mindset? Why would you want to go through life being negative? It's so much easier in theory to say that you want to be more positive, but then putting it into practice isn't so easy in reality. When you have had bad relationships or breakups, when you've been hurt, or when things just haven't gone your way in love and life, it's so much easier to just give up. It takes effort and commitment to say that you want and deserve so much more. It is something that you can undoubtedly turn around so that you are focused on what you really want. But you have to commit to that and you can't let anything interfere.

The Law of Attraction is all about your mindset and the way that you look at the world. This is something that can apply to your work life, your friendships, your financial status, your health, and of course relationships. This is ultimately mind over matter at work! This is something that you have control over, but it must be a concerted effort. Though you may be a pessimist or have a hard time with positive thinking, you do have the ability to control this of your own accord. This is most definitely something that can change your love life forever, but only if you are willing to change the way that you look at this aspect of your life and change it for the better. Let's take a look at how you can use the Law of Attraction to change your love life forever!

Stop The Bad Patterns

It's not to say that you are in your current situation due to any fault of your own. It's not a matter of fault, but rather it's about you learning to identify and then avoid the bad patterns. This may be a series of bad decisions that you have made in your life. It may be more about your relationships always going in a certain direction. It may be behavior from you or it may be about picking the wrong person. Whatever it is, there are certain patterns that have brought you to this point and it's time to break the cycle.

If you want to change your mindset and learn to really embrace a positive way of living, then it's all about stopping these bad patterns. It's time to break free of the behaviors and choices that have been holding you back. In order to usher in the positive, you absolutely must get rid of the negative. These patterns have been holding you back, and though it takes you outside of your comfort zone, it's time to put a stop to them for good. You can do this, but it requires an honest assessment and the ability to make effective changes!

You have to take inventory here and focus on the things that didn't work for you in the past. What didn't work in past relationships? Why did you find yourself in the same horrible situation over and over again? Did you ever wish that things were different? Do you know how to fix what went wrong in the past? These are the types of questions that you need to answer before you can move forward with the life that you are meant to have. There is something that was holding you back in the past and now it's time to fix it so that it is no longer a factor moving forward.

Once you identify the problem areas, you will be amazed at how you can move forward in a more cohesive and positive manner. Once you know what sort of bad choices kept you from getting what you want, you will see that there is so much more to gain. It's not always easy, but it is very satisfying when you determine the best path to move forward with. You almost feel the energy of the Law of Attraction in your life, and you want to embrace this positive change.

You start to see just how impactful it can be and you want this to be your new way of living. You are ready to accept the love that you were meant to have, and this is how to get to it once and for all. Once you break free of the bad patterns and get rid of them for good, then you can start to focus on what will make you happy for the long term. This is about the time that you learn to take care of yourself and to change the way that you think about love and life—it's very liberating!

Take Care of Yourself and Set the Scene First

If you want that happily ever after, then you need to put in the work to get it. That means that you must start by taking care of yourself first and foremost. In order to get to a positive mindset and usher in the Law of Attraction, you must learn to put yourself and your priorities first. Set the scene for this next great love and prepare yourself for it. Let yourself feel that excitement and positive energy, for this is what you will apply to your life from this point forward. It won't happen overnight and it may take some real focused effort to accomplish, but it will be worth it.

We talk so much about self-care, and it starts here. If you know that you are worthy of great things, then you have to believe in that. You have to love yourself and feel the positive energy coming at you. It's essential for you to KNOW without a shadow of a doubt that you are going to get the things that you want out of your relationship. Start by giving yourself some love and really learning to take care of your feelings, your mental attitude, and you're very being. If you don't do it then nobody else is going to do. If you don't believe that you are worthy of love, then nobody else is going to either. When you put yourself first and really start to take care of this great person that you are, then the wonderful things can start actually happening.

Change Your Mindset and Put the Right Vibe Out There

You can almost feel this sort of shift and it's tangible. You can feel yourself transform to this way of thinking and it's actually incredible. You have this positive vibe that you are putting out there to the universe, and it's going to respond to you big time. When you make the conscious choice to make that mindset shift, then great things lie ahead. You do have a choice here too, for it's all about the way that you view the world and the things that you want which matter the most.

Take that leap right now and just KNOW that somehow great things lie ahead. Trust the process, trust yourself, and trust the Universe to deliver big time when you send this powerful message out there. It's like flipping a switch and you suddenly realize that great things lie ahead when you do. When you make that ultimate decision to think positively and focus your energy on what you want, then it all comes together. It's impactful, it's powerful, and it's so rewarding—you will wonder why you didn't do this sooner.

There is great power in our mind and the thoughts that we have, and this becomes very apparent in this moment. Having a loving relationship is just going to be the beginning, but it will be a welcome change from what you have dealt with in the past. The best is yet to come, and you smile thinking about your future here—all because you changed the way that you think and feel about things!

Understand and Embrace How the Law of Attraction Can Work for You

Yes, it really is as simple as saying that you put a certain message out to the Universe and it responds exponentially. Yes, it really does happen that quickly where you get the power back over your relationships and your life. Yes, you can feel this positive impact in your life when you are ready to embrace this. Now are you ready to flip the switch? Start to think of how different things would be in your life if you were to use the Law of Attraction. It's all within your reach, and now you just have to put it to good use.

This isn't to say that you are always going to have a positive mindset. There will be good days and bad, and there will be great relationships and some that are more disappointing. At the end of the day though, if you have a good attitude it makes a big difference. It ensures that you feel good and engaged with what you are doing. It means that you are learning to flip the script and put the good messages out there.

Embrace this powerful concept, and even if you have days where you fall off track, you can get right back on again. Think of the relationships that you've had and what you would do different. Feel the power of positive thought and emotion within you and see how that comes to a productive point. See how well balanced and in tune you feel with this new way of viewing the world. This can apply to anything in your life, but start with your love life.

Start to really envision what this great love will look like, how they will make you feel, and what this relationship is like. Let yourself be in that moment and let this positive emotion overtake you. Be in this moment to really allow yourself to enjoy what a healthy and positive relationship feels like. Use this power of thought to create the ideal vision of who you want and what you want to be loved like.

There is nothing off limits, so put yourself into this body, mind, and soul. When you can create this positive image in your mind, it will have no choice to come back to you. This is when the good stuff happens and when you can really let go and enjoy yourself. This is when that great love comes to you, almost as if they were magnetically drawn there. You are probably smiling just reading that, and this is testament to what lies ahead—so let yourself go there and experience this once and for all!

Chapter 12

Why Men Are Afraid of Commitment

Do you feel as if every time you get close to a man he runs for the hills? Do you feel as if you are struggling trying to figure out what a man that you are interested in is thinking? Do you constantly end up being broken hearted and sad because you just went through a bad relationship? This is such a common situation for far too many women, and it's time to break the cycle. You will only benefit greatly if you can learn to understand why men are afraid of commitment. This is not a difficult thing to do, but it does take some understanding.

When you think of commitment as a woman, you probably have very fond thoughts. When a man thinks of a commitment, it may evoke different emotions. Even the nicest guy seems to have difficulty in committing to a long term relationship. This may be something that you see more in the younger years, or it may be a lifelong issue for some men. The thing that you have to remember is that if a man is afraid of commitment, there is often a very good reason as to why.

Women are generally wired to love being in a committed relationship. They love to take care of their man, and in turn they love to be taken care of as well. Women for the most part are more nurturing, and so a relationship gives them the perfect opportunity to do what they do best. This is of course a generalization, but you will often find it to be true most of the time. Women love to be loved and are more than happy to show their affection and admiration. So a relationship is a natural extension of that, and a way for her to show that she is committed.

Men on the other hand may not find nurturing to come as easily. They may not feel that same compelling need to be loved or to love somebody else. Sure men may enjoy being taken care of, but sometimes they like to do their own thing. They may feel tied down prematurely, and this can cause them to retreat. If their friends aren't in relationships, then that makes it even harder for them to want to commit. Men often like to do their own thing, be with their friends, and not have to answer to somebody about where they are all the time.

So when you look at these two contrasting points of view up close, you can see that sometimes a relationship isn't always going to be so easy. You can see that men are just not hard wired to want to be committed. This may change over time, but it can help to know why it is this way in the first place. It can help you to understand the various reasons why he may not want to be in a relationship at all. This may be an individual thing, but you can really start to understand him better when you look at the reasons. If you are wondering why relationships seem to freak him out, there's often a good explanation—let's focus on the most common ones so that you can gain some insight once and for all.

He's Been Burned Before

This is sometimes harder to see because he will often try to hide it or cover it up. If you are with a man who was burned badly in a previous relationship, then you can start to understand his hesitation towards commitment. If he has been hurt before, suffered from a bad break up, was cheated on, or fell madly in love with a woman only to have him crush his heart, then you know why he isn't so ready to jump back into a relationship head first.'

Everyone gets hurt in love sometimes, and that's how it goes. Most of us can recover from this and move on with our lives to find the next great love. This is particularly true for women, who may struggle at first but then get their lives back on track. Men however don't always talk about it, and they certainly won't open up to their buddies. So if he got hurt badly and doesn't have the support to work through it, he's not going to be very eager to go down this same path again.

Though it may not be rational, he could be holding onto the pain of his last relationship. While you may think that you can try to talk him through this, he has to deal with this in his own way. Therefore, if he was hurt, you may have to wait it out or move on. He will only be ready when he's ready, and trying to rush him through it will not work well for you in the long run.

He Wants to Strike Before He Gets Hurt

This can be related to him previously be hurt, or it may be its own issue alone. Some men want to hurt you before you have a chance to hurt him. He may be trying to deal with his own issues, and he wants to do it alone. He may instead find that he has turned himself into a more offensive "player" as he was hurt when he let his guard down. There are so many reasons why he may be this way, but he has it in his mind that he's going to prevent himself from ever getting hurt like that again.

Men like this tend to be serial daters and never really settle down into a long term commitment. They may feel as if they have to be protective of their feelings, and therefore they keep everything bottled up and to themselves. They may try to come off as cocky, arrogant, or as if they need nobody but themselves. You may be initially drawn to him, but find yourself feeling disappointed in the way he conducts himself. If you are getting a bad feeling, then it is definitely not the right time to be with a guy like this.

Hopefully he will work through his issues or previous hurt, but if he is at this stage, then it's very unlikely that you will get a commitment from him. And would you even want it at this stage of the game? Chances are that it wouldn't end well, you wouldn't get what you wanted, and a loving and lasting relationship would not be yours so it's best to be in tune with what's going on here. Sometimes you have to move on if the signs are pointing to it, and this is an instance where that may be true.

He's Afraid to Settle Down

This is the tale as old as time when it comes to men and commitments. If he is in a good place in his life right now or if he's young and free, then the last thing he's going to want to do is settle down. So many men go through years of their life where they just want to be free and have time with their buddies. The last thing that they want is to be tied down, and this is something that he will fight off as long as he can.

For some men, settling down signifies that he's getting older. He may not be ready for marriage, kids, and the white picket fence. He may know that he wants that, but he's not there yet. If he's younger or at a new phase of life, then there's a good chance that he just wants to go out with his friends. The idea of having to answer to somebody doesn't sound good to him right now. He may love to enjoy his freedom, and settling down means that is taken away. He may consider commitment for something that happens in the future, but he is definitely not there yet mentally or emotionally.

If you are dealing with a man that is afraid to settle down, it may be a bumpy ride for a while. He may really like you, but being in a long term committed relationship freaks him out. It signifies his need to grow up, and he doesn't want to do that yet. It may mean to him that he has to move forward to the next phase of his life, and he's just not ready. He may even stay with you for a while, but in a more casual way. You are never going to rush a guy like this into a committed relationship, and you honestly shouldn't want to. Recognize if this is the type of guy that you are dealing with—and then decide if he's worth waiting for or if you need to move on.

Commitment Just Sounds Scary and Out of Reach

He may have friends in committed relationships, and he only sees the bad side of that. He may have come from a family where his parent's relationship just didn't work. He may be at the beginning of the rest of his life, and he has certain goals for himself. Whatever the reason, for guys like this, commitment just sounds downright scary. He is afraid of it, and he may feel as if he will always have that fear. This is really hard to break through as a woman, and it may not end well.

Some guys get over it and move past this phase. It may take the right woman or the right relationship to make that happen, but he will get to the finish line. Some guys may struggle with this their whole life, particularly if this is a deeper issue for him. Fear of commitment can be very real for a man, and there's not much you can do to change his mind. He may have always been in short term relationships or just enjoyed dating so much that he never really felt that a long term relationship was within his grasp. Again, this can change with the right time, person, and circumstance.

Sometimes men need to see what relationships are and are not. Sometimes they need to see that the fear is bigger than themselves, and that they need not worry about what the future holds. Fear is a wild thing as it can get bigger than it needs to, and this is often the case for men and relationships. Be patient with him and it just might work out!

Chapter 13

The Keys to Relationship Happiness

There are some very distinct keys to relationship happiness, and they aren't as difficult to comprehend as you might think. They are real life experience based keys that can lead you to long term relationship happiness. If you are realistic about it, there is a good chance that at some point in time, you may need them. Though things may be good now and everything feels strong in your relationship, there may come a point where you want to look into these.

Even the best of relationships have their ups and downs. It's important to remember that, because even the greatest love story has points where they may struggle. It can feel frustrating when you are going through a time like that, but you have to know that it's normal. That's why it can be helpful to consider what the five keys are to loving and lasting relationships. That's why you want to try to stay ahead of this, and ensure that you are focused on what can keep you both happy in the long run.

If you think of the ideal state of your relationship, what does it look like? What does it mean to be truly happy together? How do you perceive relationship happiness? What do you want or expect out of your partner? These are things that you want to consider so that you know how to work towards what you want in your relationship. That's something important to remember too—relationships are work! They are worth it and sometimes it's easier than others, but they are work nonetheless. So if you know that you love the person that you're with and you want to make it work long term, you have to think ahead and put in the work.

Though each of these keys to relationship happiness are quite different, they are all intertwined. They all work in perfect harmony to create that relationship that you have always dreamt of. They help to pave the road to long term happiness and the things that you want to be present in your life that help you to be a better person. Happiness is what you make it to be, and therefore it's up to you and your partner to define.

These keys are a good fundamental structure by which to base your relationship on. They will help to define what it takes to enjoy long term happiness. They help you to stay on track, and to put in the work in the right areas at the right time. Though you are going to experience the ups and downs in a relationship, these keys will help you to remember what is important—they are at the very foundation of a loving relationship and if you are mindful of them then you can make things work in the most effective way possible. Love will be yours forever!

The 5 Keys to Love and Relationships

Forget about what you thought you knew to work in a loving relationship. You can reflect upon what went wrong in the past, but you want to learn from each experience. Though you are going to have good days and bad days, these keys can help you to refocus your efforts. They help you to remember how it all works, and what is truly important. Sometimes just being able to hit that reset button and get back on course is all it takes.

You will find conflict much easier to work through. You will find that you appreciate each other more, even your differences and areas of arguments in the past. You will learn to truly compromise and to remember what matters to your partner. You will feel like you wish that you knew about these sooner, but you will utilize them to help you to remain a dedicated and loving partner moving forward.

Mental Key—The Importance of a Mental Connection and Effective Communication

There is a certain way that you think about things. There is a way that you see the world around you. There is a way that you feel about things. There is a way that you consider the events and circumstances around you. All of these things work together in perfect harmony to create your mental state and the key to your own happiness. Think about what those are, and then turn your focus to their own mental key.

Together you want to try to find harmony in this very important mental key. But you must first consider how your significant other views and thinks about things too. You aren't going to see things the same way on everything. You are going to have profound differences, and that's okay. It's part of life and it's important to recognize that, because you never want to try to change somebody. You want them to be their real authentic self, and you want to be the same in the relationship.

The mental key is all about the way that you think about, view, and handle the world around you. It's also very much about how you handle and see things about your relationship. This covers so much such as the way that you view arguments, what you perceive to be relationship bliss, how you think about the long term, what you put into a relationship, and so much more. This sets the foundation for your ability to be happy with this person into the long term.

There is another important aspect to the mental key, which is the way in which the two of you connect. This may involve face-to-face time, conversations, time alone together, how you communicate, and what it means to even connect with each other in the first place. This is such an important aspect to a relationship. Again this doesn't mean that your definition of connection will be the exact same. It is healthy and normal to have differences within a relationship and that is nothing to be afraid of. It's just a matter of how you find ways to connect with one another, and to facilitate communication in an effective way.

Connection and communication will help the mental key to be alive and well in your relationship. This may take some trial and error to get it just right. It may evolve over time, and it may be a struggle at times. Sometimes you may not even know where your mental state is at, much less that of your partner. You have to remember that this will come together for you, for your partner, and for your united front.

Life circumstances may change the way that you think about and view things, and you will learn how to pivot to adapt to that. This is about being mentally invested into your relationship and your life with this person. So while you may not necessarily have recognized the importance of this in the past, you now see it and can hopefully remember it. The way that you think about things matters, and the way that you communicate matters, and all of this helps you to connect with one another—and this is the essence of the mental key to happiness.

Spiritual Key—A Spiritual Connection to Unite You Together Forever

There is something to be said for spirituality. It's not necessarily a one size fits all type of thing either. It's not just reserved for your religion either, though that is an aspect of spirituality for many. This is connection on another level. This is the two of you becoming one. This is the joining together of two individual to become one cohesive unit. This is about so much more than just the religious views that you have, for this is a spiritual connection all your own. This is something that you almost can't put into words.

This is the way that the two of you have a language all your own. It's your own little world together, and one that nobody else can truly understand or be a part of. This is the unspoken words and nonverbal communication that you share. It's the rituals that you develop together, and the traditions that are born out of the love that you have for one another. It's connection on such a deep level that it can almost take your breath away sometimes. Though you may not necessarily see it at first, you feel it after you have been together for a while.

This is natural and organic, and it develops over the course of time. It is the way in which you both hold each other dear, and how you want to be in each other's lives. It's how you want to make plans and spend time with one another. It's settling in with one another after a busy day or week, and then being able to be your true self. This spiritual key is how your relationship grows and evolves over time. There is so much to this key and much of it is unspoken or just exists between the two of you.

The spiritual key does have something to do with the religious, ethical, or life views that you both hold. When you are on the same page with this, it makes life so much easier and neat. When you are at opposing points of view, it can cause some chaos within the relationship. It doesn't mean that the relationship can't work, but it makes things more complicated. You don't want to try to convince one another to see the world in the same way, because sometimes that just isn't possible. You do however want to find a way to recognize those differences, and hopefully they are something that you have discussed all along.

It is when the differing points of view come up as a surprise that you have issues. When you are caught off guard with having contrasting views. Hopefully this is something that you discussed all along so that you know how the other person feels. It is also when the views shift or become more extreme in nature that you tend to have problems. It can happen and it's something that you want to be prepared for and talk through as a couple.

The spiritual key is how you connect with one another, and it's also about good strong communication. If you have differing views on spirituality, it's all about how you work through those. You never want to compromise who you are or how you feel, but you also don't want this to become a problem in your relationship. So if you can find a good middle ground and work through this issue, it will make life and love easier. It will ensure that you can celebrate each other's differences and appreciate each other for who you are. Differences can keep life interesting, but staying connected can ensure long term happiness.

Physical Key—Why Is It Important to Have Beauty in The Eyes of the Beholder?

Appearance matters. It just does, and we don't want to deny it. Physical attraction is real and it's an important component of every relationship. It's not to say that physical is the only thing that matters, because that's not the case. However, you do need to be mindful that the physical aspect of things matters and it is at the core of every relationship. If you didn't care about how you looked, then you wouldn't put any time into your appearance. If you didn't care at all about looks, then you wouldn't be interested in attraction. It matters, and it's a part of the process.

The physical key isn't just about sex, though that is something that we will focus on later. The physical is the way in which you put yourself out there to each other. In a relationship, you want to maintain an attraction to each other. This will change over time and become about things much deeper than appearance. However initially it's about the attraction that comes about through physical attraction. So this is something that you want to put emphasis into and put your best foot forward so to speak. You don't want to stop caring about how you look, and you don't want that from your partner either.

The physical key is a direct correlation to the sexual key, and they are closely intertwined. One doesn't usually exist successfully without the other. So in order for you to enjoy success in both areas, it must be an emphasis. When a partner stops caring about how they look or how they appear in front of their significant other, it's like a bad reflection into their thoughts and feelings in the relationship. The way that you present yourself to this other person demonstrates the bond that you have, and that you want the feelings to continue moving forward. It's making each other a priority, and it's putting time into the way in which they see you.

This isn't intended to be a shallow thing. It's not to say that you have to look a certain way to be attractive. It's not implying that physical attraction is the only thing that matters, as that's certainly not the case. It is however saying that you put time and thought into being your physical best, and that you want them to see you. It's putting the best version of yourself out there for the person that it matters to the most. You want to see and be seen in a way that is revolutionary, and which helps you to be your very best at all times.

The physical key is an important part of any relationship, and it ensures that you maintain that connection with each other. It says that you want to put in the effort and that you care about how you look and how you two see each other. It also ties into our very next key to relationship key, for the sexual key is very closely connected to the physical attraction that you want to maintain moving forward.

Sexual Key—The Necessity of Being Sexually Satisfied

This is about sex and the way that the two of you interact in this capacity. Physical attraction ties into a healthy sex life, and yes the two both matter to your overall relationship happiness. You want to be sure that sex is a priority, and that the two of you have similar views on it. You want to be sure that sex is not something that just goes away as life gets busy. Making time and effort for sex means that you are making each other a priority in a very personal way. This is something to consider if it feels like your relationship isn't quite on track, and therefore you may need to reassess.

This sexual key is about much more than just the act. It's about intimacy in every possible sense. That is to say that it's about the way that you feel attraction towards each other and nurture that. It's about intimacy in an elevated sense where the two of you are connected and the ways in which you show that to one another. This may be through the simplest and subtlest of physical touch. It may be the way that you sit together and talk at the end of the night. It may be cuddling or sleeping close to one another. Physical intimacy involves so many things beyond just sex, though that is at the core of it all too.

The way in which you nurture and care for one another in this way is all part of it. You do want a healthy sex life, where you are making this a focal point in your relationship. It's what you do to build that excitement and the anticipation that factors into it. This can be the way that you kiss each other or flirt with one another. It's any amount of effort that you put into making the other person feel desirable.

That's what it comes down to—that you desire each other and want to be close in the most intimate and physical way possible. Sex definitely matters in a relationship, and it should never be treated as a chore or imposition. You must remember that even when life gets busy and you may not necessarily feel like it. This is your way of connecting as a couple in a very intimate and important way. It is your expression of love towards one another, and it helps you to remain as a cohesive unit through the twists and turns that life may throw at you.

Financial Key—No Romance Without Finance and Why It Matters

There is the necessity to talk about finances. You have to discuss this area that is often taboo or dreaded within so many relationships. It doesn't have to be, but you do need to talk to one another about your thoughts and feelings. We all have different points of views and goals when it comes to money. We were all brought up differently in this sense, and we have all lived through a variety of different circumstances surrounding this part of life too. So recognize that you may come from different thought patterns, and then focus on how to make this work cohesively.

If one of you is a spender and the other is a saver, then this is something to address. If one of you has big financial goals in the future and the other does not, then take that into consideration. You can avoid fights about finances if you talk about things up front and all throughout. Sure you want to save for the future, but you also want to be sure to enjoy life in the here and now. It's all about finding the perfect balance that you are both comfortable with, and then making the most out of it.

Financial insecurities and arguments occur when one partner is keeping something from the other. They can occur when one person is spending too much and not being mindful of how the other person feels. There can be so many different reasons about why couples fight about money, but they can all be avoided with open honest communication. You want to be sure that you are both in places that you are comfortable with, and that you can work through the places that you may disagree.

Focusing on the financial key matters because it says that you take each other's views and philosophies into consideration. It really says that you care about your future together in this sense. You may have conflicting views on finances, but you work together to find peace and harmony. You work together to find common ground. This is when you see the financial key working in your relationship, and when you can avoid arguments about this that may unnecessarily come up.

So if you can get to this place, it will be a welcome change from what you may have experienced in the past. If you can learn to really embrace what it means to work together as a team, particularly in an area that so many people argue over, then you will have good times ahead. This will make a huge difference in how you deal with each other, and in how you learn to navigate the uncomfortable aspects of living together as a couple. This is an important life skill that helps to unite and strengthen you as a couple. These keys all work together in harmony to help you to be your best, and it's magical when they do!

Chapter 14

Embrace Each Trimester While Dating!

"A great marriage is not when the 'perfect couple' comes together. It is when an imperfect couple learns to enjoy their differences."

Dave Maurer

Marriage is more than a mere ceremony; it's a sacred commitment between two devoted souls. The glitz of a lavish wedding, the presents, and the esteemed guests will not guarantee a lasting union. Certain relationships naturally progress toward marriage, but before diving headfirst into the future, essential aspects of married life demand thoughtful contemplation. It is not just about the destination; it is about the journey that two people undertake together. The type of marriage you envision and work towards is the one you will experience. Your attitude towards marriage significantly influences its outcome. By dedicating yourself to building a strong foundation for your future together, you will reap immense rewards in the years to come. Every effort you invest in preparing for your marriage will bear fruit, while negligence or carelessness will have its consequences.

I sincerely urge you to pay meticulous attention to the entirety of this book. Marriage is not an area where you can afford to play games; it demands earnest commitment and thoughtful preparation. Every addition to your life is not an asset in your life. Just because you get somebody does not mean you got better. Dating is exploration: collecting data to make the right decision and self-discovery to know what you will tolerate and not settle for. Just because someone shares your faith doesn't mean they share your values. Do not develop a physical connection with a person before you get some clarity on who they are; don't do it! First, gather data, understand your needs, and discern if the data actually meets your needs! Don't learn the hard way - when people show you who they are, believe their actions, not just their words. Authentic love requires vulnerability, and vulnerability puts you at risk for pain. Your heart can be attached to something that isn't good for you. Pursue emotional health before pursuing a partner! If a person is emotionally/relationally fatigued, easily triggered, or has unhealed trauma or baggage from prior relationships, it's best not to be dating until they heal.

Love, like a blossoming flower, unfurls its petals in three breathtaking trimesters. In the symphony of dating, each stage presents its melody of emotions, experiences, and revelations, from the thrilling sparks of infatuation to the tender depths of emotional connection and, ultimately, the profound commitment to a shared future. There are stages in dating that exist as a natural progression to help individuals get to know each other better and navigate the complexities of forming a romantic relationship. These stages allow couples to build a strong foundation, establish compatibility, and explore their feelings before making long-term commitments.

The Journey of Finding Partner: Trimesters While Dating!

Embracing each trimester while dating refers to navigating the different stages of a romantic relationship with understanding, patience, and open-mindedness. Dating can be seen as progressing through distinct phases, each with its unique characteristics and challenges. Here's how you can embrace each trimester while dating:

1. First Trimester - Early Dating:

The exploration phase is the beginning of a romantic relationship where two individuals get to know each other better. It's a time filled with curiosity and excitement as both people discover common interests, values, and goals. During this phase, you may engage in various activities together to learn more about each other's likes and dislikes.

➔ **Shared Interests:**

You spend time together doing activities you both enjoy, such as going to the movies, trying new restaurants, attending events, or exploring hobbies. This allows you to bond over shared experiences and interests.

Don't hesitate to discuss any topic with your fiancé, even if it might lead to conflict. Now is the opportune moment to face potential conflicts head-on, understanding that resolving them beforehand strengthens your bond and fosters a harmonious future together. In First Corinthians 12–14, the apostle Paul encourages us to embrace and value individual differences. He uses the analogy of the "body" to emphasize that each member is essential and should not be despised or excluded because of their uniqueness. Likewise, in your marriage, your partner's personality might be distinct and occasionally challenging to navigate. However, God's intention is not to let these differences create division. Instead, they should be seen as opportunities to grow and appreciate the beauty of diversity within your relationship.

➜ Values and Beliefs:

Through conversations and discussions, you learn about each other's core values, beliefs, and life perspectives. Understanding your partner's values is essential to see if your principles align and if you can build a strong foundation for the relationship.

➜ Future Goals:

You talk about your aspirations and future plans. This helps you gauge whether your life trajectories are compatible and if you see yourselves supporting each other's ambitions.

→ **Patience:**

In the early dating phase, practicing patience can be demonstrated by taking the time to understand and respect each other's journey while allowing the relationship to grow naturally.

"Love is patient; love is kind. It does not envy; it does not boast; it is not proud. It does not dishonor others, it is not self-seeking, it is not easily angered, and it keeps no record of wrongs. Love does not delight in evil but rejoices with the truth. It always protects, always trusts, always hopes, and always perseveres."

(1 Corinthians 13:4-7)

Patience is an essential aspect of love, especially in the early stages of a relationship.

Love is patient; love is kind: True love demonstrates patience and kindness toward the other person, giving them the time and space, they need to grow in the relationship.

It does not dishonor others: Patience involves respecting the other person's boundaries, desires, and pace. It means not pushing them into uncomfortable situations or demanding more than they are ready to give.

It always trusts, always hopes, always perseveres: Patience in early dating involves trusting that the relationship will evolve naturally, having hope for the future, and persevering through any challenges that may arise.

→ Time to Build Trust:

Trust is the foundation of any healthy relationship. It takes time to build trust, and you both need to be patient with each other's vulnerabilities and insecurities.

→ Emotional Connection:

Allow the emotional connection to grow naturally. Building a deep emotional bond requires time and shared experiences.

→ Avoiding Pressure:

It is essential not to pressure your partner or feel pressured to move the relationship forward faster than what feels comfortable for both of you. Enjoy the process of getting to know each other without feeling rushed.

2. Second Trimester - Building Connection:

The "Second Trimester" can be seen as the middle stage of the partnership, where the initial excitement of early dating has evolved into a more profound emotional connection. It's a phase characterized by deeper intimacy, increased trust, and the strengthening of the bond between the partners. Let's explore some key aspects of the Second Trimester of a relationship:

➜ Deepening the Bond:

By now, you might have a more substantial connection. Embrace this phase by fostering emotional intimacy and supporting each other's growth.

The best way to do this is to take time to have regular heart-to-heart conversations where you both share your thoughts, feelings, and dreams. Discuss your hopes for the future and what you envision for the relationship.

"Let your speech be always with grace, seasoned with salt, that ye may know how ye ought to answer every man."

(Colossians 4:6)

Speak Love and Truth.

By all means, express the truth, but do it with love.

This means:

(a) Use caution when expressing what you have to say.

(b) Use caution when expressing what you have to say.

"A word fitly spoken is like apples of gold in pictures of silver."

(Proverbs 25:11)

➔ **Vulnerability:**

Share your fears, dreams, and vulnerabilities. A deeper connection often comes from being authentic and genuine with one another. Imagine that your partner is the most dynamic and capable person you know. Now, assume that person said something foolish or snapped at you. Would you hold a grudge? Would you find their actions unforgivable? Of course not.

You understand that everyone is imperfect, including this remarkable individual. You recognize that they have both good and bad days, flaws, and moments of weakness. However, these imperfections don't define them in your eyes and mind. Instead, you remember and cherish their moments of triumph, their shining achievements, and the love and light they bring into your life.

Vulnerability means having strong confidence in the darkest days of your loved ones.

➔ **Compromise:**

Recognize that both of you are unique individuals with different needs and wants. Embrace compromise and find ways to accommodate each other.

"Be devoted to one another in love. Honor one another above yourselves."

(Romans 12:10)

Let me explain to you; this verse calls for a profound and unwavering commitment to love one another within relationships. Devotion in love implies wholehearted dedication to the well-being, happiness, and growth of your partner. It goes beyond mere feelings of affection and extends to actively showing care, support, and affection through actions and words.

To "honor one another above yourselves" means placing the needs and interests of your partner above your own. It involves selflessness and a willingness to prioritize the happiness and fulfillment of your significant other. This doesn't imply neglecting your own needs but rather a mindset that seeks to serve and uplift your partner, valuing their well-being as highly as your own.

3. Third Trimester - Commitment and Future:

The "Third Trimester" can be seen as the phase where the couple has deepened their bond, established a strong emotional connection, and is now seriously considering a long-term commitment and envisioning a future together. It's a pivotal stage that involves discussions about commitment, shared goals, and making significant decisions for the future. Let's explore the key aspects of the Third Trimester:

➔ Solidifying Commitment:

If the relationship has progressed well, you may be considering a more committed future. True commitment entails unwavering support for your partner, regardless of the challenges that come your way. It means navigating the highs and lows hand in hand, weathering every storm as a united front.

If you find yourself lacking in any of these areas, take a step back and reassess your readiness for marriage. Open and honest discussions about mutual commitment should top the list of conversations couples have before embarking on this lifelong journey together.

➔ Support:

Be supportive of each other's ambitions and endeavors. Discuss how your individual life plans align and how you can support each other in achieving them. Mutual understanding and emotional support serve as the cornerstone of a healthy partnership. When your partner is struggling, your natural tendency could be to jump in and help out right away.

Remind your partner that you are a team and that you are in this together when things are difficult. Ensure them that you will always be there for them, supporting them no matter what. It's vital to avoid assuming that your partner knows you will be there for them, even in long-term relationships. Spend the time to express your commitment in words and show by your actions that you truly mean it.

➜ Long-Term Future Planning:

Embrace discussions about your future together. Couples should discuss and align their long-term goals, such as career aspirations, financial objectives, and personal ambitions. This ensures that both partners are moving in the same direction and support each other's dreams.

Be Sure Before Serious Commitment – Know Your Direction!

Be clear on who you are and what you want before you commit to a serious relationship. It is okay to take it slow, to need time to process, and to not be sure. Too many people hurry into marriage with insufficient knowledge of the person to whom they wed.

Let me explain this with a very simple example; Sarah and Mark, two adventurous souls who fell head over heels for each other. They shared a whirlwind romance filled with laughter and passion. However, amidst the euphoria, doubts lingered in Sarah's mind about her long-term goals and what she truly wanted from life. Mark, though, was eager to be married and have a family. They made the decision to go slowly to give themselves time to comprehend their unique desires and aspirations since they felt the need for clarity. As they embarked on this journey of self-discovery, their love blossomed even more. They realized that knowing themselves first was the key to building a rock-solid foundation for a committed future together. With newfound certainty, they chose to take the plunge, cherishing the profound love they had nurtured through patience and understanding.

Even if you're serious about marriage from the start of your relationship, I prefer not to rush things prematurely. Take the time to build a strong foundation and get to know each other deeply before making any major commitments. It's advisable to wait at least 6 to 8 months before considering engagement or deeper involvement.

Give yourselves the opportunity to understand each other's backgrounds and perspectives. A couple of meetings are not enough to truly know a person. Avoid pressuring your partner with ultimatums like "marry me or else..." Instead, be patient, nurture the relationship, and be prepared for the possibility that things may not always unfold as you initially hoped.

From a Biblical perspective, the principle of knowing oneself and seeking clarity before committing to a serious relationship is rooted in the wisdom and teachings found throughout the scriptures. The Bible encourages individuals to be mindful of their actions, decisions, and relationships, emphasizing the importance of seeking God's guidance and discernment in every aspect of life, including romantic relationships.

"Commit to the Lord whatever you do, and he will establish your plans."

Proverbs 16:3 (NIV)

This verse serves as a reminder that we should make decisions in accordance with God's will. We can ensure that our choices align with God's plan for our lives by taking the time to get to know ourselves and seek His direction before entering into a committed relationship.

Many people remain unmarried, waiting for a divine revelation. They long to hear a divine voice or receive a prophetic dream. When asked about their decision, they often refer to teachings or guidance from various spiritual leaders they admire. God's approach is gentle and respectful; He never pushes or manipulates individuals. Instead, He leads, guides, and suggests, allowing people to exercise their free will. Surrendering one's will to God is a personal responsibility, and the timing of this surrender may vary from one person to another.

Trusting in God often entails accepting that we may not fully understand His plans or the timing of His actions. We commonly hear the saying, "God is never late," yet it is essential to realize that He may not be early either. The reason behind this is that God uses these moments of waiting to strengthen our faith and foster personal growth. Embracing uncertainty and patiently waiting on His divine timing allows us to deepen our reliance on Him and develop a more profound connection with our faith.

How God Prepares Us?

The Bible, particularly in Ephesians 5:22-33, provides insights on being prepared for marriage through five graces: love and sacrifice, submission and respect, unity and oneness, nurture and care, and faithfulness and commitment.

These qualities can be applied to modern dating by fostering love, shared values, emotional connection, a supportive environment, and open communication. By incorporating these graces, individuals can lay a strong foundation for a successful marriage.

- To be utterly and fiercely exclusive (Ephesians 5:31).

- To become one spiritually, emotionally, and physically (Ephesians 5:31).

- To submit our desires and preferences totally to someone else (Ephesians 5:21–24).

- To work hard for someone else's purity (Ephesians 5:26–27).

- To die to ourselves for someone else, even if it costs us everything (Ephesians 5:25)

The dating idea today often differs from the biblical principles outlined in Ephesians 5:22-33, which focus on marriage. In modern dating, we may not necessarily experience those specific aspects of love and commitment with multiple individuals. Instead, the intention is to cultivate those qualities within the context of a committed relationship, leading to marriage. God's design is for us to develop and experience these virtues with one person within the safety and intimacy of a marriage promise. The biblical principles guide us toward a deeper and more meaningful connection within the commitment of marriage rather than through multiple casual relationships.

God often uses various life experiences, challenges, and lessons to help individuals grow emotionally, spiritually, and mentally. These experiences can shape our character, making us more prepared to handle the responsibilities and commitments of marriage. For those who experience a period of singleness, God is using this time for your personal growth, self-discovery, and learning to be content, which can be valuable before entering a marriage.

Love's Symphony: Get on the Same Page Before Tying the Knot and Stay on it!

"Do two walk together unless they have agreed to do so?"

Amos 3:3 (NIV)

This verse emphasizes the necessity of agreement and shared direction in a relationship. Before entering into the lifelong commitment of marriage, couples should be united in their values, beliefs, and goals. Marriage, a significant milestone in the journey of life, holds the promise of a profound and fulfilling bond between two souls. Before embarking on this sacred union, couples embark on a thoughtful exploration of various aspects. Deliberately tending to these aspects paves the way for a marriage that flourishes with love and endures through time. At the heart of this extraordinary journey lies being together, where both hearts intertwine with unwavering dedication. Embracing a culture of open communication and support, they stand as pillars for each other. Together, they bravely confront any challenges that may arise, knowing that their love and unity can conquer all. With the right perspective and approach, marriage unfolds as a breathtaking adventure adorned with beauty and grace. It becomes a boundless canvas where the colors of love paint a masterpiece of a lifelong commitment, drawing them closer with each stroke of affection.

Your dream is already in progress, simmering on the stove of life. Remember the saying, "The watched pot never boils." Enjoy each day fully and do your part, but avoid trying to take on God's role. Divine timing is perfect, and only God knows when it will manifest. Honor Him by placing your trust in His plan. As you journey towards your dreams, savor the process and enjoy every moment along the way. Though the exact arrival time may remain unknown, rest assured that it will come at the perfect moment. Believe in this truth, and find peace in God's rest as you patiently await the fulfillment of your aspirations.

At times, God places people on a figurative shelf where it may seem like nothing is happening on the surface. However, in the unseen realms of the Spirit, significant transformations are taking place. This period serves as a time of growth, refinement, and deepening of faith, even when there are no visible changes or progress to observe. Embrace this season of hidden development, knowing that God is working diligently, preparing and shaping you for the greater purpose ahead.

Chapter 15

It's not just all about Compatibility, but it's about SUITABILITY!

"A successful marriage requires falling in love many times, always with the same person."

Mignon McLaughlin

In the journey of finding a life partner, we often hear about the importance of compatibility and suitability. People call it the magical connection that seems to bind two souls effortlessly. Today, people think that there is one thing that all successful relationships have in common: the compatibility of the individuals. How well do you and your partner get along? Do you observe any indicators of your partner's compatibility? For those in the early stages of a relationship, it is important to inquire, "Do my partner and I share compatibility?" Coexisting harmoniously demands specific qualities from both individuals to ensure compatibility in relationships, marriages, associations, partnerships, and more.

After dating for a considerable time, you experience a delightful flutter of excitement in your stomach whenever you think about your partner. The relationship is progressing smoothly, and now you find yourself pondering whether you both possess enough compatibility to envision a future together, possibly leading to marriage. But when you think about the bigger picture of your relationship, the butterflies go away. This is because, in contemporary times, compatibility has become a significant focus in romantic relationships. For instance, the online dating industry, in particular, revolves around the concept of compatibility, offering numerous resources from relationship experts claiming to help you find the perfect match. It's a compelling promise, and a quick Google search will reveal a multitude of romance gurus eager to share their insights on discovering the person with whom you are most compatible.

In the quest for a life or marriage partner, the concept of compatibility often takes center stage in conversations. I think handling marriage issues more maturely needs to focus on suitability instead. Let's just be one hundred about this. You can be compatible with someone that keeps you in your comfort zone. You can be compatible with someone who's an assistant to your downfall. You can be compatible with someone that cures your loneliness; they help you to avoid your emptiness. However, it's not just about compatibility because some of us have been compatible with people that were not good for us. You have to understand that because some people in your life will keep you at a level that God doesn't want you to stay at. It's not always about compatibility because sometimes we look for people who are in agreement with us because some people are congruent with the current you, but they're not suitable for the next level you. Listen, and what we don't want you to do is learn how to exist on a level that's beneath you so you'll start formulating preferences. You'll start saying you get along with these types of people God did not cosmically create for you. I want you to understand that compatibility is a part, but it's more about suitability because assignment reveals alignment if you don't know what you assigned to, you won't know who they are sent by. If you only think about compatibility and not suitability, it could make some of you go back to your ex because you're compatible with them. Never let somebody make you feel guilty because you're evolving; they're complaining and have so much criticism to say about you because they're compatible with the former version of you, the expired version of you. An ex will attempt to have you go back to your old you and old places to be compatible with them. You are evolving on the regular, and sometimes an ex comes back just to see if they have access, yes, or another season, they come back to see if you're still on the same level, but you are not.

While compatibility refers to the ability to coexist without conflict, suitability carries a deeper meaning. It pertains to being right and appropriate for a particular individual, purpose, or situation. First, understand that compatibility and suitability are two different aspects that need to be considered when evaluating something, especially when it comes to making important decisions or choosing a partner. Be very cautious of who has access to you. These days, it's a must we protect our energy and peace. We are in weird times, and many out here are moving differently. Stop chasing people who don't reciprocate the same energy level as you do. The minute you realize your worth, you shift your energy to attract new people who respect your worth. It all starts with you. Your time is valuable. You're maturing when you want to invest in deep relationships, want to understand who you actually are, and realize that other people don't need to validate your experience or opinions.

Let me guide you through this:

Compatibility vs. Suitability:

Compatibility refers to how well two individuals can get along and function together in a relationship. It focuses on shared interests, values, communication styles, and the ability to coexist harmoniously. On the other hand, suitability involves assessing whether a partner is well-suited for you in the long term, considering various aspects such as life goals, personal growth, emotional maturity, and the ability to handle challenges together.

These two words are often confused, and as a result, many relationships are on the verge of breaking up. I have often heard people saying, "We are not compatible and cannot marry."

Do Opposites Really Attract?

The question of whether opposites truly attract may seem straightforward, suggesting that people should choose their romantic partners based on personal preferences and feelings. However, exploring this matter further reveals a more nuanced perspective. There are four significant zones of couple compatibility that play a crucial role in determining the sustainability of a relationship in the long term. These fundamental differences between partners can significantly impact the viability and longevity of a relationship.

1) Shared Worldviews:

It is hard to imagine a non-conflicting, blissful relationship if you and your partner hold polar opposite ideas on life. This is not to say that having different views on life is a bad thing. It can be fascinating to have a spouse who is different from you in areas of life that are not seen to be essential for the maintenance of a relationship. However, disagreements over how to manage money, how to raise children, or how to approach politics or religion can result in heated arguments and, ultimately, the breakdown of the partnership.

2) Similar Interests:

Finding a partner with similar interests and preferred activities is essential for a successful relationship. Enjoying quality time together and engaging in fun and interesting activities strengthens the bond.

However, maintaining a couple of independent activities allows each partner to retain their individuality within the relationship.

3) Sexual Compatibility

Some of the most significant problems in relationships can be attributed to different sexual preferences between partners. It will be tricky to achieve relationship satisfaction if one partner wants sexual activity a few times per week while the other is happy with a few times each month. How much do you value sex? How important is sex to the relationship? In what circumstances should sex occur? How frequently should sex occur? Communicate with your partners, and talk about all the things you like to do during sex. Sexual compatibility is important. If you don't discuss these things, you can easily destroy your relationship.

Sexual Intercourse is something that can be learned. Barring any severe medical problems, learning to please your partner is a journey you can embark on together.

4) Basic Temperament

Having compatible temperaments is also essential for a long-term connection. Smaller temperamental differences are nice to keep things interesting, but extreme differences, such as an extremely introverted and a very outgoing partner, could eventually cause problems in their relationship due to their different social appetites.

What Does the Bible Say About It?

In the Bible, God was considerably concerned with the compatibility of the man and woman, according to Genesis 2:18. Not simply someone you can live with, but someone who is right for you is what God is more interested in when you both serve the same purpose, which is what qualifies you for someone. Being compatible with someone doesn't mean you are suitable or right for each other, but suitability implies compatibility. Compatibility in a relationship requires effort and work. When you truly believe someone is right for you or is in line with God's will, you will be motivated to strive for compatibility. Then the Lord God said, "It is not good for the man to be alone; I will make him a helper suitable for him." Genesis 2:18.

Let me make this clear that in this biblical verse, the term "suitable" actually refers to the idea of "opposites." The underlying concept aims to foster relational and marital harmony by recognizing, understanding, and appreciating the inherent differences between a man and a woman. These differences, rather than focusing on compatibility, similarity, or likeness, are seen as complementary aspects that enable them to function as a unified entity. A fitting analogy is that of a two-piece puzzle. Each piece is distinct, yet they perfectly interlock because they were designed to do so. Similarly, the man and woman are like two distinct pieces of a divine puzzle, intentionally crafted to fit together seamlessly, thereby revealing a clear and complete picture. This perspective aligns with the following verse: "Nevertheless, in the Lord, woman is not independent of man, nor man of woman…" (1 Corinthians 11:11).

Love and compatibility often share common ground, and sometimes one can transform into the other. A relationship built on compatibility offers a sense of security, and there's nothing inherently wrong with valuing that security. Feeling safe within a relationship is essential for its success. However, a concern arises when the primary reason for staying in the relationship is the fear of being single again. In such cases, being in the relationship may be driven by the wrong motivations. Do you understand why our generation chose a compatible partner over a suitable one? When you are with someone, you get more excited about outside similarities like hobbies, friends, and interests. A person is not a good spouse for you just because you can laugh together over a movie and play basketball against one another. At first glance, the average Hollywood couple appears to have it all—a seemingly perfect match, a fairy tale romance. However, as time goes on, tensions and conflicts inevitably arise. Despite their wealth and physical attraction, these external factors cannot resolve the everyday problems that emerge when two imperfect individuals come together in marriage. The reality is far from the idealized picture presented in Hollywood. A person who is right for you is more than just someone with comparable interests; they also fulfill God's plan for their life.

In Scripture, we see God's design for marriage, where He creates the woman to be a suitable partner for the man, crafted from his very body (Genesis 2:7, 18, 21–22). This interconnectedness goes beyond mere biology and establishes a call for the man to protect and cherish his wife.

He is to lead with love, never letting go of this special bond (Genesis 2:18, 24). Ephesians 5:22–33 further expounds on this, emphasizing the husband's role to love his wife as Christ loves the church and the wife's role to submit to her husband as the church submits to Christ. Other passages in Scripture also shed light on marital dynamics. For instance, Peter encourages wives to cultivate a gentle and quiet spirit, while husbands are urged to live with understanding, self-sacrifice, and tenderness towards their wives (1 Peter 3:4, 7). If it is God's will, they may raise children together, working in harmony to build a joyful home centered on Christ. The husband is called to spiritually lead his family and manage it well (1 Timothy 3:4). In this divine framework, marriage thrives as a beautiful union where both husband and wife fulfill their God-given roles with love, respect, and mutual support.

5 Questions for Singles to Ask When Seeking a Biblically Compatible Spouse:

1. **How do you know he or she willingly submits to godly authority?**

   Ladies, a guy is harmful if he is not subject to godly authority. Period. Men, if she doesn't submit to godly leadership right away, she is the kind of woman Proverbs urges you to stay away from (you, single men, are not her).

2. **How do you know he or she is teachable?**

   If someone enjoys arguing, they care more about being correct than about being made righteous. When you believe you have won a marital disagreement, you have lost. Being humble and acknowledging that you have a lot to learn for the rest of your lives is what marriage is all about.

3. How well-known and involved is he or she in the Christian community?

When you are drawn to someone and determined to be married, it is simple to put up a good front. He or she is unknown to you if they are unknown in the community. The character, honesty, and religion of the individual must be confirmed by others.

4. How does he or she speak of others?

He or she will be critical, insulting, or flippant in marriage if they are like that now in attitude and speech. You will soon bear the brunt of their rage and arrogance.

5. How does he or she respond when confronted with their sin?

Someone has a skewed understanding of the Gospel if they try to cover up, mislead, shift responsibility, justify, or otherwise rationalize their sin. We can confess our sins (I John 1:9), turn from our sins (Rom. 2:4), walk in the light (Eph. 5:8–9), and be reconciled to God because of Jesus (II Cor. 5:17–21).

One common mistake among Christian singles is that they often jump ahead to questions about marriage before understanding the dynamics of dating. Like many aspects of life, discovering God's will for your future marriage involves a process, and that process typically includes the dating season.

The courtship mentality can be unhelpful because it may lead people to only date someone they believe God is specifically telling them to marry. This approach can create unnecessary pressure on the relationship too early on, causing some individuals to avoid dating altogether. They may refrain from getting to know anyone until they are certain of compatibility for marriage. However, I believe that the dating process itself should be used to explore and evaluate compatibility.

It's essential to have enough information about compatibility with someone for the particular step forward you are taking. If you are considering dating someone, you don't need to have the same level of knowledge that you would require to take a step toward marriage.

Proverbs 3:5-6 teaches us about trusting God's guidance, which may not always come all at once. As we walk down the path of dating, trusting in God's leading, He will make our path straight in due time.

The most crucial aspect of compatibility lies in your shared faith and belief in Jesus Christ. If there is a difference in faith, it can lead to disagreements and conflicting ideologies. Thus, an unbeliever might not be suitable for you, and compatibility in faith becomes essential. When you are suitable and compatible in your faith, it becomes possible to navigate and adapt to other areas of your relationship.

How Do I Choose a Compatible Partner?

Selecting a compatible partner is undoubtedly a challenging task, one of the most significant decisions we encounter in life. Some may be fortunate to find a compatible partner effortlessly, while others invest significant effort into their relationships, only to face heartbreak in the end. However, is there truly a checklist that guarantees relationship bliss? Not quite.

Although there is no foolproof checklist, there are ways to enhance your approach to finding a compatible partner. If you repeatedly find yourself in unsatisfying relationships, consider making adjustments in your romantic pursuits. By introspecting and implementing changes, you can increase your chances of discovering a partner who truly aligns with you.

Here are some valuable guidelines to consider when navigating romantic relationships:

- Take your time and avoid rushing into committed relationships.
- Ensure that you share important life views with your partner.
- Seek a partner with whom you can be your authentic self.
- Don't mistake sexual attraction for genuine relationship potential.

- Avoid searching for identical qualities in all romantic partners.

- Refrain from expecting your partner to change to meet your standards.

- Step out of your comfort zone and get to know diverse individuals.

- Don't hesitate to seek guidance from an experienced relationship advocate.

God's deep interest and value in the institution of marriage and family were evident from the very beginning. Unlike other creations that He merely spoke into being, God took deliberate steps in forming the first human couple. He caused Adam to sleep, took a rib, and carefully fashioned Eve. Moreover, He personally presented Eve to Adam, emphasizing the unique divine origin of marriage (Gen. 2:22).

However, despite being a source of joy, pleasure, and honor in its inception, modern times have witnessed a shift in attitude towards marriage and family life. Many now view it as a necessary evil, while some even disdain it. The consequence of this changing perception is the alarming disintegration of the marriage institution and, consequently, the breakdown of families.

People inside marriages often desire to escape, while those outside may be hesitant to commit.

According to the Bible, it is stated that "Perfect love casts out fear" (1 John 4:18). While none of us may have reached a state of perfect love yet, we can still grow and develop in love. We have the opportunity to mature and become more like God in our capacity to love. It's important to understand that attaining perfection in love doesn't mean we will be flawless in this lifetime or become as perfect as God. However, we can certainly progress and mature in expressing the kind of love that God embodies. The fruit of love should begin to manifest in our lives, showing signs of growth and development.

Principles—God Gives Us Guidance for Wise Decision-Making

The phrase "opposites attract" holds true in chemistry, where it often leads to fascinating outcomes. However, in relationships, it may not always be as great as it initially appears. The allure of being attracted to someone vastly different from ourselves lies in the novelty and excitement of spending time with them. Their uniqueness complements our own, and together, we feel like a complete unit. We value and appreciate their differences, which add to the magic of the relationship. However, in the long run, these opposite behaviors and attitudes can potentially lead to frustration and challenges.

In Amos 3:3, the Bible offers wise advice, asking if two people can walk together without agreeing on the direction they are heading. As Christians, we are blessed with the Holy Spirit's wisdom, which we can apply to every aspect of our lives, including our relationships. Sound relationships are built not just on exciting feelings but on good thinking.

Whether you and your potential partner align in the direction you are heading, not only within the relationship but also in other significant aspects of life.

Consider five major topics: Purpose, Expectations, Character, Attachments, and Life Experiences. Take time to ponder your attitudes and values, and then engage in a serious discussion with your partner about these important aspects. This thoughtful reflection and communication can help establish a solid foundation for your relationship and ensure that you both are moving in harmony toward shared goals and values.

Praying for clarity and guidance is crucial, as it opens our hearts and minds to the leading of the Holy Spirit. It allows us to discern the right path and gain insight into areas that might otherwise be clouded by infatuation or confusion. For instance, when physical attraction becomes a factor, seeking the Lord's guidance helps us maintain objectivity and prevents us from being solely driven by emotions. Moreover, the Spirit can provide wisdom even in situations where physical attraction might be lacking. Through prayer, we can gain discernment to understand whether pursuing marriage with that person is in alignment with God's plan for our lives.

Also, I would advise people who are actively searching for someone to marry, to focus on personal growth and becoming the kind of person that you would want to be with. Trust in God's timing and His plan to bring the right life partner into your life. Your responsibility is to prepare yourself to be the right partner for them. Rather than trying to find someone, work on becoming the best version of yourself. Trust that when the time is right, God will orchestrate the meeting with your life partner in unexpected and extraordinary ways.

Many individuals have experienced this when they dedicated themselves to prayer and sometimes fasting, seeking God's guidance in their journey. If you feel you have reached a point of readiness, turn to prayer (possibly with fasting) as your primary means of seeking God's direction in this matter. Allow Him to lead you to the person who is meant to be your life partner. We must continue to be open to the unexpected in our journey. Some people may have a strong desire to get married, but no suitable partner ever appears in their lives. They finally come to terms with this disappointment and courageously consider how they might effectively serve God alone. On the other hand, there are people who are content with their single status and develop a successful ministry in it.

However, God might unforeseeably send them a person they immediately recognize as a fantastic life partner, which could result in an even greater mission than they could have imagined.

In all aspects of discerning a life partner, turning to God in prayer not only invites His guidance but also aligns our will with His, ensuring that we make choices that are rooted in His wisdom and leading.

The Word of God holds transformative power, capable of changing lives in remarkable ways. While it is beneficial for dating couples to read the Bible together, just as there are physical boundaries in dating, it is also wise to establish spiritual boundaries.

The concept of God revealing a spouse to us is intriguing. If He knows the plans He has for us (Jeremiah 29:11), it is good to believe that He can guide us to the right person for marriage. God employs various methods to reveal our life partner. One of these ways is through dreams. Throughout the Bible, we find instances of people receiving visions or prophetic messages through their dreams. These same methods of communication can still be experienced today. As Proverbs 3:5–6 states, "Trust in the Lord with all your heart; do not depend on your understanding. Seek His will in all you do, and He will show you which path to take." When we trust in Him and follow His guidance, we can be sure that He will show us the right way to go.

In the end, we must have faith in God's schedule for our lives. These conditions are beyond our ability to forecast or manage. Some people might find meaning and contentment in being alone, while others would enjoy the delight of meeting a partner.

Chapter 16

Divorce is One Word God Never Intended to be heard in a Marriage

"I hate divorce,' says the Lord God of Israel."

Malachi 2:16

One man and one woman existed in the beginning. For that very obvious reason, divorce and remarriage were not options in the divine plan for man.

And the LORD God caused a deep sleep to fall on Adam, and he slept, and He took one of his ribs, and closed up the flesh in its place. Then the rib which the LORD God had taken from man He made into a woman, and He brought her to the man (Genesis 2:21-24)

And Adam said:

"This is now the bone of my bones

And flesh of my flesh;

She shall be called Woman,

Because she was taken out of Man."

Therefore, a man shall leave his father and mother and be joined to his wife, and they shall become one flesh."

In Malachi 2:11, marriage is called **The LORD's holy institution, which He loves.**

Lately, it's become a trend to demonize marriage through social media, and many men and women are coming forward to discuss how stressful and unpleasant their unions are/were. I have heard plenty of stories about marriages breaking up, and people saying, "How do I know God is OK with what I am doing? Is it wrong for me to give up on this marriage? Should I go back to my spouse?"

In the passage found in Mark 10:1–12, the Pharisees approached Jesus with a question: "Is it lawful for a man to divorce his wife?" This question, which was once raised, has now shifted in contemporary times. Divorce is no longer a subject of inquiry; it has become an assumption. Today, divorce is not only deemed permissible, but it is also readily accessible and affordable. A simple online search using the term "divorce" reveals various options like "Easy Online Divorce," "Simple Divorce Online," and "No Fault Divorce," highlighting the convenience and simplicity associated with divorce procedures.

In the conversation between Jesus and the Pharisees regarding divorce, Jesus emphasizes the original intention of God for marriage. He acknowledges that Moses permitted divorce due to the hardness of people's hearts, but he points out that this was not God's original design. According to Jesus, from the beginning, God intended for a husband and wife to be united and not separated by human actions. The union between a man and a woman in marriage.

"Do not think that I have come to abolish the Law or the Prophets; I have not come to abolish them but to fulfill them. For truly, I say to you, until heaven and earth pass away, not an iota, not a dot, will pass from the Law until all is accomplished. Therefore, whoever relaxes one of the least of these commandments and teaches others to do the same will be called the least in the kingdom of heaven, but whoever does them and teaches them will be called great in the kingdom of heaven. For I tell you, unless your righteousness exceeds that of the scribes and Pharisees, you will never enter the kingdom of heaven."

Matthew 5:17-20

Jesus' critique was not directed at the Old Testament itself; rather, it was aimed at the flawed interpretations and shortcomings that many had embraced. His mission involved rescuing the Law from the distortions and misrepresentations propagated by Pharisaic and rabbinical traditions. He aimed to reveal the genuine essence of the Law, emphasizing its significance both in outward actions and within the depths of the heart. Jesus' teachings sought to illuminate God's commands with crystal clarity, cutting through the intricate web of debates fostered by contemporary rabbinical discussions. His intention was to unveil the true essence of Old Testament directives, eliminating confusion and presenting God's original intent.

Let me guide you here, Jesus pointed out, "A man shall leave his father and mother and be united with his wife" (Matthew 19:5). Even though Adam and Eve did not have parents to leave, the concept of departing from one's parental home was established as a guiding principle for all future generations. The Hebrew term underlying "united with" conveys a deep and unwavering connection – envision it as a joyous fusion rather than a burdensome one. Marriage serves as the catalyst that intimately binds two hearts, dedicatedly and resolutely committed to mutually cherishing each other, intertwined in an inseparable tie, firmly linked in thoughts, intentions, spirit, and feelings.

Not everybody is suited for marriage. People who choose to live single lives in order to dedicate themselves to serving God's kingdom are exemplified in Matthew 19:12. Similar reasons for choosing singleness are given in 1 Corinthians 7:25–35. These reasons include the difficulties of the present—such as those listed in verse 26—which give rise to new worries in one's current earthly existence. It's critical to understand that remaining single shouldn't be viewed as lesser; rather, it is a choice with merit that has certain advantages for one's devotion to serving the Lord.

Divorce conveys a significant falsehood about God, suggesting that He might be a covenant breaker.

While the institution of marriage holds significance in terms of companionship, the expression of sexuality, and procreation, its primary essence lies in symbolizing the relationship between God and His people. This analogy is evident throughout the Bible, where God often refers to His people as His bride.

Consider the Old Testament's Song of Solomon, for instance. This book showcases erotic love between a man and a woman, but its core theme is God's profound love for His people. Hosea, similarly, was tasked with mirroring God's relationship with His people by marrying. His wife, Gomer, is depicted as an adulterous woman who left Hosea for another man. God instructed Hosea to redeem her, paralleling His redemption of humanity.

In a similar vein, God addresses Israel, His unfaithful and idolatrous people, using imagery of a spurned spouse:

"I will punish her for the days she burned incense to the Baals; she decked herself with rings and jewelry and went after her lovers, but me she forgot," declares the LORD. However, this narrative takes a hopeful turn:

"Therefore, I am now going to allure her; I will lead her into the desert and speak tenderly to her…. "In that day," declares the LORD, "you will call me 'my husband'; you will no longer call me 'my master'…. I will betroth you to me forever; I will betroth you in righteousness and justice, in love and compassion."

"I will betroth you in faithfulness, and you will acknowledge the LORD."

(Hosea 2:13, 16, 19, 20)

Similarly, the connection between God and Israel is likened to a marital bond, and this same imagery of marriage is echoed in the New Testament to illustrate the relationship between Christ and His church.

Marriage Is Intended to Be Permanent

In Song of Solomon 8:7, the scripture asserts, "Many waters cannot quench love, neither can the floods drown it: if a man would give all the substance of his house for love, it would utterly be contemned." The decision to marry is influenced by numerous valid factors: to find companionship and camaraderie, to share in serving the divine purpose, to experience parenthood, and to fulfill the emotional and physical facets of love. These are all commendable purposes for which God established the institution of marriage.

Marriage is Made in Heaven

Every marriage is divinely ordained, as God is the ultimate creator and orchestrator of the marital bond. Jesus underscores this truth by highlighting that from the inception of marriage with Adam and Eve, God's hand has united every husband and wife. Regardless of human attempts to distort or disregard this divine connection, marriage remains fundamentally rooted in God's institution. Whether between believers or non-believers, irrespective of parental involvement or personal choices, marriage is first and foremost a manifestation of God's craftsmanship. It serves the essential purposes of human procreation, enjoyment, and preservation.

Regardless of the circumstances surrounding its formation—whether marked by wisdom or folly, sincerity or insincerity, selflessness or selfishness, profound or limited commitment—God's blueprint for each marriage is its enduring permanence until the passing of one spouse.

When is Divorce Allowed?

Regarding the grounds for divorce, referring back to the words of Jesus in Matthew, He continues, "Whoever divorces his wife, except for sexual immorality, and marries another, commits adultery" (Matthew 19:9). This exception is a provision for instances where a spouse has significantly harmed the marriage which is beyond repair, leading the way for separation. Jesus teaches that divorcing a partner and subsequently marrying another due to sexual immorality does not constitute adultery.

Expanding on this topic in his teachings within 1 Corinthians, Paul addresses situations that might justify divorce in verse 15: "If the unbelieving partner separates, let it be so. In such cases, the brother or sister is not bound."

God Leads You to Divorce When:

Infidelity, Adultery, or Sexual Immorality in marriage:

When one spouse engages in unfaithfulness or violates the marriage covenant through extramarital affairs, it raises issues of infidelity. The perception of infidelity varies, as it involves actions that breach loyalty and trust, potentially involving a third party.

"He answered, "Anyone who divorces his wife and marries another woman commits adultery against her. And if she divorces her husband and marries another man, she commits adultery."

(Mark 10:11-12)

Any betrayal of the marital vows, especially through physical or sexual wrongdoing, causes the deceived spouse great suffering and hardship. Such offenses have serious repercussions and gravely damage the foundation of the marriage. However, God's main focus is on encouraging forgiveness, restoration, reunification, and ultimately the revival of the marriage. The Bible permits the loyal spouse to consider divorcing the misbehaving spouse if they refuse to repent and seek reconciliation.

Individuals perceive infidelity within a marriage as a subjective matter rather than an objective reality. Consequently, when a married person engages in unfaithful behavior, they might participate in discussions or receive insights regarding the implications of their actions. Such interactions can lead to a deeper understanding of the concept of infidelity and its potential repercussions.

God won't make your spouse change for you. It's challenging to embrace this idea. It's what we always cling to when things in marriage get tough.

God will not change your spouse for your exclusive benefit, but He can change them for the purpose of His glory. Let me explain further. Many times, when conflicts arise between spouses, our prayers tend to be self-centered.

We might pray, "God, make my husband more attentive to my needs." Or, "God, help my husband become a better provider."

"Notice me more."

"Give compliments."

"Find a better job."

Perhaps even, "motivate him to be more proactive."

What's the common thread here? It's all about "me."

Certainly, God cares deeply for you. He desires your happiness and a fulfilling marriage where you are treated with the respect you deserve – a principle He emphasizes in His teachings. Yet, God also desires that you treat your spouse with the respect they deserve. This begins with desiring what's best for them. Desiring change in your spouse should not be solely for your benefit, but genuinely for their well-being. Your aspiration should be for your spouse to draw closer to the Lord, not just to make your life easier, but to enrich their life profoundly. Your role involves seeking God's highest good for your spouse, rather than focusing solely on how the relationship can be optimized for your comfort.

Feel free to pray earnestly for your marriage, maintaining a continuous and unwavering connection with God through prayer. However, it's essential to understand that while God desires to fulfill your requests and respond to your prayers, His foremost priority is your heart's alignment. He values prayers marked by selflessness and genuine intent. God holds marriage in high regard and acknowledges its sanctity. He values the mutual growth of your relationship with both Him and your spouse, thereby reinforcing the ties that bind your marriage.

"But if the unbeliever leaves, let it be so. The brother or the sister is not bound in such circumstances; God has called us to live in peace."

(1 Corinthians 7:15)

Paul guides individuals who find themselves in a marriage with a nonbeliever, advising spouses to leave when the relationship does not reflect God's intended purpose.

Matthew 5:32 addresses concerns that may arise when contemplating divorce from a nonbelieving partner. It highlights that God recognizes certain circumstances that warrant divorce, allowing for such a course of action. God's intention is not for you to bear the weight of your spouse's transgressions but to live in a state of tranquility. He encourages you to find solace, allowing your hearts to be at ease and finding peace through your connection with Jesus Christ.

Is divorce a permissible option if I'm unhappy in my marriage? People often ask this question. While one might experience profound discontent within a marriage, it's essential to recognize that this dissatisfaction may not always align with the typical grounds for divorce, such as infidelity or abuse. There might be instances where none of these specific circumstances are present, yet the unhappiness persists.

It's crucial to consider two key points:

Happiness as Cultural vs. Biblical:

The concept of happiness is culturally ingrained but doesn't find direct mention as a "fruit of the Spirit" in the Bible. Jesus himself often referred to believers as "blessed," focusing on attributes like peace, contentment, and joy, which stem from a connection with God rather than external conditions.

The apostle Paul, for instance, emphasized finding contentment regardless of circumstances (Philippians 4:12).

Seeking Fulfillment in God:

Instead of placing undue expectations on our spouses for our joy, it's vital to reflect on where we seek our inner peace and contentment. Relying on our partners to fulfill roles that only God can truly satisfy can lead to disappointment. By deepening our reliance on God for joy, our reliance on marital happiness diminishes. This perspective doesn't reduce the importance of addressing marital challenges or seeking counseling. Even if working through difficulties or undergoing counseling proves challenging, it's important to remember that a perfect marriage isn't a prerequisite for experiencing true joy in Christ.

A marriage founded on mutual devotion is the only foundation for both long-term satisfaction and enduring strength. An unbreakable bond is formed when two Christian folks sincerely love one other selflessly and spend their lives in humble accordance with God's Word and each other. This relationship is impervious to the onslaught of temptations, failures, and difficulties brought by both worldly challenges and evil forces. In such a relationship, they become not just lovers but also staunch comrades, a level of intimacy that non-believers and those who wander from the road of faith find difficult.

How Does God Provide Comfort in

Times of Divorce?

God serves as a source of solace and resilience for those navigating the aftermath of losing a loved one. His presence offers multifaceted support, enabling individuals to find solace amid their grief.

Nurturance Through Scripture

Within the pages of the Bible, verses brim with hope and solace, fostering a sense of trust in God during moments of hardship. Isaiah 41:10 assures, "So do not fear, for I am with you; do not be dismayed, for I am your God. I will strengthen you and help you; I will uphold you with my righteous right hand.

Guidance through Prayer

Prayer emerges as a potent tool for coping with the departure of an individual. Through prayer, emotions can be expressed, and entreaties for divine assistance in processing these sentiments are made. Moreover, prayer facilitates moments of repose and contemplation, allowing individuals to cherish fond memories of the departed.

Connecting with Fellow Believers

Grief frequently unfolds as a solitary journey, underscoring the significance of seeking camaraderie with fellow believers for those grappling with loss. Engaging in conversations and sharing personal narratives with individuals who comprehend your emotions can offer solace during the trying phase. The presence of companions who offer encouragement, intercede in prayer and reaffirm God's sovereignty can be profoundly reassuring.

Empowerment Through Resolute Faith

Divine presence remains unwavering, providing the fortitude to persevere through the most arduous circumstances. Hebrews 11:1 asserts, "Now faith is the assurance of things hoped for, the conviction of things not seen." This verse serves as a poignant reminder that our faith can serve as an anchor when confronted with the challenge of coping with loss. Faith entails believing in a greater design, even in moments of inexplicable perplexity.

Divine Devotion: God's Profound Love for marriage

God holds a deep affection for marriage. In a clear and direct manner, the compassionate Creator of our world conceived marriage as a lifelong dedication shared by two individuals. This sacred bond, formed between a man and a woman, signifies a holy connection in the presence of God. His plan for marriage is a magnificent and selfless connection that is meant to last a lifetime.

At the end of all things, when God's people are gathered and the Kingdom fully comes, Revelation describes the celebration as a marriage supper.

"Hallelujah! For our Lord God Almighty reigns. Let us rejoice and be glad and give him glory! For the wedding of the Lamb has come, and his bride has made herself ready. Fine linen, bright and clean, was given her to wear." (Fine linen stands for the righteous acts of the saints.) Revelation 19:6b-8

When God releases you from your marriage, you may experience the ache of parting, whether via divorce or the loss of a partner. Such times can be emotionally and spiritually taxing, filled with doubts and questions about the path ahead.

Keep in mind that God's love endures even if He allows your marriage to end. Despite the grief, you can begin a road of recovery and self-discovery in your newfound single position. God's direction can lead you to a rejuvenated feeling of joy and a new purpose in life via prayer and patience. Divine mercy and grace are accessible to all, irrespective of their relational circumstances. God empathizes with the challenges inherent in marriage and extends His presence to console us during times of disappointment when our expectations go unmet. Above all, God's desire is to secure the utmost well-being of His children. While comprehending why God might permit divorce can prove perplexing, His unwavering commitment to us, as emphasized in Deuteronomy 31:8, assures that He will never forsake us.

Chapter 17

Wife Duties at Girlfriend Prices

I'm good enough to cook, clean, and have sex but not for marriage. Of course, marriage is necessary. Not getting married and living together has made relationships full of doubts and challenges. I have often heard people say, "I will date to get married." But do they really get married after knowing each other? It's okay to date even if you are interested in getting married in the future. Don't make meaningless commitments out of concern for losing a woman. It's not wrong to date, even if you are not looking to get married.

Speaking of the latter, it appears that an increasing number of couples are choosing to forgo the official vow exchange ceremony. But offering wife duties at girlfriend prices is quite problematic. No need to have a relationship like this. It accumulates baggage. Life is not a laboratory to keep on experimenting, and your life is not a guinea pig to try.

A girlfriend and a wife are two very different things. Far too often I see women confuse the obligations of the two. If you do not have a ring on your finger and a marriage license in your name then, ladies, please act accordingly. Likewise, if you are still in the girlfriend phase it's important to remember you are single until married. If no formal commitment has been made then…you know, act accordingly.

As a girlfriend, you are not obligated to do anything you don't feel like doing. As a girlfriend, your main focus should be becoming the best version of yourself and developing your relationship skills. We don't live in a vacuum. We have thoughts and feelings that can be confusing. Everyone has personal needs and desires. I was once told that individuals are akin to glasses of water. If we neglect our own self-care and fail to keep our glass full, we might end up relying on others, inadvertently leaving them with less.

Wives' Duties Vs Girlfriend's Duties

A relationship requires equal effort and time from both people in order for it to be successful. Even though they are not yet married, there are some situations where women tend to assume a more major role, even going so far as to perform wife chores. At the same time, this gesture of generosity and love can seem commonplace to some.

Women should be wary about going over the top and taking on too much responsibility because doing so could have a negative long-term effect on the relationship. A lot of women "play house" with men these days, which kills a lot of a man's motivation to move towards marriage. If she lives with you, cooks, cleans, puts his tongue in your mouth (French kissing), and has sex with you, why tie yourself into a marriage? Hence, you have a ton of 5+ year boyfriend/girlfriend relationships that have yet to tie the knot.

Go over the reasons why women shouldn't act as their partners' wives and how it might jeopardize their relationships.

It's pretty simple:

"Do things together

Support each other emotionally

Know when to put your foot down

Fight fair, avoid the blame game."

So, Why Should You Stop Taking on your wife's responsibilities as a Girlfriend? Roles Shouldn't Blur!

Numerous duties come with being in a relationship. Although it's instinctive to look out for our partners, there are occasions when we can go overboard and end up doing things that are not our job. Women must always keep in mind that we are only our partners' girlfriends, not their moms or wives. There are some things that girlfriends should not do for their boyfriends, even though we should love and support our lovers. Otherwise, he might consider you to be a given.

Being A Mother Figure

Motherly duties, such as keeping an eye on the boyfriend's habits and activities, are never appropriate for women to perform. Cooking and cleaning frequently, and constantly reminding them to complete tasks. Keep in mind that your partner should be self-reliant and accountable for their own adult responsibilities. Even if you might want to make your partner's life simpler, the best course of action is not to let him rely entirely on you. He's used to it, so if you do end up getting married, it will impact your relationship.

Allow the Natural Flow

"Not every potential date is destined to be a potential mate." It's important not to rush into seriousness prematurely, especially within a few weeks or months of knowing someone. If you used to find yourself thinking, "If the date went well, maybe he's the one," or you would get caught up in defining the relationship status too quickly. There are instances where it hinders positive outcomes by trying to force situations, and this approach can sometimes discourage people. Instead, just let the conversations and the organic evolution of the relationship take their course. This doesn't imply waiting indefinitely for someone; rather, when things feel right and are progressing naturally, it's wise to remain composed and let things develop naturally.

Maintain Your Independence

Centering your life solely around your boyfriend isn't healthy. Women should ensure their lives are well-structured, even without their partners. The Bible instructs young men to treat girls as sisters, preserving purity (1 Timothy 5:2). In essence, this means treating a girl as you'd want your sister treated by other men—a consistently prudent approach. Both genders should extend honor and respect and exercise moderation in interactions.

Maintaining a level of reserve or sobriety while still embracing humor is wise. It's crucial to recognize that we're more prone to excessive casualness when around the opposite sex, which can be risky. Cultivating personal interests not only nurtures individuality but also infuses your shared time with greater significance. Your partner should complement, not define, your life.

Make Healthy Boundaries

Being kind is admirable, but allowing your boyfriend to exploit your kindness isn't. Ladies mustn't cater to every desire solely to maintain their contentment. Making clear boundaries is crucial. An important reason to avoid assuming wife-like duties is the potential for an imbalanced relationship. When women shoulder these responsibilities, it can foster dependency, resulting in a power discrepancy. Boyfriends might feel redundant, while girlfriends grapple with overwhelming obligations. This imbalance could breed conflict and resentment, straining the relationship.

Avoiding Misplaced Expectations

Shouldering a wife's responsibility for a boyfriend can breed misplaced expectations, which can later lead to letdowns and misunderstandings.

A precedent form that the girlfriend is solely responsible. He may shirk accountability, which is unjust. This erosion of mutual effort can erode the relationship and culminate in separation.

Erosion of Self-Identity

Engaging in wife-like responsibilities for boyfriends can inadvertently lead women to become overly absorbed in caring for their partners, causing them to lose touch with their own sense of self. This situation can breed feelings of isolation and uncertainty as they gradually lose sight of their personal aspirations and desires. Preserving one's individuality within a relationship is paramount, as it serves to fortify the connection between both individuals.

Emotional Burden

Women often find themselves carrying the emotional weight in relationships. However, the expectation of being the sole emotional support is not sustainable. Partners should reciprocate understanding and empathy. Sharing emotions is healthy, but it's not solely the duty of one person. A quality man exhibits chivalry by holding the door for you, assisting with your coat, and offering a chair at dinner. He extends the gesture of paying the bill and shows reverence for your and your parents' values and desires. Romans 8:28 says, "And we know that all things work together for good to them that love God, to them who are the called according to his purpose."

So, are you tired of being a woman who is doing everything for a man at the girlfriend's price? There's a huge difference between making it clear you know how to do these things and getting trapped into taking care of a man who is taking advantage of you! In a relationship, initiate a conversation with your partner, revealing your tiredness and desire for clarity. Through shared conversations, understand the need for a clearer path. Whether the journey led to commitment or separate ways, the openness brought empowerment to the once-tired hearts.

Not every person has the same needs or preferences in relationships. Others rush into a relationship with marriage in mind, while some want to take things slowly and see where they go.

When a man is genuinely interested in marriage, he seizes opportunities to advance the relationship. For instance, after a year of being together, it's common to consider moving in together. If he opts to move in with a roommate or finds a new place for himself when his lease ends, rather than exploring living arrangements with you, it may signal his lack of intent for the next phase in the relationship.

Similarly, if you've spent several years together without taking trips as a couple, it's a notable indicator that marriage isn't on the near horizon. Such actions or lack thereof can provide insights into his level of commitment.

In long-term relationships, discussing future plans is a natural progression. However, if he reacts with anger or defensiveness when the topic of the future arises, it's likely an indication of inner conflict.

His response might stem from perceiving your desire to discuss marriage, causing him to feel pressured if he isn't interested in marrying. If you find yourself pondering whether he will propose but encounter repeated excuses against marriage, the answer could lean towards a negative outcome. While striving for financial stability before marriage is reasonable, consistent excuses could suggest marriage isn't part of his intentions. Initially, he might cite financial concerns, yet if each barrier is overcome and new excuses arise—like homeownership or a destination wedding—it hints at his reluctance to propose. A sequence of excuses often implies avoidance rather than genuine intentions for marriage.

What to Do When He Doesn't Want to Marry You?

When faced with a situation where your boyfriend is not inclined towards marriage, it's important to remember that his decision is influenced by factors beyond your worthiness. His perspective on marriage is shaped by his own values and preferences, and his choice isn't a reflection of your value or capacity for love. Men may decline marriage due to several reasons, such as commitment fears, negative past experiences with marriages, or personal beliefs against the institution. These factors are independent of your qualities.

Recognizing that his stance is a result of his personal considerations, not your shortcomings, empowers you to make informed decisions.

If marriage aligns with your aspirations and he remains hesitant due to minor issues or concerns, consider seeking professional guidance such as counseling or relationship coaching to work through these obstacles together.

However, if significant time has passed without a proposal and marriage remains a priority for you, address the importance of marriage to you, expressing your feelings and desires. If he doesn't foresee marriage in the near future, it might indicate fundamental differences that need addressing.

Before having this discussion, seeking advice from trusted friends or family can provide valuable insights. Remember that your happiness and goals matter, and a candid conversation can help determine the best path forward for both of you.

While the desire for marriage might appear inherent, it's crucial to pause and reflect on what precisely you're seeking. What motivates you? Is it a quest for security, validation, acknowledgment of your partnership, or the simple privilege of saying "husband" or "wife?"

Dig deeper into these questions: What does marriage symbolize to you? What influenced this perception—personal beliefs, family values, societal or religious teachings? What unique elements would marriage offer that you currently lack, and are these exclusive to marriage? If your relationship is already committed and marriage feels like a formality, your focus might be on added security or the customs tied to marriage, like weddings and anniversaries.

Explore your motivations if your current relationship is less stable. Are you looking to mend it through marriage? Are external expectations influencing your decision? Do you seek marriage as a prerequisite for having children?

Don't be the Girl with "Over Thirty and Worried" Mindset

Entering your thirties often triggers a shift in your perception. There's an inexplicable urge to assess our lives and scrutinize our progress in relationships, careers, and family matters. This inclination can stem from societal pressures or be self-imposed. However, it's essential to recognize that this mindset isn't confined to a specific age bracket. It's not limited to being thirty; it can manifest at any age—20s, 30s, 40s, 50s, and beyond. It's characterized by an excessive fixation on finding a partner or perpetual sorrow stemming from being without one. This mindset leads to desperation, compromise, or overwhelming sadness as the focus shifts away from appreciating what we have to dwelling on what we lack. We've all encountered, embodied, or experienced a version of this mindset.

Don't Think of Him as a Piece of Clay

Avoid the misconception of treating him like moldable clay,

shaping him to match your desires. Questions like "How can I make him go to church?" or "How can I make him settle down?" might arise. While people can evolve over time, true change is driven by individual empowerment, not coercion. Rather than force change, respect the unique path and pray for him. Conversations and guidance played a role, but the choice for change was ultimately his.

Persistently expressing intentions without evident changes might signal a need to reconsider your role. Redirect your energy from altering them to assessing your involvement. If his commitment is genuine, his actions—not just words—will reflect it. Remember, authentic change originates within, not from external pressures.

Let Go of People

This principle applies to two categories: 1) Dead Weight - those causing harm or negativity, and 2) Pop-ups - inconsistent individuals who appear when it suits them. Unless you are content with these patterns or not seeking stability, you'll find yourself waiting or pursuing in vain. I've personally used the "block" and "delete" functions to break the cycle and prevent relapse. Taking drastic measures underscores your commitment to moving on and severing ties.

Don't Confuse Lust with Love

"I made a covenant with my eyes not to look with lust upon a girl."

(Job 31:1 - TLB).

Several relationships crumble or face heartbreak due to misconceptions that physical intimacy equates to love. While physical attraction, sex, and intimacy hold significance, they shouldn't overshadow other aspects. The past pain often stemmed from either rushing intimacy or believing love would follow physical connection. Distinguishing between personal pleasure and genuine compatibility is crucial. True love offers both elements, but that isn't guaranteed with every partner. Don't sacrifice future well-being for immediate gratification, and avoid conflating love and lust. Recognizing these distinctions safeguards against heartache and paves the way for healthier connections.

Nothing Occurs Instantaneously, Processes Demand Time

For some, it takes numerous attempts, months, years, or even a lifetime. Love can't be hurried; the journey from singlehood to marriage wasn't an overnight shift. The path encompassed pain preceding joy and heartache before happiness, eventually leading to genuine love. It might sound cliché, yet what's destined for you will materialize as per God's plan—whether it's marriage, being single, or other aspects of life. Through personal encounters and others' stories, I have understood that often, when we cease fretting and searching, that's precisely when things fall into place.

Finding the Person

"How do I get into marriage?" is the first question you must ask. The answer is in Proverbs 18:22:

"Whoso findeth a wife findeth a good thing, and obtaineth favor of the Lord. "Whoso findeth..." not, "Whoso prayeth or fasteth," or "Whoso his father giveth a wife..."

Finding a life partner is an intentional endeavor that requires active participation. It's not a result of mere slumber or fantasy; rather, it involves entering marriage with heightened awareness. This entails consciously embarking on a search by remaining receptive and observant to identify the person with whom you can share your lifetime. This search is a pragmatic undertaking rather than a spiritual one.

Courtship can be broken without confusing it with divorce. The Bible does not dictate that courtship is an unbreakable commitment. Instead, it serves as a phase for gauging compatibility. If compatibility is lacking, it's appropriate to conclude the relationship at this juncture rather than prolong it. When ideas and values do not align, practical reasoning suggests ending the relationship.

Your single status shouldn't be a barrier to personal growth. Seize the moment to invest in your self-development and nurture your connection with God. Devote time to enhancing your career, shaping your future, and building your personal brand. Take deliberate steps to care for your physical, mental, and emotional well-being. Embrace opportunities for enjoyment, such as travel and exploration. This doesn't mean these opportunities vanish when married, but as 1 Corinthians 7 reminds us, an unmarried person can wholeheartedly dedicate themselves to spiritual matters. Utilize this period to focus on your present possibilities as a single individual.

Satan's Attack

Is it any wonder that Satan slithered up to assault the union of Adam and Eve and continues to do so now after we discover the potent yet utterly lovely experience of being one in marriage and with our Lord? Is it any surprise that Satan is trying to undermine our relationship with Christ Jesus? He is attempting to stop two things: "And he said unto them, I beheld Satan as lightning fall from heaven." LUKE 10:18.

The opposite of what Satan desires is the rebirth of sinners, freedom from oppression and demonic possession, maturation of new believers into the full stature of Christ, the edification of the Church, and the establishment of God's kingdom. Satan can easily infiltrate any organization, partnership, union, marriage, or church. He began his assault on the woman in the Garden of Eden. He had already pursued God and failed; therefore, he was unable to do it again.

Numerous temptations in the realm of sexuality confront us in our times. The Bible portrays Satan both as a fierce lion eager to consume and as a cunning serpent seeking to mislead. Recognizing the susceptibility of young individuals, he targets the domain of sex to ensnare and devastate lives. Our protection rests in practicing self-discipline and remaining perpetually watchful. Even within this arena, the adage holds true: "eternal vigilance is the price of liberty."

The purpose of marriage is to amplify the truth, value, beauty, and magnificence of God. It's crucial to recognize that marriage doesn't serve to elevate God's significance; rather, it's God who enhances the purpose and meaning of marriage. Until this hierarchy is clearly understood and esteemed—until it's perceived and deeply appreciated—marriage won't be embraced as a revelation of God's splendor, but rather, it may mistakenly be perceived as competing with God's glory.

Marriage is not for boys in the kingdom; it is for men. If you want to enjoy the full blessings of God in marriage, be mentally, spiritually, and physically prepared for your home. Matthew 19:5 says: "...For this cause shall a man leave father and mother, and shall cleave to his wife: and they twain shall be one flesh?"

During the courtship phase, it's imperative to shield the relationship from actions that might invoke divine displeasure. Preserving your own integrity is a means of safeguarding your shared destiny. Hebrews 13:4 reminds us: "marriage is honorable in all, and the bed undefiled: but whoremongers and adulterers God will judge."

Engaging in behaviors that test the boundaries of your commitment, especially in terms of sexual matters, goes against the covenant. It not only introduces potential future shame but also risks diminishing the blessings of the divine. The covenant between partners necessitates protecting the relationship from moral impurity. The sanctity of marriage lies in preserving untarnished intimacy.

A Great Need for Caution

A crucial lesson emerges from the Song of Solomon, emphasized three times (Chapters 2:7; 3:5; 8:4): "Do not awaken nor stir up love until love itself shall please" (Berkeley Version). This cautionary message underscores the importance of waiting for God's timing in matters of love, rather than hastily plunging into impulsive infatuations.

"Above all else, guard your affections. For they influence everything else in your life"

(Proverbs 4:23 - TLB).

There is wholeness through love and marriage. It's exceedingly rare for God to summon a man to a solitary existence. God's own assertion conveys that a man finds a form of completion through marriage. Genesis 2:18, as translated by the Berkeley Version, conveys, "It is not good that man should be alone. I will make him a suitable helper, completing him." The Bible's framework further underscores this point, with marriage initiating the narrative (Genesis

2:18–25) and concluding it (Revelation 19:7–9; 21:2–10). Notably, Jesus' inaugural miracle occurred at a wedding (John 2:1–11).

When the Lord guides you towards marrying a person, He will surely cultivate love between you. The example of Isaac and Rebekah stands as a testament to this truth. Despite being strangers, when Isaac took Rebekah as his divinely chosen wife, he "loved her" (Genesis 24:67). Although most cases don't involve such a spectacular revelation, the vital lesson remains in recognizing God's chosen partner. Whether this connection occurs through parental involvement or a more direct path, if the person aligns with God's plan, a mutual and genuine love will undoubtedly flourish, much like the love Isaac felt for Rebekah.

Why Women Should Refrain from Assuming Wife Duties in Their Boyfriend Relationships?

The saying "Why buy the cow when you can get the milk for free?" may be old, but its wisdom endures. While it's natural to want to exhibit wifely qualities to our boyfriends, it's essential to exercise caution and avoid giving too much too soon. Do not freely give your time, energy, and emotions to individuals who often don't deserve it. Ideally, relationships should be a balanced partnership, with each person contributing equally.

Yet, if you give excessively without receiving reciprocal effort, he reaps the rewards while you risk losing everything. This can ultimately lead to heartache and disillusionment. Some women tend to be "all about him" rather than all about themselves. Ladies should prioritize safeguarding their autonomy, self-esteem, and personal growth by abstaining from shouldering wife-like responsibilities for their boyfriends. It's imperative that we let our partners actively engage in all facets of the relationship. A successful relationship thrives on equilibrium between both individuals' lives, rather than favoring one side.

Couples that perform the best in marriage have made their expectations clear from the beginning about the division of labor, parenthood, and money. Try not to drop everything and have sex with your partner. Feeling sexy is a good way to start, but a woman must make herself a priority. A ring is important!!! Fostering open-mindedness and effective communication within a relationship helps to work towards a future that's more fulfilling and joyful together.

While being in a relationship necessitates effort and compromise, it's essential to avoid overextending oneself. Women should steer clear of taking on wife duties for their boyfriends, as it can lead to an uneven power dynamic. Such actions can inadvertently establish false expectations, impede personal aspirations, foster dependency, and ultimately erode their sense of self.

The culmination of all things is imminent; therefore, exhibit self-control and clear-headedness for the sake of your prayers. Above all, foster sincere love for one another, as love has the power to forgive many wrongs. Extend hospitality to others without complaint. Each individual possesses unique talents, which should be used to serve one another responsibly, harnessing the diverse grace bestowed by God. Those who communicate should do so with the weight of divine wisdom, while those who serve should draw strength from God's supply. Ultimately, in all actions, let the glory of God shine through Jesus Christ. Glory and dominion belong to Him eternally. Amen. —1 Peter 4:7–11

"Every beautiful thing has a price tag. So, protect your relationship, and you will enjoy dignity at the end of the day."

Chapter 18

Could I Become One with That?

Having good looks can only get you so far in life. Sure, you might catch other people's attention and make a better first impression than others, but that tends to fade over time.

What about a good heart and personality? It is the key to living a more successful life. How you carry yourself is beneficial but have you ever thought of having a relationship in the long run?

From the time we are born, the biases hold a strong and deep connection in society. People treat each other on the basis of physical attraction.

The concept of beauty is connected with having a good body, skin, and plenty of other physical features. The moment you switch on your television, you are thrust into a world that celebrates fame and affluence. Not just on social media but the billboards scattered throughout the city are filled with beautiful people because they know how to attract the audience. But do you know what's real beauty? The real beauty lies within you. It lives within you and grows within you.

Have you heard the story of "A Very Old Man with Enormous Wings" by Gabriel Garcia Marquez? This story perfectly portrays the narration of a fallen angel, appearing weathered, unattractive, burdensome, and relegated to the status of a sideshow spectacle. Yet, there's a purpose behind this natural oddity. This celestial being was, in fact, the guardian angel who took care of a sick child but people thought that he was coming after the sick child. We, as a society, have set beauty standards that make us deemed ugly beings for judging other people based on the so-called beauty propositions. Contemporary culture seems to be driving a tendency where people to prioritize their personal preferences above all else, sometimes at the expense of valuing someone's character. While someone might align with your preferences, it's important to recognize that their true character will inevitably surface, especially within the context of a marriage. The initial attraction might lead you to say "I do" based on your preferences, but over time, their true nature will reveal itself, highlighting the significance of assessing character from the start. Before entering into a relationship, individuals often carry their own unique personalities, beliefs, and self-perceptions. These qualities are shaped by various factors such as upbringing, life experiences, and personal values. When someone enters into a relationship, particularly a significant or intimate one, it can have a profound impact on their sense of self and their worldview. Positive relationships built on trust, respect, and mutual support can contribute to personal growth and emotional well-being. In such relationships, individuals might feel validated, loved, and understood. This positivity can reinforce their self-esteem and lead to a more optimistic outlook on life. Conversely, negative or toxic relationships can indeed have detrimental effects. A "bad pick" in terms of a partner can lead to emotional turmoil, eroded self-esteem, and a distorted self-perception. If someone finds themselves in a relationship that is characterized by manipulation, disrespect, or abuse, it can gradually erode their sense of identity and create a more negative perspective on themselves and the world.

Reflecting on your emotional state prior to meeting someone is crucial. How did you view yourself and others? Unfortunately, the impact of making poor choices in partners can be profound. It can gradually alter your perspective, transforming a once-positive outlook into a more negative one. The influence of these misguided choices can taint the purity of your heart, leading to changes in personality and self-perception.

Don't fall in love too quickly. More specifically, do not fall in love if you consider beauty preferences as your top priority.

In the Bible, the emphasis is more on inner qualities, character, and spiritual alignment rather than physical appearance. In Proverbs 31:30, it is written, *"Charm is deceptive, and beauty is fleeting, but a woman who fears the Lord is to be praised."* The value of a person lies within a person's character over superficial attractiveness. 1 Samuel 16:7 states, "The Lord does not look at the things people look at. People look at the outward appearance, but the Lord looks at the heart." While physical attraction is a natural aspect of human relationships, the Bible encourages individuals to consider qualities that contribute to a healthy and God-honoring partnership. A few traits like kindness, integrity, patience, humility, and a shared faith in God are often emphasized over mere physical appearance.

Your choices reflect your perception of your own worth. The

initial stride toward making sound decisions involves defining your desires precisely. This is where your standards come into the picture. Being aware of what brings you joy, the beauty or the beast that you will be getting post-marriage? It all depends on you!!! Make the right choice.

Don't allow your feelings to manipulate you for the sake of eye-pleasing beauty norms. But you know what will happen, next?

Do Not Judge a Book by Its Cover!

The saying "Do not judge a book by its cover" is particularly relevant when it comes to finding a good partner. Just as you wouldn't assess a book's worth solely based on its outer appearance, you shouldn't evaluate a potential partner solely based on their physical attributes or initial impressions.

Infatuation is Deceptive

"Charm is deceptive, and beauty is fleeting, but a woman who fears the Lord is to be praised."

-Proverbs 31:30

Charm and beauty are words that go hand in hand. While beauty often relates to how someone looks, charm is about their outward behavior. When you combine these two qualities, they create the visible way a person presents themselves. These aspects are what others observe and sometimes use to form opinions about us. In a lot of societies, there's a strong focus on how we look.

Consequently, partners put in significant effort to improve our appearance. No matter what we buy from the skin target stores to enhance our external looks, its effects won't endure. As we grow older, our hair may become gray, our skin might lose firmness, and wrinkles will emerge. Sustaining a youthful and appealing appearance demands increasing investments of both time and money.

Although it's been quite some time since I watched "Snow White and the Seven Dwarfs," it bears relevance to our conversation. An egotistical queen possesses a magical mirror that repeatedly assures her of being the most beautiful in the realm.

On a certain day, the mirror conveys a very different message. It states that Snow White is now the fairest. This revelation triggers the queen's anger, leading her to make unsuccessful attempts to harm Snow White. This highlights how some of us, similar to the queen, struggle with the idea of someone else appearing more attractive than we do. Instead of resorting to extreme measures, we often spend even more resources in the futile pursuit of maintaining our sense of vanity.

Realizing that someone you love or married has been dishonest with you can be incredibly painful. What you will do with beauty when a person is not loyal or deceptive?

It can lead to feelings of betrayal, loneliness, and being unsure about things. When this deception happens in a relationship, the pain can be even stronger because it can break the trust you have in your partner and even in other people. Then, the lying stage begins in which people might lie to their partners because they don't feel secure when they're together. So, they lie to safeguard themselves from getting hurt or to sidestep arguments. Sometimes, it's because they're scared of losing you or they want to stay in control of the relationship.

Did you read or watch "Beauty and the Beast" during high school?

Can you imagine marrying someone solely based on their personality? If their appearance resembled that of the Beast, would you still be able to develop love? Sadly, for most people, the answer would be no. It's a sad reality. The kind of love depicted in stories like 'Beauty and the Beast' seems almost impossible in today's society. Consequently, many individuals are losing faith in the concept of love, as it frequently takes a backseat to the pursuit of someone deemed conventionally attractive. Yet, true love isn't about finding a flawless model; it's about discovering someone who ignites that special feeling within us.

"Beauty and the Beast" isn't your typical love story because it doesn't rely on physical attraction. While most romance movies involve the main characters overcoming some initial dislike, there's usually some level of attraction or romantic tension. In this case, Belle and the Beast don't experience that kind of infatuation. However, this absence of attraction serves a purpose for the Beast's growth.

Infatuation can cloud judgment and prevent seeing the real person beneath the surface. The Beast needs Belle to love him genuinely and see his true self. Likewise, he must also understand and appreciate who Belle truly is to break the spell because he needs to truly love her as well.

The person you fall in love with should be someone who's up for any crazy adventure you have in mind. Whether it's staying up late into the night sharing your deepest dreams and fears on the kitchen floor or dancing spontaneously to a catchy song on the street, they should be all in – disregarding honking cars – and just swaying to the rhythm, holding you tight.

Perhaps it's someone who can whip up pancakes without a single burn. Or someone you engage in captivating conversations with. Maybe it's a person who finds as much joy in painting on a rainy day as you do or who eagerly anticipates Saturday nights for orchestra music. Most importantly, it's someone who uplifts your strengths and provides reassurance during challenging moments. This person should make you a better version of yourself. The reality is, that our world is saturated with self-centeredness. It's a place where appearances take precedence. In this environment, a tale like Beauty and the Beast is deemed a fairy tale because we're surrounded by the notion that marrying a Beast is an act of benevolence rather than true love. Physical attraction has transformed into a hindrance, veiling us from the genuine connection and magnetic power that defines love.

You will Hear the phrase, "What did you find so attractive in her/him"

People will constantly ask you, "What did you do to get her/him?" or "You don't deserve her, or she/he will eventually go," which you might choose to ignore. But at some point, in life, you might contemplate it. They would merely laugh at you if you rejected them by telling them that you are much more than just good-looking. You find this annoying, but you put up with it!

Love at First Sight

You have probably heard of the phrase "love at first sight," which implies that you can tell you're in love with someone just by meeting them for the first time. But is this idea really true? Or is it just the physical features? Later in the relationship, you would think that the other person is intellectually not so smart, and eventually you will find beauty not important.

Love Bombing

One common red flag in relationships today is something called "love bombing." This entails a partner getting quickly and emotionally invested in the relationship's early phases. This conduct, which is frequently a method of manipulation, involves showing you an excessive amount of affection, making lofty predictions about the future, and using elaborate protestations of love. However, love bombing's true goal is to seduce you into an emotional commitment before quickly pulling away, leaving you hurt and distraught.

Trust Issues

When a relationship requires us to compromise our true selves or suppress our identity, we venture away from the reality of what the relationship truly is. Instead, we delve into an illusion of what we believe a relationship should resemble. For instance, consider a situation where a woman's boyfriend's extreme jealousy leads him to forbid her from spending time alone with other men.

Another scenario could involve a man whose partner's insecurities drive her to continually seek reassurance of his affection and attraction. Despite outwardly maintaining a façade of normalcy, these couples will likely begin to develop resentment and lose their initial interest in the relationship. Such restrictive circumstances can serve as breeding grounds for deceit. The woman might resort to hiding instances of spending time alone with a male friend or colleague, while the man might conceal emerging feelings of attraction towards another woman.

If our partners confide in us about finding someone else attractive, it can signal a level of trust that enables us to believe their assurance that they won't act on this attraction. Openness between partners contributes to healthier, more robust relationships. Conversely, embracing secrecy tends to foster a habit of progressively larger falsehoods.

In cases of infidelity, denying the reality of the situation is a deceptive tactic that upholds the illusion of everything being fine. Acknowledging when something is amiss or when there's a search for fulfillment outside the relationship is crucial information that should be shared with a partner. Emotions that arise from deception, such as suspicion and anger, have the potential to dismantle a relationship. Moreover, they can deeply wound someone by shattering their sense of truth.

Can you Love Someone who is not Physically Attractive?

Can you love someone who you don't think is physically attractive? Certainly, yes!!! To put it another way, it is possible to feel romantic love without having a sexual urge for another person.

Not all romantic impulses are accompanied by any kind of sexual desire, and even when they are, the desire might not be for sexual activity as such. Maybe just holding hands, kissing, or hugging. When I refer to "romantic" in a broad sense, I don't necessarily aim to suggest or negate the presence of passionate, enchanting, or emotionally stirring feelings. My intention is merely to differentiate this type of love from parental or sibling love, for example. This encompassing definition of romantic love can encompass emotional, sexual, and intellectual attractions. However, these connections might be intense and passionate, or they might not hold that level of intensity. It's meant to include fervent lovers as well as those individuals whose affection is calmer and more tranquil in nature.

People think that there should be a common romantic connection which, I think is not the case. Love is of paramount importance then comes physical attraction. Although our minds are naturally wired to evaluate someone's appearance and respond with snap judgments or previous assumptions. But on a subconscious level, sometimes without our awareness, this process takes place. As a result, we commonly fail to attempt to change this behavior.

For those who maintain that loving someone without sexual attraction is possible, the dynamics of this love connection function in a unique way. Individuals who have fallen for someone without sexual attraction often base their affection on a deeper intellectual and companionship-based connection.

For those who prioritize passion and chemistry in a relationship and seek that elusive spark, comprehending the opposing viewpoint might prove challenging. To them, sexual attraction is a fundamental aspect of a relationship, a sign of serious and affectionate connection. The physical presence of the person you love holds significant importance for them, and without this attraction, they believe genuine love cannot exist.

The rationale behind this perspective often hinges on the role of sex in differentiating close relationships from others. Those who deem sexual chemistry an essential component, argue that if you claim to love someone without experiencing physical attraction, what truly distinguishes that relationship from any other? As per this view, the unique chemistry is what sets apart romantic relationships from platonic ones.

Paul conveys to Timothy that while "physical training is of some value, godliness holds value for all aspects of life, promising rewards in both the present existence and the life beyond" (1 Timothy 4:8). Physical training primarily focuses on the external aspect, and it does hold significance in preserving our bodily health. However, this significance pales in comparison to the value of cultivating godliness.

Ultimately, our physical bodies will eventually deteriorate and decay, regardless of how diligently we care for them. In contrast, the essence of our inner being will persist. If we invest in nurturing godliness within ourselves (as noted in 1 Timothy 4:7), it will carry enduring worth in this lifetime and throughout eternity.

Likewise, Proverbs 5:18-19 urges individuals to embrace their partner's physical attributes. The verses convey, "May your fountain be blessed, and take joy in the wife of your youth, a charming deer, a graceful doe. May her breasts always satisfy you; may you be continually captivated by her love."

Sex – This Is Not What Makes You Human

In contemporary times, many individuals often define their identity solely through their sexuality, linking their identity with whom they engage in sexual relationships. However, the perspective presented in the Bible differs. According to the Bible, a person's identity is rooted in being a human being, made in the image and likeness of God. This implies that your inherent worth and significance are at their peak even before engaging in any aspect of life, including sex. You are an embodiment of God's image, entrusted with dominion over creation and living under His authority.

This understanding carries profound implications. Firstly, it suggests that while sex is natural for humans, it is not obligatory. A person can lead a complete, enriched, purposeful, and God-honoring life without engaging in sexual activity. Sex is positive, yet it doesn't hold the ultimate position. This concept might surprise many within numerous cultures.

The Bible underlines that marriage, sex, singleness, and celibacy are all honorable. They are valuable gifts bestowed by the Lord, granted in His wisdom and timing for His glory and our eternal well-being. We can only be grateful for this perspective and insight from the Bible.

The profound wisdom behind God's instruction to abstain from intimacy before marriage is to save us from sin. This guidance serves to avert significant harm and preserve the sanctity of what is the most cherished aspect of a relationship between a man and a woman. Don't wrap everything in romance and sex, making it challenging to prioritize and discuss crucial topics.

The more you delve into understanding each other on levels beyond the physical, the more the physical attraction will naturally evolve. This is largely because you will come to value the person for who they are beyond their external appearance, recognizing their true essence, which is their personality. That's why people often prioritize qualities like humor or kindness when seeking a partner—traits related to personality, not looks.

The takeaway is that physical attraction doesn't always materialize right away. It might need time to grow as you build a connection from the inside out. So, if you find that the level of physical attraction towards your romantic interest isn't as strong as you'd like it to be, don't worry. With time and understanding, that connection can certainly develop.

Too Beautiful to Find True Love?

Beautiful people face challenges in finding love can be attributed to factors involving both potential partners and their own mindsets. The striking physical appearance of a person can greatly hinder a genuine understanding of their character and compatibility.

This leads to biases, particularly directed at women, resulting in phrases like, "She's gorgeous but not intelligent," or, "You can't be both pretty and smart," and "Beauty without brain." Individuals who could be well-matched might shy away due to the perceived unapproachability of such remarkably attractive people.

Moreover, the obstacles in the pursuit of a suitable partner for beautiful people also emanate from their personal attitudes. Often, they're acutely aware of their exceptional attractiveness, causing them to be less willing to settle for a partner who is simply "good enough." This mindset creates a tendency to become overly selective, disregarding viable options and concentrating on unsuitable ones. Once they establish a romantic relationship, their strong belief in their desirability might lead to reduced commitment, as they may feel entitled to invest less effort in nurturing the romantic connection, assuming a privileged status within the relationship.

Society acts like a pair of malfunctioning glasses. The standards set are often incorrect for all of us, clouding our vision. Our clarity and understanding are compromised. Yet, there's a depth beyond what the eyes perceive (pardon the pun). Our eyes possess remarkable strength, capable of peering into the soul and transcending mere appearances. We should aspire for a vision that delves into inner qualities rather than surface traits, seeking genuine love instead of a flawlessly symmetrical visage.

Good Things Take Time – A Hit or Miss?

It's easy to feel love for someone without a physical attraction, its possibility is influenced by the individuals involved in the relationship. Regrettably, if you find yourself questioning whether love can develop without physical attraction, the likelihood is that, despite your hopes, a level of sexual interest or attraction might be necessary to sustain your interest in the relationship.

This situation isn't uncommon. Sex and desire play significant roles in many relationships, and people generally have a strong inclination towards sexual engagement. While the intensity of this desire can differ among individuals and evolve over time, the majority of us are biologically predisposed to value sexual attraction and satisfaction from our partners.

The concept of sex primarily centers around forming a close and intimate connection in the Bible. It involves bonding with your divinely ordained partner and establishing a deep connection. But obviously not before marriage. The notion of "becoming one flesh" signifies a profound unity. While the instruction to "be fruitful and multiply" implies a purpose for procreation, the concept of sex in the context of faith is more expansive. It's intended to be a delightful and close experience between partners. In Genesis 2:24, it's stated, "Therefore a man shall leave his father and his mother and hold fast to his wife, and they shall become one flesh."

What does the phrase "become one flesh" signify? It certainly refers to physical intimacy, but it also implies that in a relationship, two individuals' hearts and spirits can intertwine so deeply that they effectively merge into a unified whole. They collectively share the joys and challenges of life, where what impacts one also affects the other.

Nonetheless, for certain individuals, this need is less prominent and can easily be overshadowed by other factors. They prioritize a connection based on shared intellectual interests and stimulating conversations, which becomes the primary source of attraction between them.

Here's a key point to remember: love doesn't necessarily start with an immediate physical bond. While we often hear stories of people being drawn to each other intensely from the very beginning, unable to keep their hands off each other, this pattern doesn't apply to every couple. In some cases, the process of developing physical attraction might require time as you first build a mental and emotional connection. Charm and beauty are what is seen and are temporary. But what is unseen, our inner beings, are eternal. And so, we should put much more effort into growing and developing as followers of Christ than we do in prettying up our outside appearances.

Chapter 19

How to Get My Marriage off Life Support

What happens when you wake up one morning and you realize that the heart of your marriage has stopped beating? You do what any normal human being does: you perform CPR, you call 911, you rush it into the emergency room, begging the doctors to save it. For some people, their marriage has been on life support for so long that they've forgotten what it looks like, alive. Marriages can become so severely wounded by crises like verbal abuse, physical abuse, and or adultery that their survival seems impossible. But nothing is impossible with God. If both you and your spouse are willing to work with God, your marriage stands a chance - even if it's on life support. God's help can get your marriage's vital organs to function again. And, since simply returning to the way things were isn't good enough, God will breathe new life into your relationship to transform it into a healthy one. So cancel your marriage's funeral. It can survive - and thrive - if you work with God for reconciliation.

"A marriage is supposed to be enjoyed rather than endured." Well, we tend to find enjoyment in activities or experiences we like, such as the excitement of a basketball game, while we endure those we don't particularly enjoy, like waiting for an oil change in the garage. It's only natural to look forward to things that bring us pleasure and excitement and to approach fewer stimulating tasks with a sense of endurance. This simple concept aligns with our natural inclinations and preferences.

My initial assumption was that all couples inherently enjoy their marriages, especially those who have celebrated milestones like 10, 20, or 30+ years together. I believed that their commitment and longevity were signs of happiness and enjoyment in their marriage. And if you have similar thinking, then it is not true. However, I soon realized that my hopeful outlook concealed a lack of understanding regarding the possibility of enduring a marriage without truly enjoying it.

This realization led me to question why some couples, despite staying together for many years and not divorcing, might still be in marriages marked by endurance rather than enjoyment. I want to clarify that I'm not referring to high-profile Hollywood celebrity couples who may marry for publicity or power couples who view marriage as a strategic move to advance their social status. Instead, I'm interested in those couples who may have begun their unions with sincere intentions but have found themselves in marriages that feel more like obligations than sources of joy and fulfillment (Shucks Pastor). To be factual and realistic, marriage becomes obligatory when partners do not work on making the marriage work in every possible way. Marriage is a God-made institution. You cannot do marriage without God in the center of it. A main parasitic factor in destroying marriages is the use of sarcasm, name-calling, belittling, and insulting comments. Belittling someone can come in many forms. It's laughing at them for making mistakes. It's dismissing things that they find important. It's putting them down when you should be lifting them up.

This is especially harmful if you do it in front of other people, including friends or even your children. What happens behind closed doors is one thing, but if your spouse shows blatant disrespect to you in front of your friends and family, this is a sign that your marriage is on life support. Marriage is not something you can turn on and off. If you've decided as a couple or as individuals to take a break from your marriage, it means that you're not yet ready to accept that your marriage is over. It can be tempting. You two are in a constant state of annoyance and conflict with one another. You keep having the same intense fellowship over and over, and you're just tired of looking at their face at the end of a long day.

Maybe if you got some distance, you'd learn to really appreciate one another. Sadly, this is almost never a good idea. If your marriage is otherwise perfect and you don't wear your ring, you don't need to worry.

The problem comes specifically when you're going through a rough patch in your marriage, and you or your spouse take the ring off. This can be to send a message to the other person that if they don't act right, they could lose you.

Or it could simply be to stop being reminded of your marital issues every time you look down at your hands. Whatever the case, this kind of denial of your marriage is indicative of deeper issues with love and intimacy.

You might say, "Who cares? It's just a ring." But it's more than that. It's a symbol of your life together.

If you sleep in separate beds. This is a common sign of a marriage that's on life support. There's a reason they call it a "martial bed." If you don't share a bed, how can you expect to share your life? Sharing a bed is about more than just sleep. Sex is a vital part of a healthy marriage and when spouses stop sharing a bed, it's often a sign of a sexless marriage. Plus, there's a powerful psychological effect of ending and beginning each day together that you just won't get in your separate beds.

If you're not ready to share a bed with someone, you're not ready to be married to them, and all the love in the world won't change that.

There are certain situations where you can have separate beds in a happy and healthy marriage:

- *If you work drastically different hours*

- *If one of you has a medical problem*

- *If you need to leave town on business*

When Two People Meet

Here, I'm referring to marriages that follow a more traditional path. Two individuals meet, fall in love, court each other, and take the time to understand and connect with one another. They enjoy their courtship so much that they eventually become engaged and get married. These are the couples I'm discussing. Sadly, in some cases, what starts as an enjoyable marriage can transition into a situation where the couple feels they are enduring rather than enjoying their marriage.

The reason for this transformation is relatively straightforward. Marriage often transitions from being relatively easy in the beginning to becoming more challenging over time. It requires effort and work to maintain and nurture the relationship, and this process is not always as enjoyable as the initial ease and excitement of being together.

Let's understand it this way. When it comes to pets and plants, negligence can have significant consequences. If you neglect your pet, it can experience loneliness, weakness, and frailty. Without proper care, it won't be able to provide you with the same joy it once did, and it may even become gravely ill or die. The same principle applies to beautiful plants. If you fail to protect them from the elements, provide water, nutrients, and proper pruning, they too may wither or deteriorate to a point where they no longer bring you the same admiration. In both cases, the responsibility lies with the caregiver because these living beings depend on your care and attention to thrive.

Your marriage is a living, breathing entity of two fleshes transformed into one flesh (Genesis 2:24; Ephesians 5:31; Mark 10:8). If each individual is alive, then this shared entity, the marriage itself, must also be considered alive. Just like any living thing, a marriage requires protection, sustenance, care, and nurturing to thrive; otherwise, it may stagnate and eventually wither away. Therefore, in order for your marriage to remain vibrant and enjoyable for both partners, it is imperative to put in the effort and endure the necessary work. Sometimes, this work involves doing things you may not particularly like, but it is essential to do them in order to preserve and enhance the aspects of your marriage that you cherish. In essence, enduring the challenges and making the necessary investments in your marriage is what allows you to ultimately find joy and fulfillment within it.

Why Are Newlyweds So Characteristically Happy?

In the early stages of marriage, many couples find themselves living in a sort of fantasy world, experiencing what could be described as a utopian relationship. During this phase, each spouse may seem perfect, and any perceived flaws are seen as endearing quirks.

The mirth and excitement of moving in together and transitioning from a "pretend" to a real-life partnership is invigorating.

Additionally, the introduction of sexual intimacy adds a new layer of novelty, freshness, fun, and excitement to the relationship.

This phase of intense infatuation and focus on each other is often referred to as "Young Love or Puppy Love." These two young lovers become deeply enamored with each other, pouring abundant care, nourishment, and nurturance into their relationship. At this stage, their marriage revolves entirely around the two of them, and they are wholly dedicated to one another. There's no one-size-fits-all secret formula for a successful marriage. Even a happy marriage can turn into a headache if things are not settled or dealt with in the same way as they should be.

Why Is Marriage Often Challenging?

Well, first and foremost, difficulties faced in marriage are not unique to you, your partner, or your specific relationship. These challenges are a common part of the married experience, and they tend to ebb and flow over time. One significant reason why marriage can be tough is that societal perspectives on marriage have evolved over time.

Nowadays, marriage is viewed as more of a choice, emphasizing romanticism, individual fulfillment, and intimacy. This shift in expectations can lead to difficulties, as once the initial romantic and sexual excitement fades, some individuals may perceive the relationship or marriage as a failure. These changing societal norms and expectations contribute to the complexities couples face in modern marriages.

What happens when you wake up one morning and realize that your marriage is in serious trouble? Will you react like any normal person, or would you try to revive it, seeking help, and doing everything you can to save it? You may seek advice or therapy, hoping to breathe life back into your relationship. You sit by its side, holding its hand, reminiscing about the good times you once shared.

But when your marriage has been struggling for so long that you can't remember how it used to be vibrant, you might wonder if it's time to let go. Should you keep holding onto hope, wishing and praying that it can be resurrected, or is it finally time to accept that it's over, grieve for what's lost, and move forward?

Amidst the messiness of your marriage, I truly believe that there are ways that can make your marriage work.

Identify Issues and Goals

First and foremost, recognize and openly discuss issues and goals within your relationship. Additionally, it's vital to collaborate on establishing objectives to address these concerns. What might be a problem for one person may not be perceived as an issue by the other, but it's important to acknowledge your partner's concerns as matters that impact the relationship as a whole. As partners come together, acknowledge the stumbling blocks, and create a plan to establish goals that will guide you in navigating these challenges.

Take a Closer Look at Yourself – Put Yourself First

Blaming your partner for all the issues in your relationship can be a common impulse. (For instance, blaming them for spending too much time at work.) to Remember that a healthy relationship involves both partners. Instead of fixating solely on your partner's perceived faults, take an honest look at how your actions might also play a role in the problems. When you can identify areas where you can improve and suggest ways to make positive changes, it becomes easier to encourage your partner to do the same. When you ensure your own well-being and contentment, you become better equipped to attend to the needs of your partner and others.

Commit Yourselves to Reconciliation

Make a firm commitment to reconcile with your spouse. Decide that you won't end your marriage or settle for a return to an unhealthy relationship. Instead, actively dedicate yourself to rebuilding love and trust on both sides of your marriage, whether you're the one who's been hurt or the one who's caused pain. Put all your heart, mind, and effort into achieving the goal of transforming your marriage. Turn to the example of Jesus. Understand that Jesus' sacrifice on the cross serves as the ultimate model of reconciliation. Seek His guidance and rely on His strength as you work towards reconciling with your spouse. If either of you hasn't yet started a relationship with Jesus, consider doing so soon. Repent for your mistakes, accept His forgiveness, and begin living in accordance with His teachings.

Work on Intimacy

Well, I'm truly aware of the fact that life is busy. But you have to manage intimacy along with the busyness of other work. Take some time to consider how you can make your sexual relationship with your spouse more exciting and enjoyable. A fulfilling sex life is a vital component of a strong marriage, and couples who thrive put deliberate effort into enhancing their sexual experiences. Sexual intimacy is an expression of love that brings happiness and unity into a marriage. It is also the power by which married couples can "multiply, and replenish the earth" (Genesis 1:28). Intimacy is a blessing that can lead to the incomparable joy of children as part of the eternal family unit. Ecclesiastes 9:9 (NIV) suggests,

"Enjoy life with your wife, whom you love, all the days of this meaningless life that God has given you under the sun—all your meaningless days. For this is your lot in life and in your toilsome labor under the sun." Make an effort to spend quality intimate time together, creating memorable experiences and cherishing each other's company.

Good Communication

Maintain regular communication with each other. Saving your marriage often hinges on effective communication, which is a fundamental element in nurturing deep connections that can make marriages last a lifetime. Wondering how to communicate effectively in your relationship? Engage in open conversations with your spouse about your interests, dreams, goals, feelings, and even the things that bother you. Proverbs 15:1 (NIV) advises, "A gentle answer turns away wrath, but a harsh word stirs up anger." Open and respectful communication is key to resolving conflicts and understanding each other better. Practice active listening and strive to communicate with kindness and empathy. Remember that listening is equally important in communication. Create an environment where your spouse feels comfortable sharing everything, they may hesitate to discuss with anyone else. For additional guidance, explore communication exercises designed for couples.

Don't be Controlling – Stop Gaslighting

Are you frequently caught in the trap of attempting to dictate your partner's actions, and timing? Someone exhibiting controlling behavior may encounter challenges in sustaining relationships, as most individuals prefer not to be subjected to excessive oversight.

Imagine if you were to step into lukewarm water and gradually turn up the heat. Initially, you might not notice the temperature change, but over time, you could find yourself in scalding hot water. This analogy can help you grasp the dynamics of a controlling partner. Some controlling behaviors can be so subtle or develop so slowly that they're challenging to identify at first. You might even become accustomed to some of them. Then, one day, you realize that the situation has become unbearable, much like realizing the water is too hot.

But remember that not all controlling partners exhibit the same behaviors. Control can manifest in various degrees and may be seamlessly integrated into your relationship. What truly matters is how these behaviors make you feel. The line between being attentive and exerting pressure can be blurry, but if your partner consistently makes decisions for you without your input, it falls into the category of controlling behavior. This pattern of behavior can induce stress, feelings of oppression, and even border on abusive conduct, which is unacceptable for anyone to endure. Attempting to control one's partner can potentially lead to emotional abuse which can be a precursor to divorce. Sometimes, couples find themselves entangled in disputes over seemingly trivial matters, such as how to load the dishwasher or pack the car before a road trip. However, when viewed in the larger context of a relationship, these issues often appear insignificant.

Share Financial Expectations

Financial disagreements are a common source of tension in many marriages. This often arises because couples enter the relationship with varying financial expectations and perspectives. It can be challenging for each partner to fully understand the other's point of view on money matters. One key to a successful marriage is reaching an agreement on how you will manage your finances together. This involves establishing a budget, deciding on an approach to handling debt, and making a plan to ensure that your spending aligns with your financial limits. Additionally, it's essential to distinguish between needs and wants. Both are valid, but problems can arise if couples attempt to satisfy all their desires without considering their financial constraints.

Perfection is Flawed

"Your perfect husband and wife have a flaw!" So, are you too taken aback by this comment? Why was it so much easier to focus on a spouse's imperfections instead of their strengths? This is truly an "aha" moment for couples in marriage. When your partner does something that drives you nuts, it will make you think that he is quite imperfect. It is because we have accepted the perfection but not the imperfection that comes along with that person. It's a fact!!! marriage takes acceptance and it's better to work on it and improve your relationship. Don't compare who does more or keep score. A smart spouse knows when to take the lead when to move aside, and when to motivate you to keep going rather than get preoccupied with keeping track of things.

Don't Lose Sight

It may sound cliché but make it a rule to never let a disagreement linger unresolved overnight in your relationship. Resolve any conflicts promptly and ensure that no unresolved issues carry over into the next day. Remember that disagreements are a natural part of every relationship; what truly matters is how effectively you both move past them and process the emotions involved. Be cautious of your relationship during slippery situations, much like navigating a treacherous road. When you engage in an argument, it's crucial to stay focused on one specific issue at a time. Venturing into tangential or unrelated matters can obscure the core problem, making it difficult to find a resolution. By adhering to a single argument, you significantly increase the likelihood of reaching a solution. Adopting an attitude of patience and empathy allows both partners the necessary time to process their emotions and work toward a resolution without prematurely shifting to other topics.

Express Your Thoughts and Feelings

Do let your concerns and grievances with your partner accumulate and intensify over time. Instead, address them directly and honestly in a considerate manner. Begin the conversation by acknowledging your care for the relationship or you're understanding that your partner may not have intended to upset you. Then, clearly describe the behavior you'd like your partner to change and express the emotions you're experiencing, whether it's anger, hurt, frustration, or confusion. Follow this by requesting a specific change, like asking for a quieter tone or requesting your partner to wait until you finish speaking. Finally, seek agreement by asking, "Are you willing to agree to that?" Trust me, this approach promotes effective communication and resolution in your relationship.

Marriage is Hard Work, But Worth It

Altogether, marriage is tough and it comes with its own set of benefits. It can be extremely rewarding at times while on the other hand, you have to deal with certain struggles. But it's a worthwhile and blissful union.

Do you remember your marriage vows?

"For better, for worse…"

"In sickness and in health…"

"For richer, for poorer…"

"I will try with you better to understand ourselves, the world, and God; through the best and worst of what is to come, and as long as we live."

These promises presuppose tough times. We went into our marriage with our eyes open, so there's really no excuse for not bringing everything we have to the table when things – once in a while – get dicey. When one spouse in a marriage is unhappy, it often creates an atmosphere characterized by resentment, hostility, and indifference. This negativity can envelop the entire relationship. A Reddit user provided insights into why some people may find themselves unhappy in their marriages, stating, "I'm not unhappy, but I think I know why some people might be. It takes effort to maintain long-term marital happiness; it doesn't happen automatically." Problems are a part of life, but their significance is adaptable. We have the power to determine what these challenges mean to us by how we choose to perceive and evaluate them. When a marital rift arises between a husband and wife, resolving the issues typically necessitates the joint efforts of both individuals. If one person is actively trying to mend the rift while the other shows no interest or concern about bridging the gap, it reflects a high degree of insensitivity and indifference. In other words, saving a marriage becomes nearly impossible when one party has no intention of actively working toward resolving the issues. When there is a problem, try solving it as soon as you can. The longer you let a problem breed, the deeper its effects remain in the relationship. But don't let trivial problems become parasites in your marriage either. Take a step forward and talk to each other and speak out about your unhappiness without blaming the other.

Get Your marriage Groove Back- Clear the Clutter!

Your marriage can be likened to an abandoned, dilapidated mansion like Hollywood Hills. Despite its current state of disrepair, it retains its original structure and the potential to be restored to its former grandeur. However, restoring it will require effort and dedication.

The pivotal question is whether you are willing to clear away the clutter and neglect that has accumulated in your marriage over time. Are you prepared to endure the necessary work to rekindle the joy and vitality within your relationship? Similar to the neglected mansion, your marriage has remained fundamentally the same as it was when you first experienced the euphoria of "Young Love." It's a matter of redirecting your attention and effort to breathe new life into it. And speaking of "Young Love…" Proverbs 5:18 tells us to rejoice with the wife of thy youth. In simple words, it doesn't matter how long you have been married, however, what really matters is how you have maintained and how long it can run. It is entirely plausible for individuals to rediscover the joy and connection they once shared with their spouse, even as they grow older and their marriage matures. This notion is supported by the Bible, which suggests that we can continue to find the qualities and essence of our youthful love within our lifelong partners.

Ecclesiastes 9:9 encourages us to wholeheartedly relish the beauty of our marital relationship throughout our lives. This implies that not only can we maintain our love for our spouse, but it may even deepen with the passage of time. The Bible's teachings emphasize that our love has the potential to endure and flourish over the years, allowing us to see and appreciate in our long-time partner the same qualities that initially captivated us during the early days of "Young Love."

If your marriage is facing challenges or issues, it's likely a result of neglect over time. Just like a garden overrun with weeds and unwanted growth, your marriage may require some dedicated effort and endurance to restore it to its former vitality. Similar to the abandoned Hollywood Hills mansion, your marriage might have lost its sparkle and appeal, but the potential for rejuvenation exists.

The key is to be willing to put in the necessary work to bring your marriage back to its former glory and enjoy it once more. And once you've achieved that, it's crucial to prioritize maintenance. Just as a living entity requires constant care, your marriage, as emphasized in Genesis 2:24, Ephesians 5:31, and Mark 10:8, should be nurtured, fed, and watered to keep it alive and thriving. Consistency and commitment are essential to sustaining the beauty and vitality of your marital bond.

In the end, staying together will always be better, best, and gratifying—and smart. It is not about happiness. There is a lot of comfort, love, and satisfaction, though, and yes there is happiness, but that is not the end all, be all. Whatever hell we thought we were going through can be worth it. You can breathe, be still together, like warriors, and wear badges. With honor, you will be married.

Chapter 20

We Had to Break-Up

There's that old saying that *"breaking up is hard to do."* Well, not only is it hard to do, but it's hard to handle the aftermath and the emotional complications that burp up out of us when we're in such a vulnerable state.

Sadness overwhelms you as you are ready to say goodbye to a close friend, the person with whom you shared "good morning" and "good night" messages every day. Sometimes you must acknowledge the truth that it's not working out, and then end it. However, the reality is that you may second, third, fourth, and maybe fifth-guess yourself and end up excusing all of your partners' faults to justify giving them another chance after another chance. The pain becomes worse with each passing day. Breaking up with someone you love is terrible. Breaking up with your partner is the best thing to do if you feel like you're not happy anymore, and the relationship is just pulling you down instead of pushing you up. That could be the greatest red flag.

When you break up, suddenly you will find yourself without the person who was always around. This is hard for your brain to deal with, so it will tempt you into "just checking in" on your ex. Essentially, you're just fueling your brain's need for this person, and you're prolonging the process of getting over them by stalking them on social media. There have been significant studies that show that our brains literally become addicted to our partners. But our relationships also have an emotional attachment. Oftentimes our partner fulfills some kind of void. Maybe we want to know that our partner will put us first or will never leave us, or maybe we want to feel that we are worthy of being loved unconditionally. These wants make it difficult to go through with a breakup—even when it's for our own good. To have a healthy separation, we have to understand that breakups are huge obstacles to overcome, and have compassion for ourselves as we navigate the intense emotions.

It's important to know yourself and what you need to do to move forward. Even then, it can prove difficult to remain steadfast. Breakups can re-open deep wounds that evoke powerful emotions.

Flip-flopping in relationships is a sign that we aren't clear on what is best for us or how to give ourselves what we need. We're dealing with the intensity of feelings and the brain's addiction, so we have to learn how to gain and maintain clarity for ourselves. The back and forth shows that there is doubt and uncertainty and it will cause feelings to remain open the back and forth can be exhausting and a little embarrassing. It shows that you aren't abiding by your own truth and respecting your own boundaries. Having boundaries is an act of respect for yourself. It shows you and the person you're in communication with that you value yourself first and foremost.

You might be dating a perfect partner but as the years progress, things become endearing. You had been planning the future together but later decided that you might not be compatible. It sounds ridiculous but certainly, at times, it might not be true. There might be no chasm— just an explosion and two people couldn't be together anymore.

The most challenging aspect of ending a relationship with someone you love is convincing yourself that it's the right thing to do. While you may understand that this choice is in your best interest, it doesn't make the process easy.

"As soon as you trust yourself, you will know how to live."

~Johann Wolfgang von Goethe

Relationships aren't easy. But most of the best things in life aren't supposed to be. Perfection is elusive, and life won't always be a constant stream of positivity. There will be challenging times, moments of uncertainty, periods of complacency, and instances of fear that you will encounter along the way.

How Do You Know When It's Time to Break Up?

→ **Breaking Up and Getting Back Together**

Do you remember those middle school days when it felt like everyone you knew was constantly breaking up and then getting together again? You'd often question why they even remained in those relationships. Such on-and-off behavior may have appeared entertaining in our youth, but as adults, trust me, it's not alluring at all and doesn't sound practical. It's OK to drift away from a relationship that has made your life miserable.

If you find yourselves repeatedly splitting up and reuniting, it might indicate that neither of you is addressing the deeper issues causing these recurrent breakups.

→ Bearing the Brunt of all Sacrifices

In every relationship, there's always a need to make compromises and sacrifices for mutual support. This could be minor choices like letting your partner decide on a restaurant or which TV show to watch. However, in some instances, these compromises might extend to more significant decisions, such as relocating for a job opportunity. When you consistently find yourself making sacrifices for your partner without receiving the same level of reciprocity, it can lead to an unequal power dynamic, ultimately fostering lasting discontent and bitterness.

→ You Don't Like Yourself

You have a negative self-perception when you're with your partner. Experiencing self-doubt or a lack of self-esteem in your partner's presence can gradually erode your well-being. A thriving relationship should inspire and encourage your personal growth. If you sense that your partner tends to amplify your negative qualities or behaviors, it's likely an indicator that the relationship has taken an unhealthy turn.

→ You Think About Breakup All the Time

When you and your partner first entered into a relationship, you might have connected due to shared interests. But if you're now considering advancing the relationship or considering a breakup, it's important to reflect on whether both of you also share common values.

It's natural for partners to wonder what the future holds for their relationship from time to time. However, it's concerning when thoughts of being apart from someone take over your mind consistently. Preferences in daily life will change, but core values will likely not change. This will trigger a reality check – would you really want to spend your entire life with a person with whom you get consistent thoughts of getting apart? If your answer is no, then take it as a sign that you are heading in the right direction ending the relationship. Having hope that your partner will change is not good for a relationship.

→ Nothing New Anymore

All relationships go through a cycle of phases that includes newness, excitement, stability, dullness, and slower periods. It's okay to feel like the relationship has lost its spark because things have become the same every day. If this is your primary concern with your partner, consider injecting some fresh experiences into the relationship by trying new activities together or exploring new aspects of your intimacy.

It's also possible that you might need more personal time to foster your individual growth within the relationship. If, despite these efforts, you still find yourself leaning towards being single and on the dating market, then perhaps that's the right decision for you.

→ **Persistent Uneasiness**

You experience a persistent sense of tension and unease in their presence. Feeling consistently on edge when you're around someone is an indication that you don't feel completely secure. There could be various reasons for this, such as a constant fear that they might react angrily if you upset them or a worry that making a mistake could lead to them leaving. In healthy relationships, we should all feel safe enough to express ourselves and communicate our needs without the constant fear of facing volatility, retaliation, or abandonment.

→ **Right Focus**

When we are in a committed relationship, each partner's actions are filtered through the lens of our own personal experiences. We build impressions of their personality based on their actions, and then we try to apply those impressions to ourselves. This is normal, but it becomes problematic when our judgments of their actions lead us to make personal attacks on them.

Your partner's motives may not be what they seem, and they may be completely oblivious to the problem you're having. That's why it's so important to stay focused on the issue at hand rather than making value judgments or attacking the person's character. When emotions get heated, it's hard to have a rational discussion about what's really at issue. Avoid attacking the other person personally and instead focus on the problem at hand and possible solutions to it.

What if There is No Specific Reason?

Sometimes, there might be no specific reason for the breakup, but over time, you don't feel the same way as in the beginning. Not having a reason to stay is a good reason to leave. That's okay. Things change, and feelings change as the years progress.

Having the desire to end a relationship is a valid and sufficient reason to initiate a breakup. The fundamental aspect of any relationship is the genuine desire to be in it. If that desire has faded, it's a sign that it's healthier to move on. However, making the decision to end a relationship and actually going through with it are two distinct challenges. Even when you're certain that a breakup is the right choice, it doesn't diminish the sadness or emotional pain that can come with it. You may still hold affection or love for the person, and the thought of losing the positive aspects of the relationship can be difficult.

Having a "conversation about ending the relationship" can be challenging. Unless the other person shares similar feelings, they may feel bewildered if there isn't a clear reason provided. Therefore, taking some time to reflect on how to articulate your emotions in a way that respects your own feelings and addresses the other person's likely concerns about their actions is beneficial. Maintain honesty with yourself while also being empathetic to the other person's emotions when communicating challenging news. Every relationship is unique, and ending a relationship is best done with thoughtful consideration.

Avoid It? Or Get It Over With?

In the aftermath of your breakup, "just get it over with." Think through things and make yourself clear about how you will get over with the breakup phase. Don't rush into troubling conversations if you are not prepared well or you might regret it afterward.

I'm surprised by the people saying that they got separated since they were blindsided by the breakup. Relationships don't just dissolve in a single moment. It takes at least a little time for things to fall apart. So, once you're feeling like things are getting a little off track, you owe it to the other person to give them a chance to ponder on it and then focus on the implementation.

DO:

Think twice or thrice about what you want: Reflect on your desires and the underlying motivations behind the breakup. Take ample time to contemplate your emotions and the rationale behind your decision. Stay true to yourself and your needs. Even if your choice may potentially cause some emotional distress to the other person involved, it's acceptable to prioritize what is best for you. However, it's crucial to handle the situation with care and sensitivity.

Anticipate the Reactions: Consider what you want to convey and anticipate the possible reactions of the other person. Will your boyfriend or girlfriend be taken by surprise? You both may experience sadness, anger, hurt, or perhaps even a sense of relief. Empathizing with their perspective and emotions can help you approach the situation with preparation.

Have Good Intentions: Let the other person know that the decision to break up took place for the mutual benefit. It's important to have truthful and good intentions, expressing that the other person holds significance in your life. Your kindness, honesty, and respect matter a lot while you speak.

Be Honest but Don't Be Brutal: You don't have to be brutal or cruel while communicating with the other person. Appreciate their qualities and the things they did for you. Later, with a soft and light tone, explain your reasons for wanting to end the relationship. Each and every word uttered from your mouth must be filled with a gentle and considerate manner instead of being harsh or critical. Instead of dissecting the other person's qualities as a means to highlight what isn't working, focus on expressing your feelings kindly and compassionately.

DON'T:

Avoid Dragging:

Don't dodge the other person or postpone the necessary conversation. Prolonging the situation only makes it more challenging in the long term, both for you and your boyfriend or girlfriend. Additionally, delaying the conversation can result in information being revealed through other means. It's crucial to ensure that the person you're ending the relationship with hears it directly from you rather than than learning about it from someone else.

Don't Disrespect:

Speak about your ex-partner (or soon-to-be ex) with respect, avoiding any form of gossip or negative comments. Consider how you would want to be treated in a similar situation, as you'd hope your ex would speak positively about you once the relationship has ended. Furthermore, it's worth acknowledging that your ex could potentially become a friend in the future, or circumstances might lead to the rekindling of a romance.

These guidelines for respectful communication aren't limited to break-ups; they can also apply to situations where someone expresses interest in you, but you're not reciprocating those feelings. In such cases, maintaining kindness and consideration can help you let the person down gently and minimize any potential hurt feelings.

Why Is Breaking Up So Hard to Do?

If you're contemplating ending a romantic relationship, it's common to experience a mix of emotions. After all, you and your partner came together for a reason, so you might find yourself asking questions like, "Is there a chance for things to improve?" or "Should I give this relationship another shot?" The decision to break up is not an easy one, and it often requires careful consideration. Even if you feel confident in your choice, initiating a breakup conversation is challenging and uncomfortable. The person you're ending the relationship with may experience emotions, including hurt, disappointment, sadness, or even heartbreak. As the one initiating the breakup, you likely want to handle it in a way that is respectful and compassionate. Your aim is to minimize the pain for both parties involved, ensuring that neither you nor your partner feels unnecessarily hurt or upset.

Know Your Worth and Move on for Good

Staying in a relationship when the emotional connection has faded is unfair to both you and your partner. If you're eager for a new chapter in life, don't wait for change to happen on its own. Recognize and address the warning signs early on. Save yourself from unnecessary heartbreak, try to move forward, and heal yourself. If the prospect of finding love again feels daunting, don't worry. Take some time for yourself, and do things that make you happy and satisfied. But healing is essential.

When You Don't Heal Right!!! You Don't Pick Right

I think the biggest mistake people can make is when they are in pain, to actively seek out and engage the other person. This happens when you don't allow God to heal you, you will go back and keep picking what you used to have. It's possible to continue to pick the same person but have a different name and face.

Ultimately, relationships and dating are trial and error. Who you think may be the perfect match for you might not actually be "the special one" for you. Verbal compatibility or written on a piece of paper doesn't equal compatibility in real life. When you get together with the personality twin, it doesn't mean the relationship will be a happy one. Would that be a deal breaker for you?

Dating people with identical personalities can lead to a sense of stagnation in personal growth and development. You may not be challenged to adapt or learn from different types of individuals. Not all personality types are compatible with each other.

If you consistently date the same personality type, you may miss out on potentially better matches with personalities that complement yours more effectively. Do you know what can happen in the latter stages of your relationship? If you have a predisposition for a specific personality type, you might be less likely to recognize red flags or problematic behaviors because you're focused on familiar traits and characteristics.

The Bible does address the idea of making wise choices in relationships. For example, in the context of marriage, it advises believers to consider the character and values of a potential partner. While it may not use the specific phrase *"Continue to pick the same person,"* the concept of learning from past mistakes and making better choices is a recurring theme in the Bible. Proverbs 12:15 (NIV): "The way of fools seems right to them, but the wise listen to advice."

The LORD will do what you CAN'T, not what you WON'T... Peace comes when we let go of what HE didn't send. The Bible often emphasizes the need for faith and trust in God to provide for our needs and guide our lives. It suggests that God can accomplish what may seem impossible to us. "I can do all this through him who gives me strength."

Philippians 4:13 (NIV). The Bible encourages believers to seek God's will in their decisions and to trust His plan for their lives. It suggests that finding peace often involves surrendering our desires and trusting in God's wisdom. "Trust in the Lord with all your heart and lean not on your own understanding; in all your ways submit to him, and he will make your paths straight." Proverbs 3:5-6 (NIV).

God Heals Broken Hearts!

A comedian once said, "If broken hearts were commercials, we'd all be on TV." In some strange way, he was saying we each have a broken heart, not physically I hope, but inside, where no one else can see.

"How can you stop the rain from falling down? How can you stop the sun from shining? What makes the world go round?"

Individuals experience heartbreak for many reasons, ranging from the loss of a loved one, divorce, job loss, loss of social status, health decline, betrayal by a friend, and even the loss of one's childhood. It can leave a person emotionally shattered. Let me ask you what actually a wound is. When you have suffered an injury or a deep cut, you're well aware of the intense pain and sensitivity that follows. In many ways, sorrow and loss can be likened to deep wounds, causing an excruciating ache that feels impervious to relief. At times, the anguish is so overwhelming that finding the right words to express it seems impossible, and it appears that nothing can ease the pain. Similar to a deep physical wound, a broken heart doesn't heal overnight. Just as certain medicines can cause a burning sensation when applied to a skin wound. No one wants to pour rubbing alcohol on an open wound. Instead, we seek soothing ointments to apply gently and cover with a Band-Aid, providing comfort and protection. The same principle applies to healing a broken heart—we require the right emotional support and care to facilitate the healing process.

The saying "time heals all wounds" often refers to physical injuries, but what about the wounds that are hidden within us? We can't simply visit a doctor and say, "I have a broken heart, can you fix it?" So, where do we turn when we're dealing with a broken heart, and does anyone truly understand our pain?

The good news is that God heals the brokenhearted, so don't give up. Through Jesus, it is possible to mend your damaged heart. There are many sorts of broken hearts, and Christ is good at healing them all.

The Scriptures also consider the brokenhearted blessed. The Bible addresses matters of the heart, including the experience of a broken heart, in various passages. While it may not use the phrase "broken heart" explicitly, it provides guidance and comfort for those who are experiencing emotional pain and heartache. "The Lord is close to the brokenhearted and saves those who are crushed in spirit." This verse assures that God is near to those who are hurting emotionally and is there to offer comfort and healing. Psalm 34:18 (NIV). The Lord will guide our hearts when we are lost in a storm. Whatever you're going through, God's love and power will get you through it. "Trust in the

Lord with all your heart and lean not on your own understanding; in all your ways submit to him, and he will make your paths straight." Trusting in God during times of emotional pain can help bring clarity and guidance. Proverbs 3:5-6 (NIV)

The enduring pain from past wounds can exert a powerful influence over many lives. It lingers, stifles personal growth, and on occasion, renders a person emotionally paralyzed. Nonetheless, God has the power to heal these wounds. He stands ready and willing to soothe our deepest pain, provided we open ourselves to His intervention. It's akin to a divine exchange, where we surrender our hurt to Him, and in return, He offers us His healing grace. God, often referred to as the "Great Physician," possesses the ability to renew us to the state of perfection, purity, and holiness in which He originally created us, reflecting His own image (Genesis 1:27). This restoration is a promise that the Lord extends to each one of us. "Blessed are those who mourn, for they will be comforted." (Matthew 5:4 NIV) When faced with adversity, it might be difficult to make the right choice; but it is precisely during these times that our faith is reinforced. However, Jesus acknowledges the pain of mourning and offers the promise of comfort for those who are grieving.

It is written in 2 Corinthians 5:7, "For we walk by faith, not by sight." It is up to us to make the decision to actively seek God and to obediently obey God's will. This verse encourages believers to rely on their faith in Christ rather than their physical senses or the visible circumstances around them. It underscores the idea that Christian life should be guided by trust in God, even when situations may seem difficult or challenging. Believers are called to have faith in Christ Jesus and Heavenly Father, understanding that they have prepared a way for them.

God's Way of Healing People

Pouring out our hearts to God and entrusting Him with our cares is crucial for the healing of our hearts. This is because healing can only begin when we acknowledge the need for it in the first place.

Sometimes, due to feelings of shame, pride, or guilt, we are tempted to deny our brokenness when our hearts are hurting. In an attempt to appear strong, we may pretend that we are not vulnerable or in pain, avoiding any display of weakness to shield ourselves from further hurt. Understand that pretending not to need healing does not lead to actual healing. A hard heart cannot become a healed heart. One of the gifts God offers us in our relationship with Him is the freedom to be honest, both with ourselves and with Him. We can bring all our shattered pieces to His presence and invite Him into the most fragile parts of our hearts.

Another way in which God facilitates the healing of a broken heart is through the power of forgiveness. You might be wondering how forgiving the person who caused your pain can help in your healing. Forgiveness is not primarily for the benefit of the other person but for your own well-being. Forgiveness enables you to release the burden of offense and move forward in your life. Conversely, harboring unforgiveness leads to bitterness, resentment, and prolonged anger, which only perpetuates your own suffering. Here are some important points to remember about forgiveness:

* God calls us to forgive as we have been forgiven: (Ephesians 4:32) It is God's desire that we remember our own need for forgiveness and extend the same grace to others.

* God will fight our battles for us: (Romans 12:19) It is often wiser to allow God's justice to prevail rather than seeking revenge on our own. Trusting in God's justice can bring peace and healing.

* Forgiveness is a process: It doesn't occur overnight but is something we experience as we seek God for strength and empowerment to let go of the hurt.

* Forgiveness is directed toward ourselves: There are instances where we need to forgive ourselves, and God's grace is available for that too. Self-forgiveness can be a crucial step in healing and moving forward.

The third way God facilitates the healing of a broken heart is through gratitude. Bitterness and pain can often blind us to the blessings and goodness of God, even in the midst of our heartache. A relevant example is that of Naomi in the book of Ruth, who, after experiencing the loss of her husband and sons and returning to Israel from Moab, asked to be called "Mara," meaning bitter. She expressed her feelings, saying: She said to them, "Do not call me Naomi; call me Mara, for the Almighty has dealt very bitterly with me. I went away full, and the LORD has brought me back empty. Why call me Naomi, when the LORD has testified against me and the Almighty has brought calamity upon me?" (Ruth 1:20-21 ESV) Amid her bitterness, Naomi overlooked the blessings that God had bestowed upon her. She had a faithful daughter-in-law, Ruth, who stood by her side, ensuring she wasn't alone. They arrived in Israel during the harvest season, so they were not hungry. Additionally, Naomi had a home to return to, so she was not lost and without shelter. It's natural to find it challenging to focus on the positive when everything around us seems dark. When our hearts are broken, negative emotions like jealousy, resentment, bitterness, and defensiveness can take hold. However, when we pause and intentionally reflect on how God has been moving and protecting us, even in the midst of our heartbreak, we can shift our hearts toward gratitude. Gratitude allows us to see the blessings and positive aspects of our lives, which can help mend our broken hearts and move us toward a place of healing and restoration.

The fourth way God brings healing to a broken heart is through His love. Often, our broken hearts result from the loss of human love or relationships. While the pain of such loss can be profound, it's important to remember that even when we lose the love of people, we will never lose the love of God. This divine love is something we should cherish and never take for granted. God's love is distinct from human love.

As stated in Numbers 23:19, He is not like humans; He keeps His promises, remains faithful, and demonstrates extraordinary patience, forgiveness, kindness, and gentleness. The ultimate proof of God's love for us is seen in Christ's sacrifice on the cross. Through this sacrifice, we are assured of God's unwavering love. No matter what others may do or say, God's love for us remains constant and unchanging. It is a love that can mend even the most broken of hearts and provide solace and healing in times of pain and loss.

The fifth way in which God brings healing to a broken heart is by infusing it with purpose. When our hearts are shattered, life can seem devoid of meaning, and we may question the worth of our experiences, especially when pain is so prevalent. If you feel like you're walking on broken glass, you aren't alone, and God won't leave you this way. Most often, healing is a process that He uses to teach us more about Him and about ourselves. God has the ability to transform our brokenness into something beautiful and our pain into a powerful purpose.

Not only can God heal us, but He often utilizes our stories and testimonies to aid others on their journeys. You are not alone in experiencing this kind of heartache, and you won't be the last. By placing our trust in God for healing and wholeness, we become a source of hope for others who are navigating similar dark seasons, showing them that they too can find their way out. While I may not understand the specific reasons behind why God allows certain heartbreaks, I do know that when we lean into Him for healing, He possesses the capacity to turn any situation around for His glory and our benefit, as stated in Romans 8:28. His Word is a testament to His unwavering truth, and it reminds us that there is always the potential for redemption and purpose, even in our most challenging moments.

The sixth and final way in which God brings healing to a broken heart is through the gift of hope. Hope reminds us that our current circumstances won't last forever. Romans 15:13 offers this encouragement: "May the God of hope fill you with all joy and peace in believing, so that by the power of the Holy Spirit you may abound in hope." (Romans 15:13 ESV)

Hope serves as the guiding light that assures us that the darkness, we're currently in is not permanent. It gives us the strength to continue walking through difficult times, believing that there is light at the end of the tunnel, even if we cannot yet see or feel it. Hope prevents us from becoming stagnant and encourages us to have unwavering faith in the best outcomes, urging us to keep moving toward the light.

For believers, God is that light. He provides us with a reason to wake up each morning and maintain our belief in a brighter future. The fact that God has granted us another day to live means that He is not finished with us yet, and hope fuels our optimism for tomorrow.

Life's Greatest Teachers: Love Relationships and Broken Heart

Relationships serve as valuable learning experiences. Whether they endure for an extended period or are relatively short-lived, each relationship offers unique insights into ourselves, our partners, and our preferences for future relationships. They provide an opportunity to develop empathy and experience the mutual care and affection that comes with being in a relationship. Even break-ups can be opportunities for growth and learning, although they are undeniably challenging. But sometimes leaving someone is for our own better.

Continuing to stay in a troubled relationship will likely prevent you from finding inner peace. If your fear of being alone is the only thing keeping you in an unfulfilling and painful relationship, it's crucial to recognize that being in such a relationship is detrimental. A relationship that is inherently doomed cannot be repaired. Its negative impact extends beyond your love life and can also harm your professional life, as well as strain your relationships with family and friends. So, if you find yourself unable to envision a future with your boyfriend that excites you rather than fills you with apprehension, it may be time to consider ending it. Healthy relationships should inspire enthusiasm about what lies ahead. Don't delay; instead, take the necessary steps to move in a different direction.

Parting ways with someone allows us to practice respecting their feelings and engaging in honest and compassionate communication. In essence, ending a relationship, despite its difficulty, contributes to our ability to navigate tough conversations with kindness and integrity.

Regardless of the troubles and despair, God has something better planned for you. He will use the bitterness and troubles to restore your life into something so much better than you could've imagined. Though suffering is never a small thing, God is always greater, and this Psalm is a promise nothing can touch you except what has been carefully filtered through His fingers. Whatever heartache He allows, it's because He has a purpose and a plan.

Chapter 21

From Chaos to Calm: A Guide to Blended Family Harmony

The formation of a blended family or stepfamily, encompassing individuals from previous relationships, presents a unique set of challenges and opportunities. This chapter delves into the intricacies of these family structures, highlighting the importance of establishing healthy boundaries for promoting individual well-being and fostering a harmonious environment.

Defining Blended Families and Stepfamilies

A blended family or stepfamily is comprised of individuals from previous relationships, united through the marriage or long-term partnership of two adults. This can involve:

Stepparents

Individuals assuming a parental role for their partner's children from a previous relationship.

Stepchildren

Children residing with and adjusting to a new family structure, including a stepparent and stepsiblings.

Stepsiblings

Children who are related through their parents' new marriage but do not share a biological parent.

The Ever-Evolving Landscape of Parenthood

In today's dynamic world, navigating the complexities of parenthood can feel like a constant uphill battle. The constant pressure to raise well-adjusted, happy children can be overwhelming, especially as cultural norms and expectations continue to evolve at an unprecedented pace. Whether you're a parent, grandparent, co-parent, or a single parent raising a child solo, the sheer number of decisions you face on a daily basis can be daunting. We all grapple with the same fundamental questions: when to say "yes" and when to say "no," how to encourage independence while fostering safety, and how to guide our children through life's inevitable challenges.

The complexities of parenting are further amplified when dealing with children who are not biologically your own or when faced with the unique challenges of raising an adult with childlike needs. Each child presents a unique set of circumstances and requires a tailored approach, making the journey of parenthood a highly individual and ever-evolving experience. Despite the inherent challenges, the rewards of parenthood are immeasurable. The joy of witnessing your child learn and grow, the unconditional love and support you share, and the profound impact you have on their future are just a few of the countless blessings that come with raising a child.

While there may be no definitive answers to the myriad questions parents face, embracing the journey with love, compassion, and a willingness to learn can make all the difference. By sharing our experiences, supporting one another, and drawing strength from the collective wisdom of parents across generations, we can navigate the challenges of parenthood together and ultimately create a better future for our children.

Understanding the Challenges

In the depths of Ephesians, nestled within Chapter 4, verse 32, the timeless wisdom whispers gently: "Be kind to one another, tenderhearted, forgiving one another, as God in Christ forgave you." This verse, as penned in the eloquence of the English Standard Version, resonates with the grace of a forgiving heart, urging us to embrace kindness and tender compassion toward each other, echoing the divine forgiveness bestowed upon us through Christ.

Blended families face unique challenges, stemming from the complex dynamics of merging individuals from diverse backgrounds and adjusting to new roles and expectations. Children may experience:

- Uncertainty and anxiety regarding their place within the new family structure and concerns about their relationship with their biological parents.

- Loss of identity and displacement as they adapt to new family dynamics and potentially navigate changes in their previous family structure.

- Sibling rivalry and resentment towards stepsiblings, especially when vying for attention or experiencing differing expectations and discipline.

Understanding the Dynamics

Blended families and stepfamilies are characterized by the merging of individuals from different backgrounds, each carrying their own experiences, values, and expectations.

In Romans, within Chapter 12, verse 16, a profound harmony resonates: "Live in harmony with one another. Do not be haughty, but associate with the lowly. Never be wise in your own sight." This verse, scripted in the essence of wisdom, beckons us to coexist in synchrony, eschewing pride and embracing humility. It calls upon us to intertwine our lives with others, recognizing the folly of self-assuredness and the beauty found in genuine connection and shared understanding.

This dynamic can lead to a range of emotions, including:

Excitement and anticipation

The prospect of a new family structure and renewed love can bring joy and optimism.

Uncertainty and anxiety

Children may feel worried about their place within the new family, their relationships with their biological parents, and adapting to new rules and expectations.

Loss and grief

Children may experience sadness and anger over the loss of their previous family structure and the changes it brings.

Sibling rivalry and resentment

Stepsiblings may struggle to build relationships and navigate competition for attention, resources, and affection.

The Enemy's Grip on Families and the Power of Faith

Families are the cornerstone of society, and their strength and unity are essential for individual well-being and societal progress. However, this very strength makes them a target for forces seeking to weaken and destabilize them. One such force is often referred to as "the enemy" or "evil," which seeks to bind families in shackles of defeat.

Just as a demon-possessed man in the Bible was held captive and prevented from experiencing a new life, the enemy wants to keep families isolated and trapped within their struggles. He thrives on discouragement, hopelessness, and a distorted view of the future. He wants families to believe the worst, fueling negativity and despair, instead of fostering hope and the potential for growth.

While every family faces challenges, some common issues are particularly prevalent in today's world. According to a recent study by Lifeway Christian Resources, the top ten challenges facing families include:

Anti-Christian culture

The prevailing cultural values often clash with traditional Christian beliefs, creating tension and confusion for families.

Divorce

The breakdown of marriages leaves families fragmented and struggling to cope with the emotional and practical consequences.

Busyness

The fast-paced and demanding nature of modern life leaves little time for families to connect and build meaningful relationships.

Absent father figure

The absence of a strong male role model in the home can have a significant impact on children's development and family dynamics.

Lack of discipline

Inconsistent and ineffective discipline can lead to children developing poor behavior and struggling with authority.

Financial pressures

Financial worries can create stress and conflict within families, impacting their overall well-being.

Lack of communication

Poor communication skills can lead to misunderstandings, resentment, and a breakdown of trust within families.

Negative media influences

Constant exposure to violence, negativity, and unrealistic portrayals in the media can have a detrimental effect on families.

Balance of work and family

Finding a healthy balance between work and family can be challenging, leading to neglect and resentment.

Materialism

Focusing on material possessions over relationships and spiritual values can create dissatisfaction and emptiness within families.

Despite these challenges, families have the power to overcome them through faith and commitment. By drawing strength from their beliefs, relying on prayer and community support, and prioritizing family time, families can build a strong foundation and navigate life's challenges together. Just as the chains were broken and the demon-possessed man found freedom in the Gospel, families can find hope and healing through Jesus Christ. By recognizing the enemy's tactics and clinging to their faith, they can transform their homes into beacons of hope, resilience, and love, defying the darkness and experiencing the abundant life that God has promised.

In the profound passages of Luke, chapter 14, verses 18 to 19, a stark contrast unfolds: *"Satan brings shackles - Jesus wants your family in freedom!"* These verses, in simple words, depict the struggle between bondage and liberation. They illustrate Satan's snares, the chains that seek to confine us, while Jesus, in His infinite grace, yearns for our families to revel in freedom from these shackles.

Challenges for Parents

Colossians 3:21 - "Fathers, do not provoke your children, lest they become discouraged."

Here, the guidance is clear and straightforward. It speaks to fathers, imploring them to nurture their children with tenderness and understanding, steering clear of actions that might dishearten or disillusion the young ones they hold dear.

Parents in blended families face their own set of challenges, including:

Developing new roles and responsibilities

Stepparents need to navigate their role within the family while respecting the established relationship between the biological parent and child.

Balancing loyalties

Navigating conflicting loyalties between their new spouse and their biological children can be difficult.

Communicating effectively

Learning to communicate effectively with all family members, fostering open dialogue, and addressing concerns constructively is crucial.

Managing expectations

Setting realistic expectations for the family and individual members is essential to avoid disappointment and frustration.

The Power of Boundaries

Healthy boundaries are essential for promoting individual and family well-being in blended families. These boundaries serve several functions:

Provide a sense of security and stability

Clear boundaries define roles, expectations, and individual space, creating a sense of predictability and comfort.

Facilitate healthy communication

Boundaries allow for respectful interactions, reducing conflict and fostering open and honest communication.

Empower individual expression

Respect for individual needs allows family members to express themselves freely and pursue personal interests without feeling overwhelmed or controlled.

Promote individual well-being

Healthy boundaries help individuals maintain a sense of self and identity within the family system, contributing to their overall well-being.

Proverbs 4:23 - "Above all else, guard your heart, for everything you do flows from it."

This simple but profound message reminds us that our actions and thoughts flow from our inner core. Just as a garden needs tending, our hearts need nurturing to ensure our actions bloom with kindness and good intentions. So take care of your heart, for it is the wellspring of your being.

Strategies for Building Healthy Boundaries

Establishing healthy boundaries requires consistent effort and open communication. Here are some key strategies:

Open and honest communication

In the treasured verses of Proverbs, residing within Chapter 15, verse 1, a pearl of wisdom gleams brightly: *"A gentle answer turns away wrath, but a harsh word stirs up anger."* These words, spoken in the simplicity of wisdom, carry the profound truth that kindness and gentleness possess the power to diffuse anger and conflict. They remind us of the potency found in responding gently rather than with harshness, guiding us toward peace amidst turmoil.

Encourage open dialogue about concerns, expectations, and individual needs. Actively listen and empathize with all family members.

Hold regular family meetings:

Dedicate time to open and honest discussions about concerns, expectations, and feelings. Encourage active listening and respectful dialogue.

Create a safe space for individual expression:

Ensure all family members feel comfortable expressing themselves freely without fear of judgment or criticism.

Utilize "I" statements:

Focus on personal feelings and perspectives rather than accusatory language to avoid defensiveness and promote understanding.

Actively listen and empathize:

Demonstrate your willingness to understand different perspectives and validate everyone's feelings.

Clear expectations and roles

Define roles and responsibilities for each member, including stepparents, biological parents, and children. Ensure everyone understands and agrees to these expectations.

Discuss and establish family rules together:

Encourage family members to participate in creating clear and consistent rules for behavior, chores, and responsibilities.

Define roles and responsibilities for stepparents:

Be clear about the level of authority and involvement expected of stepparents in discipline, decision making, and daily routines.

Ensure all members understand the rules and expectations:

Review and discuss rules regularly, ensuring everyone is aware and understands the consequences of non-compliance.

Be flexible and adjust expectations as needed:

Recognize that children may need different approaches depending on their age and individual needs.

Consistent discipline and rules

Develop fair and consistent rules for behavior and consequences for infractions. Apply these rules equally to all children.

Develop a consistent disciplinary approach:

Establish clear guidelines for addressing misbehavior and ensuring all children experience consistent consequences for similar actions.

Communicate consequences clearly and consistently:

Ensure children understand the expected behavior and the associated consequences beforehand.

Avoid favoritism or comparisons:

Treat all children with fairness and avoid comparisons between stepsiblings or biological children.

Focus on positive reinforcement:

Encourage and reward positive behavior to promote cooperation and compliance.

Respect for individual needs

Acknowledge and respect individual needs for privacy, space, and time alone. Encourage individual pursuits and hobbies.

Create individual spaces:

Provide each family member with their own space to relax, reflect, and pursue individual interests.

Respect privacy needs:

Knock before entering another person's room and respect their need for personal space and belongings.

Schedule alone time:

Encourage individual activities and hobbies to allow for self-expression and personal development.

Recognize and address emotional needs:

Be sensitive to individual emotional needs and provide support and understanding when needed.

Positive reinforcement

Focus on praising positive behavior and celebrating individual achievements to create a supportive and encouraging environment.

Encourage open communication with the non-resident parent:

Facilitate open and positive communication between children and their other biological parent.

Be respectful and supportive of the other parent's role:

Avoid criticizing or undermining the other parent's relationship with their children.

Cooperate on parenting decisions:

Work together with the other parent to establish consistent rules, expectations, and discipline across both households.

Focus on the child's best interests:

Prioritize the child's well-being and avoid engaging in conflicts that may negatively impact their relationship with either parent.

Flexibility and adaptability

Recognize the need to adjust boundaries and expectations as the family evolves and children grow. Remain open to feedback and compromise.

Recognize that blended families evolve:

Be prepared to adjust boundaries and expectations as children grow and family dynamics change.

Be open to feedback and suggestions:

Encourage open dialogue and welcome constructive feedback from all family members regarding existing boundaries and rules.

Be willing to compromise:

Acknowledge that different individuals may have different needs and be willing to find solutions that accommodate everyone's perspectives.

Seek professional help if needed:

Don't hesitate to seek professional support from therapists or family counselors specializing in blended families.

Seeking professional support

When needed, seek guidance from therapists or family counselors specializing in blended families. They can provide valuable support and resources. Navigating the complexities of blended families can be challenging. Seeking professional support from therapists or family counselors specializing in blended families can be invaluable. These professionals can provide guidance on:

- Effectively communicating and resolving conflicts.
- Developing strategies for managing individual needs and expectations.
- Establishing and refining healthy boundaries within the family structure.

By implementing these strategies, blended families can create a healthy and supportive environment where everyone feels respected, valued, and empowered to thrive.

Building a Thriving Blended Family

Creating a successful blended family requires dedication, patience, and a willingness to embrace the complexities of this unique family structure. By prioritizing communication, establishing healthy boundaries, and demonstrating commitment to individual and family well-being, blended families can overcome challenges, foster harmony, and build a fulfilling future together.

Remember, each blended family is unique. The specific strategies needed to achieve harmony will vary. However, by prioritizing open communication, establishing healthy boundaries, and remaining flexible and adaptable, blended families can create a loving and supportive environment where everyone feels valued, respected, and empowered to thrive.

Parents in blended families also face challenges, including:

- Establishing new roles and responsibilities as stepparents, navigating their relationships with their stepchildren while balancing responsibilities towards their biological children.

- Managing conflicting loyalties between their new spouse and their biological children, ensuring both feel loved and supported.

- Developing effective communication strategies to foster open dialogue within the new family unit, addressing concerns and building trust.

The Significance of Healthy Boundaries

Boundaries are crucial for promoting individual well-being and ensuring a harmonious environment within blended families. They define roles, expectations, and individual space, allowing for:

- Increased sense of security and comfort as individuals understand their place within the family structure and expectations for behavior.

- Improved communication and conflict resolution by providing a framework for expressing needs and resolving differences respectfully.

- Enhanced self-esteem and confidence as individuals feel respected and empowered to express their needs and opinions.

From Division to Reconciliation

Family is the cornerstone of society, yet its intricate web of relationships can be easily frayed by the threads of division. These divisions, fueled by conflicting ideologies, unresolved conflicts, and external forces, leave families fractured and vulnerable. Satan, often depicted as the embodiment of negativity, eagerly exploits these vulnerabilities, thriving on the discord he sows. His aim? To isolate us from God and each other, weakening the very foundation of our social fabric.

But amidst the shadows of division, a beacon of hope emerges: the transformative power of Jesus Christ. His message of reconciliation and peace echoes through the ages, serving as a potent antidote to the venom of discord. The cross, a symbol of his ultimate sacrifice, stands as a testament to the possibility of bridging the chasm between humanity and God. For those seeking to be a blessing to their families, the path of peacemaking beckons. This journey, however, begins with an inward transformation, finding personal peace with God through the redemptive grace of Jesus Christ. This newfound inner peace then becomes the wellspring from which flows a spirit of empathy and understanding, permeating every interaction within the family unit.

But the complexities of blended families demand a deeper understanding of the unique challenges they face. A 2023 study published in the Journal of marriage and Family sheds light on the interconnected nature of relationships within these families, highlighting the specific difficulties encountered by stepparents. Often struggling with undefined roles and grappling to establish their place as parental figures, stepparents face an uphill battle, often experiencing less positive connections with their stepchildren compared to parents in traditional families. This lack of clarity can further exacerbate the challenges faced by stepchildren, who may find themselves navigating a sea of uncertainty and ambiguity regarding their new family structure. Incomplete or contradictory information from their biological parents can further cloud their understanding of their stepparent, creating a barrier to building meaningful bonds.

Left unaddressed, these feelings of isolation and disconnect can manifest as anger, frustration, and resentment, negatively impacting individual mental health and the overall family dynamic. As parents, fostering a supportive environment where healing and connection can flourish is paramount. Two key strategies can guide parents through this process:

Open Communication and Setting Realistic Expectations

Initiating open and honest conversations about the changing family structure is essential. Prioritizing the children's needs and feelings during these discussions and creating a safe space for expressing concerns without judgment fosters trust and understanding. Additionally, attentiveness to non-verbal cues helps parents tap into unspoken emotions that children may struggle to articulate.

Respectful Integration and Unifying the Parental Team

Maintaining an environment of respect for all family members is crucial. This creates a space where individuals feel comfortable and safe, allowing them to get to know each other at their own pace. By avoiding forced interactions and allowing genuine bonds to develop organically, parents foster a more positive and supportive family environment.

Research consistently underlines the importance of a unified parental team in shaping healthy blended family dynamics. A 2022 study highlights how positive parenting is often dependent on factors like individual characteristics, the quality of the romantic relationship between partners, and the unique needs of each child. Children thrive in predictable and stable environments. When parents present a united front, communicating openly and consistently about parenting philosophies, values, and expectations, they provide children with the stability they need to flourish. This applies across various domains, including daily routines, screen time limits, homework expectations, and consequences for behavior.

Cultivating Self-Care and Investing in the New Relationship

Prioritizing self-care and actively nurturing the new relationship is vital. A healthy and happy parent is better equipped to nurture their children and contribute to a thriving family environment. By attending to their mental health and actively nurturing their relationships, parents can create a foundation for lasting peace and joy within their families.

Ultimately, navigating the labyrinth of blended family dynamics requires a commitment to healing, understanding, and unity. By embracing the principles of reconciliation, open communication, a unified parental team, and self-care, parents can transform their families from fractured entities into sources of strength, resilience, and love. This transformation, however, starts with a personal choice: to reject the divisive forces that seek to weaken families and embrace the transformative power of Jesus Christ, who offers a message of hope and a path towards lasting reconciliation.

Building a Thriving Blended Family

Building a successful blended family is a journey, not a destination. It requires commitment, patience, and a willingness to overcome challenges along the way. By understanding the unique dynamics of these families, establishing healthy boundaries, and seeking support when needed, blended families can cultivate a loving, supportive, and thriving environment that fosters individual well-being and happiness for all members.

Here are some key takeaways to remember:

Embrace the Uniqueness:

Each blended family is unique with its own set of challenges and opportunities. Embrace the differences and celebrate the diversity within your family unit.

Open Communication is Key:

Prioritize open and honest communication. Encourage active listening, respectful dialogue, and the expression of feelings and concerns without judgment.

Boundaries Build Harmony:

Establish clear, consistent, and fair boundaries for roles, expectations, communication, and personal space. These boundaries provide a sense of security and promote healthy relationships within the family.

Consistency and Fairness Matter:

Implement consistent discipline and decision-making across the family. Treat all children with fairness and avoid comparisons or favoritism.

Respect Individual Needs:

Acknowledge and respect the need for individual space, privacy, and personal development. Encourage individual pursuits and hobbies while fostering a sense of belonging within the family.

Nurture Biological Parent Relationships:

Encourage and support continued positive relationships between children and their non-resident biological parent. This promotes a sense of security and stability for children and fosters healthy family dynamics.

Be Flexible and Adaptable:

Blended families are dynamic entities, and boundaries and expectations may need to adjust as the family evolves. Be open to feedback, compromise, and seeking support when needed.

Never Stop Learning and Growing:

Embrace the continuous learning process involved in building a successful blended family. Seek knowledge from books, online resources, and professional support if needed.

Remember, building a thriving blended family is a collaborative effort. By working together, prioritizing open communication, establishing healthy boundaries, and demonstrating commitment and patience, blended families can create a loving, supportive, and fulfilling environment where everyone feels valued, respected, and empowered to thrive.

Psalm 133:1 - "Behold, how good and pleasant it is when brothers dwell in unity!"

These words, expressed with pure simplicity, celebrate the beauty and joy that arise when people come together in harmony and solidarity. They paint a picture of goodness and delight in the shared bonds of unity, reminding us of the profound blessings found in togetherness and mutual understanding.

Chapter 22

She Comes With Favor

You too have a choice today, married or single: let your loneliness drive you to wallow or to worship. Many young women find themselves transitioning from one relationship to another, initially enjoying the honeymoon phase but later experiencing a sense of restlessness. With the ability to constantly explore new dating options, people often grapple with fears of choosing the wrong partner.

Some people can't help but ponder whether there might be a more fulfilling relationship out there. They pose questions such as, "Is there a chance I could find someone I'd love even more? What if I ended this relationship only to later realize it was the best I could ever have? What if I'm always uncertain, regardless of who I'm with? How can I ensure I'm making the correct choice?" And what if you married a person of your choice and still feel lonely?

Single Girls: marriage Will Not Cure You're Loneliness

Marriage, and a man, will not make you 'complete'. Stop feeling like a man's arrival is an upgrade in your life. A man's presence will not cure loneliness, it will expose it.

The loneliest women I have encountered aren't necessarily those who are single; rather, they are often women in challenging marriages. Loneliness is a significant concern for married women, regardless of the quality of their marriage. A key part of this issue is that they experience loneliness but believe they shouldn't. After all, wasn't marriage meant to provide companionship and connection? Many of us carry this expectation, and then we enter into marriage. Even in genuinely fulfilling marriages, a sense of incompleteness can linger, leaving us wondering, ***"What's missing From Life?"***

Women feel unable to discuss this loneliness with anyone because they fear it might be perceived as a betrayal of their spouse. Alternatively, they might experience guilt for feeling lonely when they have what seems to be a great husband. Consequently, they often find themselves unsure of how to address these feelings. In contrast, a single woman may find it more socially acceptable to discuss her loneliness with friends, and it's often expected that she might experience moments of solitude. However, for married women, this isn't always the case. This is one of the reasons why loneliness can be a complex issue within marriage, particularly for some women.

Feeling Lonely? Waiting for a Man?

Loneliness is a universal feeling. Humans are social animals. When we find ourselves isolated from others, it's natural for feelings of aloneness or loneliness to emerge.

Are you postponing your dreams of traveling the world until you find that special someone? Maybe you're saving your first drive-thru cinema experience for a romantic date night. Or perhaps you've compiled a list of thoughtful, romantic gestures that you're eagerly waiting to use as soon as a partner enters your life. If you've answered yes to any of these questions, then I can relate. The exciting part is that you should now see a much more fulfilling and adventurous path ahead, where you live life to the fullest, regardless of whether you are in a relationship or not.

"The Lord is close to the brokenhearted and saves those who are crushed in spirit."

Psalm 38:9 (NIV)

During times of emotional distress or heartbreak, remember that the Lord is near to you. He never leaves your side, and His presence is just a prayer away. Reach out to Him in prayer, immerse yourself in His words, sing uplifting songs, and maintain a positive outlook to find solace and strength.

Take comfort in the belief that the same God who led the children of Israel will neither abandon nor disappoint you. He is compassionate and empathetic, serving as your guiding light in moments of darkness. Remember the encouraging words:

"Be strong and courageous. Do not be afraid or terrified because of them, for the Lord your God goes with you; he will never leave you nor forsake you"

(Deuteronomy 31:6).

There is no need to feel lonely or depressed because when you think you have lost everything and everyone you are sure that you will never lose the love of God.

I wholeheartedly believe in love, and there's a strong possibility that, at some point, we will cross paths with someone who deeply connects with us. However, the challenge lies in not knowing when or if this will occur. So, if we defer our dreams and aspirations in anticipation of that moment, we might find ourselves waiting indefinitely – perhaps even until the end of our lives. Instead, we have the opportunity to embrace life to the fullest and nurture the relationships we currently have. There are countless reasons why we should stop waiting and start living now. Everything is a process!!!

The Clock Ticks Louder for Girls!

Our time on this Earth is fleeting, like a short breath.

In some cases, time may feel more pressing and urgent for certain individuals. As a man, there's often a perception of having more time at your disposal. Your 20s are typically viewed as a period for exploration, your 30s for establishing yourself, and your 40s for witnessing the fruits of your efforts. It's often said that men can remain attractive to women throughout these years, extending into their 50s and beyond if they take care of themselves. This perspective is rooted in our biological nature, as one of our fundamental drives is the urge to reproduce. Organisms that don't reproduce eventually age and perish without leaving descendants. This drive is deeply ingrained in us.

Women, to some extent, depend on male attention. Many of a woman's actions are influenced by the desire for male approval and companionship.

Even when women critique male behavior, they often seek support or intervention from other men. Few women want to face the prospect of becoming an older single woman with only cats for company, while their peers find partners and start families. It's a daunting thought.

Of course, there are exceptions to this narrative. Some women may have ambivalent feelings about reproduction, and a small minority may not desire children at all, going to great lengths to ensure they don't conceive. Asexual and aromatic women exist as well, although they represent a minority. Such women have unique perspectives and desires. For many women, time is a ticking clock, not just in terms of biological reproduction but also in the realm of finding a compatible partner. It's a race against time to secure a suitable mate before the music stops, or they risk facing a future of navigating life alone with increasing difficulty in finding a compatible partner.

"Commit to the Lord whatever you do, and he will establish your plans."

Proverbs 16:3 (NIV)

Jonathan Devon Bryant Sr.

"Many are the plans in a person's heart, but it is the Lord's purpose that prevails."

Proverbs 19:21 (NIV):

There's nothing wrong with making plans, but be open to God's guidance and course corrections. While it's perfectly acceptable to plan with the knowledge that we've been given the ability to make decisions, we should always remember that God holds ultimate authority and may alter our path when necessary.

God thinks about us in a positive manner and this is the same way we should think about ourselves. We should look at the future with hope, think positive thoughts, and make plans for our lives with confidence and optimism.

Men Love the Chase

Human biology often plays a significant role in our preferences and behaviors. One common aspect of human psychology is the tendency to value the rare and unique over the commonplace. This principle can be seen in various aspects of life, such as the greater desirability of a Porsche 911 compared to a Renault Clio.

In the realm of relationships, this concept holds true as well. Men, in particular, often find excitement and satisfaction in pursuing and winning over a woman they initially thought might be unattainable. The challenge and uncertainty can add an element of intrigue and interest to the process.

First, when you've just met someone, you don't truly know them yet. Being overly available or committed too quickly can come across as premature and may raise questions about authenticity. Moreover, people are often drawn to individuals who already have fulfilling lives and interests of their own. Being in the company of someone who is independent and self-assured is typically more appealing than someone who seems to be waiting for someone else to complete them. In essence, it's about individuals who bring their own well-rounded lives to the table, rather than seeking fulfillment solely from a romantic partner.

A Less-Than-Ideal marriage

Another reason why loneliness can become a factor in a marriage is when a woman finds herself married to a husband who falls short of her ideal expectations. No one has a perfect spouse, and marriages often go through challenging seasons. Issues such as betrayal, distractions, or a wife feeling neglected can arise. In these situations, the marriage may not live up to the expectations she had held.

During such times of turmoil, a wife might wonder where to turn and what steps to take. This is an opportunity for her to realize that her marriage to her husband, while significant, is ultimately designed by God to symbolize a deeper connection – her belonging to the body of Christ. The church is metaphorically referred to as the bride of Christ, and in this broader spiritual context, her marriage to the Lord takes precedence. Her earthly marriage serves as a symbolic representation of the more profound relationship she shares with the body of Christ.

The Lord God said, 'It is not good for the man to be alone. "I will make a helper suitable for him."

Genesis 2:18

God's declaration that it was not good for man to be alone implies that Adam experienced loneliness and a sense of incompleteness in solitude. His very creation indicated the need for human relationships, as it is impossible to fully experience companionship in isolation. When God created Eve, Adam found joy in loving and being loved by another person. The Bible is distinctive in its portrayal of women as valued and complementary companions. In the ancient texts of the Middle East, there is no other commentary on the creation of women like that found in the Bible. The Scriptures emphasize the significant role women have played since the inception of humanity. Genesis 1:27 underscores the equality of man and woman in being made in the image of God: *"So God created mankind in his own image, in the image of God he created them; male and female he created them."*

Can I Trust Love at First Sight to Last?

There are couples who have experienced an immediate sense of rightness within hours of meeting, and their relationships have thrived and remained successful. Strong relationships require dedication and effort, with each partner actively supporting the other's growth and development through both the highs and lows. They continuously learn from one another and are open to acknowledging and rectifying their mistakes along the way. These couples keenly observe other relationships, analyzing what led to breakups and what contributed to longevity, and adjust their own relationship accordingly whenever possible. They recognize early on that there are aspects they can influence in their partner, while also understanding the limits of change and the importance of respecting individual differences. They confront potential deal-breakers head-on and are committed to resolving them to sustain their connection. Perfection is not their expectation, but they wholeheartedly commit to continuous improvement. They are aware that temptations may arise, but they prioritize their bond and would never jeopardize it by yielding to such desires. Rather than viewing their differences as obstacles, they see them as opportunities that keep their interest alive.

"Nobody Likes Me"

Few thoughts can be as emotionally distressing as the belief that *"Nobody Likes Me."* It's a readily available feeling to embrace and obsess over, often serving as a self-critique when we're experiencing moments of loneliness, depression, anxiety, or insecurity. Despite its pervasive presence in our minds, this thought is largely disconnected from reality and serves no constructive purpose other than to harm us emotionally, undermining our self-esteem and obstructing our pursuit of goals. Astonishingly, this very thought is something that both introverted and extroverted individuals commonly grapple with.

Feeling Left Behind

Today, many individuals are actively choosing to embrace the single life, unburdened by the potential stigma, judgment, or unwarranted pity from others. They are making a deliberate decision to lead a different life, one focused on their careers and personal interests, rather than tirelessly searching for "the one" or raising children.

However, there's a contrasting experience for those who are not single by choice. Spending your teenage years and twenties with friends can be an exciting period filled with fun and adventures. But what happens when your friends begin to find their own partners, and one by one, they prioritize their blossoming relationships over your plans? Do not feel excluded when everyone around you is entering into relationships?

I know that suddenly, loneliness or even jealousy can creep in. There may be a sense that if you don't initiate plans to see your friends, you might lose touch altogether – especially when they start building their own families and having children.

Instead,

➤ Engage yourself in meaningful activities and focus on the present moment. In general, your happiness depends more on your mindset and how you choose to spend your time than on your relationship status.

➤ Not all your thoughts should be considered as facts. Frequently, negative thoughts creep into our minds without our awareness, and over time, we can internalize them as undeniable truths. Consider the opposite of these negative thoughts. For instance, if you're thinking, "I'm not good enough for that person," try adopting a perspective like, "I won't settle for a relationship with someone who doesn't value me."

⋏ Don't postpone pursuing your goals until you're in a relationship. Often, we mistakenly believe that our lives will truly begin only once we're married or living with a partner as if we're in a state of limbo until then. Take a moment to reflect on how your life would change once you're in a relationship. Perhaps you'd travel more, explore the idea of buying a home, or start considering parenthood. Many of these aspirations can be pursued independently, even without a partner.

You can't predict the demands of marriage until you're in it, so don't squander your single years by living passively. This is your opportunity to cultivate strength and learn that dependence on Jesus is essential, regardless of your life stage. Jesus isn't just there for your single years and then replaced when you say 'I do.' He is the constant companion you need more than any husband or friend. He alone can mend a lonely heart. If you're looking to marriage to "fix" something within you, you're approaching it with the wrong perspective.

Marriage isn't a solution for self-improvement; it's a mirror that reflects our weaknesses. It highlights the selfishness that we may have been able to overlook as single individuals. This process is a part of sanctification, a journey towards becoming more Christ-like.

If you're currently single, use this time to practice the same attitudes and qualities you'll need in marriage. Embrace the opportunity to cultivate resilience and learn to find joy in the midst of disappointment. This is a part of your sanctification process, preparing you for the future.

Entering marriage with the expectation that it will fill an inner void or emptiness is a setup for disappointment. No human being can satisfy such a profound need. It's neither fair nor healthy to place this level of expectation on human relationships.

So if marriage won't cure the lonely – what will?

→ "Be strong and courageous. Do not be afraid or terrified because of them, for the LORD your God goes with you; he will never leave you nor forsake you." (Deut. 31:6)

→ "For the sake of his great name the LORD will not reject his people, because the LORD was pleased to make you his own." (1 Sam. 12:22)

→ "Turn to me and be gracious to me, for I am lonely and afflicted." (Psalm 25:16)

→ "And surely I am with you always, to the very end of the age." (Matthew 28:20)

→ "So do not fear, for I am with you; do not be dismayed, for I am your God. I will strengthen you and help you; I will uphold you with my righteous right hand." (Isaiah 41:10)

→ "A father to the fatherless, a defender of widows, is God in his holy dwelling. God sets the lonely in families, he leads forth the prisoners with singing…" (Psalm 68:5)

Signs of Being Married and Lonely

Living with another person doesn't automatically eliminate loneliness. It's the sense of connection with your spouse that prevents feelings of isolation within your relationship.

Signs that you might be experiencing loneliness in your marriage can include:

⇨ Feeling lonely even when you're physically together as if there's an unexplained emotional distance between you.

⇨ A lack of communication, where you feel your spouse isn't interested in your conversations, or you're hesitant to share the details of your day, resulting in feelings of isolation and disappointment.

⇨ Finding reasons to avoid spending time with your spouse, such as working late, staying occupied elsewhere, or using social media to evade interaction.

⇨ Infrequent or non-existent sexual intimacy, which not only reflects a lack of emotional connection but also a shortage of physical intimacy.

These factors can contribute to a sense of loneliness within the marriage. Loneliness may affect one or both partners in the relationship, leading to feelings of disconnection and detachment from each other.

Why Are People Married but Lonely?

Here's a list of a few reasons:

Work and family Responsibilities:

One of the primary reasons married couples may sense a growing emotional distance is the demands of work and family life. When both partners are caught up in busy schedules that involve childcare, work responsibilities, and other commitments, it can lead to a sense of passing each other by. As a result, couples may feel they have limited time to spend together, which can foster feelings of drifting apart.

Stressful Life Events:

Couples face challenging situations that strain their relationship. Stressful or traumatic events can test even the strongest marriages, and if these events reveal weaknesses or exacerbate existing issues, it can make the situation even more challenging. For example, losing a job can be particularly difficult if you feel unsupported or sympathized with by your spouse. In such cases, you may find yourself experiencing a sense of abandonment and loneliness even after the stressful event has passed.

Unrealistic Expectations:

Sometimes, the source of loneliness in a marriage may not directly involve your spouse but rather unmet needs in other areas of your life. For instance, if you have poor relationships outside of your marriage, you might expect your spouse to fulfill all your social needs. However, when you place such unrealistic expectations on your partner, it's not surprising to feel dissatisfied because they cannot reasonably be expected to meet all those needs.

Lack of Vulnerability:

Another factor leading to feelings of isolation is a lack of emotional openness with your partner. This means not sharing the personal and intimate aspects of your life, including your dreams and fears. When you withhold these deeper emotions, it becomes challenging to feel truly understood and connected to your spouse.

Social Media Comparisons:

Drawing unrealistic comparisons between your own relationship and those portrayed on social media can also contribute to loneliness. Research from 2017 showed that individuals who spent more time on social media platforms tended to report higher levels of loneliness, as they were often exposed to idealized representations of relationships that didn't reflect the complexities of real-life partnerships.

Favor Is the Divine Act!

"He who finds a [true and faithful] wife finds a good thing and obtains favor and approval from the Lord."

Proverbs 18:22

Finding a good, faithful, and virtuous spouse holds tremendous value. It portrays a wife as a precious blessing from the Lord, bringing favor and approval from God to the one who discovers such a partner.

Marriage is not a human invention but a divine concept that originated from God. It goes beyond being a societal construct; it is a creation of God to fulfill humanity's need for companionship and unity. This union involves a three-dimensional oneness, encompassing the physical, emotional, and spiritual aspects of a couple's relationship. Additionally, marriage serves as God's ordained plan for procreation and parenting.

Remarkably, the Bible commences and concludes with wedding events, signifying God's intimate involvement in the institution of marriage. The proverb cited highlights God's favor in the discovery of a virtuous wife, emphasizing her worth as a gift from God. When a husband and wife perceive each other as divine gifts to be cherished and received with gratitude, they begin to experience the profound oneness that God intended within the marital bond.

A wife is like a precious gift, beautifully wrapped. When you unwrap this gift with love and care, you receive blessings that exceed your wildest expectations. However, if you handle this gift with cruelty and mistreatment, you may incur the disapproval and consequences of God. A wife plays a crucial role in supporting her husband, especially during terrible work situations and challenging circumstances. She serves as a source of encouragement, reminding him of his inherent abilities and talents, and reinforcing his identity as a man of God.

A wife's support empowers her husband to achieve greater feats, transforming recklessness into boldness and insecurity into confidence. The presence of a godly woman in a man's life is truly remarkable, as she offers unwavering support and encouragement.

This is what favor refers to, a divine act of receiving special and preferential treatment from God, serving as your guide and source of protection. Under the influence of favor, you attract attention effortlessly, without actively seeking it.

Ephesians 2:8 tells us, "For by grace you have been saved through faith, and that not of yourselves; it is the gift of God" *(NKJV)*.

Divine favor is a term that signifies the supernatural blessing, grace, and endorsement bestowed by God upon a person or situation. It represents an expression of God's kindness, mercy, and generosity toward His followers. Divine favor isn't something attainable through human effort alone; rather, it is a gift given by God out of His love and benevolence towards us. When someone encounters divine favor, they may find themselves presented with unique opportunities, favorable circumstances, protection, provision, guidance, and success in various aspects of life. It serves as a tangible manifestation of God's steadfast goodness and loyalty as He intervenes in our lives to bring about positive outcomes and blessings.

Divine favor can manifest in diverse ways, tailored to an individual's specific needs and circumstances. It can impact relationships, careers, financial stability, health, spiritual development, and other facets of life. Above all, it serves as a constant reminder of God's presence and His unwavering desire to abundantly bless His children. God's favor is a transformative force in our lives. Its significance goes beyond our eternal salvation; it encompasses our deliverance, protection, preservation, healing, and overall well-being.

The all-encompassing nature of God's favor is evident in how it addresses every facet of our existence—our spiritual, emotional, and physical needs. His supernatural grace is so immense that it is said to require endless ages for Him to reveal the full extent of His grace and kindness through Christ Jesus (as noted in Ephesians 2:7).

Some might think they need to wait for the afterlife to fully experience God's favor, but the truth is, that He is pouring out His favor upon us right here and now. Even before our spiritual transformation, God was extending His favor toward us. Even when we were in rebellion, He demonstrated His profound love by sending Christ to die for us (Romans 5:8).

It is God's grace that enabled us to be born again, and from that moment, His favor has been continuously at work on our behalf. Being born again marked just the beginning of His favor in our lives, and He will keep pouring out His grace and favor if we are open to receiving it.

If you haven't made Jesus the Lord of your life, you can do so now through a simple prayer.

Psalm 5:12 declares that the righteous are blessed and surrounded by God's favor as with a shield. This scripture speaks directly to those who have embraced Jesus as their Lord. Through Jesus, we have been made righteous, and His shed blood made righteousness and God's favor available to all. As born-again believers, we are constantly enveloped in God's favor.

God Is Searching for Someone to Bless with His Favor

Regrettably, there are times when we are slow to embrace God's favor. We may think we're waiting on Him, but in reality, He is waiting for us to receive His blessings. The truth is, that God has already provided everything we need for a fulfilling life on this earth – blessings like health, prosperity, peace of mind, joy, deliverance from sin, and all that contributes to our well-being (2 Peter 1:3).

Additionally, He promises us eternal life in heaven when our earthly journey ends. It's all part of His divine favor, and all we need to do is remain open to receiving it.

In fact, escaping God's favor is impossible. Second Chronicles 16:9 reminds us, "The eyes of the Lord run to and fro throughout the whole earth, to show himself strong on behalf of them whose heart is perfect toward him..." (KJV). "Perfect" in this context doesn't mean flawless; it signifies someone who is loyal, devoted, and faithful. Such a heart is always prepared to accept the blessings that God's grace offers. God is perpetually in search of individuals to bless – it's inherent in His nature. He is rich in mercy and compassion, and His favor seeks out those who are willing to trust Him, those who are ever ready to step out in faith to receive His blessings.

So, are you that kind of person? Are you trustworthy, ready, and eager to embrace God's favor and blessings?

For me, hearing the Word of God in Matthew 6, which assured me that the Lord takes care of His people and provides for their needs, ignited my faith and led to my spiritual rebirth. I developed a profound love for God's Word, and my faith continued to grow. Even today, I enthusiastically declare, "Here I am, Lord. I'm ready. Just reveal it to me in Your Word, and I'll accept it. I'll believe it, act on it, and receive everything you promise!"

Chapter 23

Stop the Wedding Preparation Right Now

Wait! What? Are you getting married? Your most awaited marriage is happening soon? Congratulations! You have decided to tie the knot with the person you love and couldn't be happier. But while The Beatles may be able to sell, "all you need is love," the wedding industry sings a very different tune.

So, is your decision to get married primarily influenced by your partner's physical appeal, financial status, or material possessions?

Let's be honest, beauty is inherently unequal. Not everyone is fortunate enough to have exceptional genes or possess perfect symmetry from birth and that's okay. A conventionally attractive appearance, often described as "Enticingly Average," is not within everyone's reach.

Attractiveness is influenced by numerous factors, and some of these factors may be within our control and some of them aren't. Attractiveness is an asset but does that mean to get married someone if one is good-looking or is financially stable? It doesn't work like this! Sure, love is mysterious, but, in some ways, attraction is not.

"Love is patient, love is kind. It does not envy, it does not boast, it is not proud. It does not dishonor others, it is not self-seeking, it is

not easily angered, and it keeps no record of wrongs. Love does not delight in evil but rejoices with the truth. It always protects, always trusts, always hopes, and always perseveres."

(1 Corinthians 13:4-7)

Our feelings about attractiveness are conflicted. We are often advised not to make snap judgments based solely on appearances, with sayings like "don't judge a book by its cover" and "beauty is only skin deep" cautioning us against this tendency. However, despite these admonitions, our natural inclination is to evaluate people based on their looks and to favor those who are appealing.

Proverbs 31:30 from the Bible verse draws attention to the idea that charm and physical beauty are fleeting and can often be deceiving. In the context of a marriage or any relationship, relying on a person's external appearance or superficial charm may not lead to a lasting or fulfilling partnership.

"Charm is deceptive, and beauty is fleeting, but a woman who fears the Lord is to be praised."

Proverbs 31:30 (NIV)

You have been made in the image of God, and He doesn't create YOU without purpose. Just like snowflakes, each individual is entirely unique. In the eyes of God, you are considered a work of art, and when you gaze at your reflection, He desires you to have complete confidence in that knowledge.

Here's a beauty suggestion: Start your day by looking in the mirror, and saying Psalm 139:14 with a smile. You could even place the verse on your mirror as a daily reminder!

Moving forward, the question arises: where do you invest more of your time and effort, in enhancing your external appearance or nurturing your inner self?

"But the Lord said to Samuel, 'Do not consider his appearance or his height, for I have rejected him. The Lord does not look at the things people look at. People look at the outward appearance, but the Lord looks at the heart.'

1 Samuel 16:7

God's message to Samuel was a reminder that He doesn't make judgments based on external attributes like physical appearance or height, as humans often do. Instead, God looks deeper, into a person's heart and character. As you grow older, you will find boys and girls finding the perfect attire, achieving flawless skin, and striving for an ideal body. But what is that for???

While there's nothing wrong with wanting to look attractive but maintaining a balance is essential. God values and encourages us to prioritize developing inner beauty, which means fostering a deep connection with Him through prayer and studying His Word, the Bible.

Ultimately, God values the kind of person who is spiritually enriched on the inside, a beauty that radiates from within. As time goes by, physical beauty naturally diminishes, so if your primary concern is your outward appearance, you may find yourself discontent when wrinkles appear and the number on the scale increases. Interestingly, the signs of aging can begin to manifest as early as one's twenties.

This is why God encourages us to have a deep "fear" of Him. It doesn't mean being afraid of Him, but rather holding Him in profound reverence and awe for all that He has accomplished. To put it simply, if you were to place two girls side by side, one being Miss World or Universe with beauty primarily centered on physical attributes and the other an average-looking girl who wholeheartedly loves the Lord, the latter is considered more beautiful in the eyes of God.

Stop Binge Purchasing Beauty in a Partner

Here's the thing: "Do you know when looks matter in a relationship, it becomes the source of frustrations and difficulties?" Appearances do matter in relationships, and of course, financial stability as well. Everyone has their own insecurities, and no one is perfect. I have keenly observed that couples often bring their unresolved problems and unaddressed issues into the marriage relationship, which can lead to challenges in building a healthy and strong partnership. Usually, they neglect important aspects like compatibility, communication, and emotional connection. This can result in dissatisfaction and frustration within the marriage.

The Scripture offers guidance on various aspects of relationships, including marriage, and the importance of addressing issues and priorities before getting into a union.

"For where your treasure is, there your heart will be also."

(Matthew 6:21 (NIV)

Our priorities and values should align with what is truly valuable in the long term, such as character and virtues, rather than materialistic or superficial concerns Your marriage is meant to follow the greatest love story of all time: Jesus pursuing the world (followers of Jesus — His bride, the church) to the point of laying down His life for them and offering them salvation. If you follow Jesus, you are dearly loved and called to follow His example by humbling yourself and living in a way that demonstrates that love in your marriage and other relationships. Loving each other unconditionally, following the example of Jesus who loved and sacrificed himself for us, is undoubtedly challenging. However, when we strive to love as Jesus did, it creates a foundation for establishing and maintaining a healthy marriage.

In the words of Paul Miller from "A Loving Life: In a World of Broken Relationships"

"When we realize that our spouse, like ourselves, is inherently imperfect, our tendency is to withdraw, assuming that everything is fundamentally flawed. A troubled marriage often arises when neither partner is willing to put in the effort required for love. But when one partner commits to practicing steadfast and unwavering love, the troubles in the marriage start to dissolve."

This doesn't mean that the relationship or marriage suddenly becomes effortless. Nonetheless, when personal agendas are set aside, and there is a genuine desire to love, even in the face of difficulties, it becomes an opportunity to beautifully manifest God's love in the relationship.

Many couples later had to sacrifice truth for fine, sexy, handsome, money and or a big butt and a smile. Marriage brings about significant transformations in your life. It's not merely about cohabiting or sharing expenses, as those aspects can be achieved without marriage. What sets marriage apart are love, understanding, and care.

"Above all, love each other deeply, because love covers over a multitude of sins."

1 Peter 4:8 (NIV)

Everybody has a beauty to them and you have to try to capture it. Beyond major life choices, there's lots of love, honesty, trust, and good times. Before coming together in marriage, both partners must be willing to open the books and be honest about any past and present troubles that may come to bear during the marriage.

The Expensive Wedding vs. the Cheap marriage: What Truly Matters?

Marriage is a covenant, and maintaining this covenant requires a consistent dedication of two committed individuals. The extravagance of your wedding, the gifts received, or the guests may not be the sole determining factors in a successful marriage. Sustaining a marriage requires more than just a celebratory event, and there are crucial aspects to contemplate before embarking on the journey of marriage.

After 3 or 4 decades of marriage, it's not uncommon for some couples to find themselves stuck in less-than-ideal routines. Starting out young, and energetic, they might have experienced moments of happiness, endured challenges, and stress, and built a family. Over time, they might feel that they argue often, have infrequent intimacy, and experience emotional distance together in the same room.

"Hey, I've been unhappy for a long time and I don't want to be."

"We really don't know each other."

"I have a hard time dealing with my marriage."

Don't worry, I have got you covered here. If you are having the same thoughts and feelings before getting married. The following are a few things that you should consider:

1. *Emotional Compatibility:*

Emotional compatibility is an essential element in every marriage, as couples should be capable of providing emotional support to one another, whether in moments of joy or adversity. For instance, when one spouse is facing challenges, the other should be ready to offer comfort and emotional assistance.

"Carry each other's burdens, and in this way, you will fulfill the law of Christ."

Galatians 6:2 (NIV)

Recognizing the actions that foster a sense of love and connection in your partner can lead to increased satisfaction for both of you. If you feel most loved when your partner expresses affection through hugs and kisses, but your partner feels most loved when you take care of household chores like taking out the trash or emptying the dishwasher, it might indicate a disparity in your expressions of appreciation. Talk about it!!!

2. *Choose to Love:*

At times, it can be quite challenging to fully grasp someone's perspective or where they are coming from. However, this should not serve as a reason to withhold love and compassion. Whatever the circumstances might be, choose to love and care, and do not think negatively about them. Jesus exemplified love for those who opposed Him, and likewise, we can choose to love those we may find it hard to relate to or comprehend.

3. *Open Communication:*

As I always say, effective and open communication is the cornerstone of a joyful marriage. It's vital for couples to communicate openly, honestly, and effectively, regardless of their stage in married life. For instance, when one person is upset or facing an issue, it's important for them to express their feelings to their spouse so that both partners can understand and navigate challenges together.

4. *Conflict Resolution:*

Conflict resolution is an inevitable aspect of any marriage. Couples must possess the ability to address disagreements in a harmonious and constructive manner prior to exchanging vows. This involves active listening to each other's perspectives, identifying common ground, and reaching compromises. For instance, in situations where one partner prefers city living while the other prefers the countryside, they must work together to find a mutually beneficial compromise that takes both their desires into account.

5. *Personal Growth*

Personal growth is an integral aspect of the marital journey. Partners should commit to each other's individual development and progress. This entails offering support to one another in pursuit of their dreams and aspirations. For instance, if one partner expresses a desire to return to school to pursue a degree, the other partner must be supportive of that decision.

"Do nothing out of selfish ambition or vain conceit. Rather, in humility, value others above yourselves, not looking to your own interests but each of you to the interests of the others."

Philippians 2:3-4 (NIV)

Marriage should be a milestone in a person's life, and it

necessitates a careful examination of various factors before entering into it. Through thoughtful consideration of these factors, couples can enhance the prospects of a successful and enduring marriage.

6. *Spending Habits Are Different*

It's no surprise that money often becomes a significant source of tension in marriages, particularly when it comes to differing spending philosophies. However, there's still hope even when one partner is financially cautious while the other follows a more liberal approach.

"For the love of money is a root of all kinds of evil. Some people, eager for money, have wandered from the faith and pierced themselves with many griefs."

1 Timothy 6:10 (NIV)

The Bible clarifies that money itself is not inherently bad, but the love of money is where the problem lies. It's essential to recognize this distinction. Money, in essence, is merely a tool that facilitates transactions and enables us to acquire goods and services without the need for bartering. Much like a hammer, money can be employed for both positive and negative purposes. Your partner is not a mind-reader and you have to tell them about your financial goals. It's not always easy to talk about what you need. For one, many of us don't spend enough time thinking about what's really important to us in a relationship but you have to do this in order to avoid future conflicts.

In your money talk, make sure you discuss short-term and long-term goals. Examples include buying a house, having children, long-term savings, and retirement accounts.

Don't expect family and friends to bail you out of your financial inconveniences. However, I have mentioned a few guidelines for you which can help you out.

A Few Guidelines!!!

So, here's a list of some guidelines for initiating a conversation about finances with your partner:

Schedule a Specific Time: Avoid discussing finances in the heat of the moment, especially when emotions are running high. It's beneficial to set clear time boundaries for the conversation, specifying when it starts and ends.

Examine Future Goals: Choose a specific topic or theme to discuss. This could involve holiday spending, examining future financial goals, or deciding on a major purchase, such as a new vehicle.

Choose A Refreshed Time: Opt for a time when both of you are feeling refreshed and not stressed. For instance, a Sunday morning might be a more suitable choice than a weekday evening after work when exhaustion and tension may be high. Ensure you are not hungry, angry, or under the influence of substances during the discussion.

Consider a Good Place: Holding the conversation in a public setting like a coffee shop or library can help reduce the likelihood of heightened emotions or raised voices. Being in a neutral environment can also eliminate potential triggers, such as bills on the desk or household issues.

A Positive Intention: Instead of approaching the conversation as a conflict, set a positive intention. For example, aim to find creative compromises to address recurring financial conflicts, with the goal of fostering a more peaceful and harmonious relationship.

7. *Children and Parenting*

Children and parenting are crucial topics that couples should not overlook in their discussions before marriage. Surprisingly, some couples may assume rather than discuss these issues, only to encounter significant differences in their views a few years into their marriage. Couples should have conversations about the number of children they plan to have before starting a family. They should consider how factors like financial stability and career choices might affect their plans for expanding their family. Additionally, it's valuable to explore the possibility of alternative options, such as adoption, if health issues prevent pregnancy.

"Children are a heritage from the Lord, offspring a reward from him."

Psalm 127:3 (NIV)

Parenting styles often stem from a person's own upbringing, and spouses may bring different experiences to the marriage. It's wise to address some fundamental topics related to child-rearing. For instance, after a child is born, will one partner become a full-time stay-at-home parent? Is the use of daycare while both parents work an acceptable option? How will discipline be handled—jointly as a team or primarily by one parent? Believe it or not, these discussions can help establish clarity and alignment on parenting roles and expectations.

8. *Household Tasks*

Household tasks and how they will be managed should be a topic of discussion. For example, if one spouse grew up in a home where hired cleaners handled regular chores, while the other lived in a family where daily cooking and cleaning chores were shared with each member, then what's the solution? How to deal with it?

"Whatever you do, work at it with all your heart, as working for the Lord, not for human masters."

Colossians 3:23 (NIV):

Every day in marriage presents opportunities for learning and growth. While it's impossible to anticipate all potential sources of conflict, it's likely that most of the topics mentioned above will come up at some point in a marriage. Instead of assuming your future spouse shares your plans and preferences, engage in honest discussions with them. Find out the solution and choose the best option as per the circumstances.

But, avoid *"Winning"* your primary objective when dealing with issues. If you approach your partner with the mindset that everything must go your way or there will be no compromise, finding common ground becomes difficult. This attitude may stem from unmet needs in your past or years of built-up resentment in the relationship, which has now reached a breaking point. It's perfectly acceptable to have strong convictions, and equally important to listen to your partner and respect their perspective. Treat the other person with courtesy and acknowledge their point of view.

Don't Buy a Big Ring!

Believe it or not, a diamond ring should always be seen as a crucial element in a marriage. I wholeheartedly believe that your love, care, and understanding for your partner will play a big part in the sustainability of your marriage.

"He who finds a wife finds what is good and receives favor from the Lord."

Proverbs 18:22 (NIV)

"Husbands, love your wives, just as Christ loved the church and gave himself up for her."

Ephesians 5:25 (NIV)

Just as a pair of scissors needs two halves to function properly as a whole, so does marriage. We have seen that Paul is very fair and balanced in the way that he addresses the people involved in these relationships. For instance, he talks first to the wives, then to the husbands; he talks to the children, and then he talks to the parents. Paul delivers the

Christian Gospel message, conveying a radical idea for the time to women, slaves, and children. He emphasizes that they are equal to men. Paul reminds them that they are creations of God, recipients of His love and that Christ's sacrifice is for them as well. They have the opportunity to be reconciled with God, filled with the Holy Spirit, and become integral members of the Body of Christ, leading lives of eternal significance. Paul's primary aim is to guide these new believers in shedding the secular values they've absorbed and adopting a fresh, Christian perspective on life and culture. This challenge remains relevant today, as we navigate a secularized society while professing faith in Christ.

Many young couples hope to tie the knot one day, but some are spooked by high costs. You want to share your happiness with all of your friends and family and that's understandable! But it's unnecessary to spend thousands of dollars. Why not simplify your scheme? But you really don't have to do that. Marriage is not about how "Money Talks." You need money to pay for everything in your life. The problem is we talk about love and we don't know what it is! Fortunately, the Scriptures don't leave it up for grabs.

Life can often feel like a series of battles, and perhaps none are as intense as those within the realm of marriage. Marriage is a serious commitment that should not be taken lightly. While success may come more easily in other aspects of life, achieving a thriving marriage demands significant effort and dedication. Neglecting your marriage can have costly consequences. It's true that the choices and efforts you make in your marriage lay the foundation for its future. Failing to establish a strong foundation can jeopardize the entire structure of your marriage.

The type of marriage you ultimately experience is closely tied to the choices you make and your attitude toward it. If you invest sincere effort and meticulous planning in establishing a strong foundation for your future in marriage, you will undoubtedly reap substantial benefits in the years to come.

Align Yourself with God

When you align yourself with God, you become an invincible team, capable of triumphing over the challenges of marriage. Even complex issues can be effectively addressed with divine wisdom. Your home will be a place of happiness and peace, and failure or casualties will not be part of your story. God will be your constant source of help and intervention when needed. You will receive the guidance to make your marriage shine brilliantly and stand out as the best.

Understand that a successful marriage requires you to assemble the necessary components. The first crucial step is to initiate preparations centered on prayer. In the journey of a godly marriage, battles are inevitable. From the outset, the forces of darkness often attempt to wage battles, and as the journey progresses, these battles intensify. Recognize that knowing and aligning with God's will is accompanied by these battles because the devil seeks to thwart your success. The more prayer effort you put into your marital plans, the more you will succeed at reaching the peak of marital bliss.

Chapter 24

My Marriage Was Made In Heaven but Lived On Earth

You have probably heard the statement, "Oh, that's a match made in heaven." Well, marriage was made in heaven, an institution created by God. It is meant to be a loving, intimate, selfless relationship between a man and a woman that lasts for eternity. God's original plan for marriage is found in the words of Jesus when He said, in Mark 10, "From the beginning of creation, God made them male and female. For this reason, a man shall leave his father and mother and shall be joined by his wife. What God has joined together, let no one tear apart." (Mark 10:6-9, King James Version)

Without commitment, there will be no improvement in either love or romance in a marriage. A husband and wife must be committed to improving love and romance in their marriage. They must work to have a marriage in which love and romance exist.

In the scriptures we read, we find the ideal of commitment. In Genesis 2:24, King James Version, it says, "Therefore, shall a man leave his father and his mother, and shall cleave unto his wife: and they shall be one flesh." In Genesis 2:24, we see "leaving" and "cleaving." The decision has been made to leave father and mother, and the commitment has to be made to become either a husband or a wife. The decision to leave one relationship (parent/child) and the commitment to begin a new relationship (husband/wife). The word "cleave" means "to be cemented together." In Ephesians 5:31 (KJV), the word "joined" means "to be glued together." Both carry the same idea. Two people, a man and a woman, enter into a relationship called marriage, and thus become husband and wife. As husband and wife, they enter into a relationship that is meant to become such a strong bond that it is inseparable. They become like "one flesh."

Now, let me say this glue is not the fast-drying kind of glue. As we all know, a couple can have a wedding and say their vows, but not be cemented or glued together. This "cleaving" and being "joined together" is a process. It is a process achieved because a couple is committed to having this extraordinary bond between them. Listen to me; it is much simpler to be pronounced husband and wife than to become husband and wife. The pronouncement takes only minutes; the becoming takes years. Marriage is a university we enroll in, not a single class we complete as soon as we say, "I do," and then graduate.

If a marriage fails, it is either because the people in it were ignorant of God's purposes or unwilling to apply themselves to the marriage and the Word of God. There must be a commitment to a loving marriage!

Again, the words "cleave" and "joined together" speak of a relationship so bonded together that it is inseparable. With this thought in mind, Jesus said in Matthew 19:6 (KJV), "Wherefore they are no more twain, but one flesh. What therefore God hath joined together, let not man put asunder." Jesus was saying that no one or nothing should be able to divide the marriage relationship. A couple should enter marriage with the attitude that this is for the rest of their lives. Those who are married should say, "We are going to make this marriage last." For those who have had a bad marriage and are in a second or third marriage, they should say, "This marriage is not going to be like the last one. We are going to make this one work."

For many who have been married, there may be periods when they don't like their partner. Yes, I said "like," not "love." What does a person do when those initial feelings fade? Do they work through it, talk about it, and choose their partner? Or do they seek external validation? Many are experiencing this right now with their partners. Everything they say and do gets on their last nerves, and they don't enjoy spending time together anymore. They are constantly and consistently agitated and angry. Some are so sad until their feelings are dying, and they don't know what to do. Most people go the route of seeking external validation because, at their core, they are programmed to be unstable and insecure, so they constantly need something to feed their ego and make them feel good. While cultivating self-awareness and discipline serves as a promising initial step, it is equally vital for individuals to reprogram themselves, fostering emotional stability and diminishing these inclinations.

When a man and a woman come together as husband and wife, they are expected to have entered a better way of living. Ecclesiastes 4:9 (NKJV) says, "Two are better than one because they have a good reward for their labor."

Although marriage was made in heaven, it has to be lived on earth.

The man has to take care of the woman. She is catered for, cherished, and nourished by him. He brings material possessions while she, in turn, creates a harmonious and beautiful home environment. Both partners invest their time, energy, and finances to ensure the well-being of their household.

I hope these revisions help your text flow more smoothly. If you have any further questions or need additional edits, please feel free to ask.

However, when a relationship lacks a strong foundation rooted in shared values and principles, the initial joy, enthusiasm, and contentment experienced by the couple tend to be short-lived. This happiness gradually fades away, much like the appeal of a new car that loses its shine over time. As newer models enter the market, the once-new car no longer excites the owner, prompting a desire for the latest versions. This phenomenon occurs because the old car no longer holds the same allure. When God is at the center of a marriage, you find that instead of growing tired of each other, your excitement and satisfaction increase as the years go by, making the relationship go from good to better and from better to the best!

God is the greatest author of all marriages since the beginning, as seen in His creation of Eve specifically for Adam and His role in bringing them together (as described in Genesis 2:22). The union of Isaac and Rebecca, depicted in Genesis 24, epitomizes a heavenly union, characterized by divine presence, blessings, joy, harmony, and even signs and wonders. "And Isaac brought her (Rebekah) into his mother Sarah's tent, and took Rebekah, and she became his wife, and he loved her: and Isaac was comforted after his mother's death." (Genesis 24:67)

Are all marriages Made in Heaven?

The next question is: Are all marriages made in heaven? If yes, why have so many marriages today become hellish, not heavenly? Why is the divorce rate so high? Sadly, instead of asking for God's guidance, we look for God-like qualities in our future partner. Women want Mr. Romancer, the man who showers them with money, candies, kisses, and flowers, but later, these materialistic things become empty. Likewise, men tend to choose Miss Perfect with good looks, ready to show off like a shiny car but later realize that it wasn't a wise decision.

There should always be a deep sense of "one and only" that accompanies your decision to spend the rest of your life together. "But seek ye first the kingdom of God and His righteousness; and all these things shall be added unto you" (Matthew 6:33). Everyone who has a wedding is looking for one thing: a marriage made in heaven! I just want you to know that while some marriages may have been made in heaven, they still have to be lived out here on earth. That tends to make most of them less than perfect.

God's Part in the marriage

God designed marriage to involve the spirit, soul, and body so that the blessings marriage carries are expected to affect your spirit, soul, and body. When God blesses the union of a man and a woman, certain things follow.

Spiritual Strength:

A married couple is expected to experience spiritual growth and strength greater than what they had individually when they were single. When two individuals unite in matrimony, they form a powerful bond in the spiritual battle against the forces of evil. This union has to be potent enough that it can cause a remarkable dispersion of adversity, symbolized in Deuteronomy 32:30 as the fleeing of ten thousand devils. Consequently, the couple becomes a formidable threat to the forces of darkness, surpassing their individual spiritual strength. Nevertheless, many individuals, particularly women, express concerns about feeling less spiritually active post-marriage. It may be because of the increased responsibilities that come with married life, such as caring for a husband and children and managing household tasks. These duties can sometimes challenge their ability to engage in spiritual practices as fervently as they did before matrimony.

The Power of Prayer:

Marriage offers the couple unity so that when they offer prayers to God on any issue at all, He honors their request. Why? "If two of you shall agree on earth as touching anything that they shall ask, it shall be done for them of my Father which is in heaven" (Matthew 18:19). A couple can agree on issues more easily than any two close friends. For instance, if they both firmly believe in God and ask for the fruit of the womb, God is obligated to grant their request. Thus, when a man and his wife agree, there is tremendous power released; and if they disagree, their prayers are hindered (1 Pet. 3:7).

Divine Favor:

"Whoso findeth a wife findeth a good thing and obtaineth favor of the Lord" (Proverbs 18:22). Once divine favor graces your life, it becomes an enduring and irrevocable blessing. This favor is so profound that even those who may have been opposed to you are compelled to regard you with kindness and love. It is said that when an individual's ways align with the divine will, God creates circumstances in such a way that benefits you.

God's favor elevates you to extraordinary heights, to the point where others might envy your life. Your marriage serves as a shining example of a harmonious union, and when you and your partner step out together, people can't help but remark, "Look at them; you'd think they just got married yesterday." This, in turn, makes marriage an appealing and aspirational institution, as it should be.

Taking a glimpse at the first family, that of Adam and Eve, one can discern that even after their transgression, God's favor continued to envelop them. Although they had initially tried to cover their shame by sewing fig leaves together, God, in His special favor for the family, looked past their betrayal. Instead, He provided them with clothing made from animal skins, thereby concealing their nakedness and relieving them of shame. This act exemplified the enduring grace and compassion that God bestows upon families.

Companionship:

Iron sharpeneth iron; so, a man sharpeneth the countenance of his friend. (Proverbs 27:17)

When a husband and wife work together to make decisions that may influence their family, they will have better clarity. For example, there are some choices that you would have made that would not have been advantageous to the other; however, because you have the honor of being married to your husband, a man of integrity who is real and godly, such mistakes will be avoided. You should have family-related discussions. God has made provisions for "iron to sharpen iron" within the union. However, there's no way two pieces of iron can sharpen each other unless they both come together in contact. Thus, this provision only works when you are united as a couple.

Finally, be ye all of one mind? (1 Peter 3:8)

Physical Fulfilment:

God ensures that a man and his wife enjoy and are fulfilled by each other's bodies in order to honor their physical marriage. In addition to avoiding temptation, both the husband and wife fulfill their sexual desires. They are given appropriate channels through which to satisfy their sexual urges.

Because your mate should be enough to please you, God disapproves of infidelity. I frequently quip that your mate has everything that any other man or woman does. You only need to be content with your partner to benefit from marriage.

Fruit of the Womb:

They have a good reward for their labor. (Ecclesiastes 4:9)

One such reward is the fruit of the womb.

Lo, children are a heritage of the Lord: and the fruit of the womb is his reward. (Psalm 127:3)

The institution of marriage, in accordance with God's original plan (Genesis 1:26-28), is intended to be a source of procreation, leading to the joy of having children. When this natural process is hindered, it can often result in grief and frustration. It was the fall of Adam and Eve that first introduced the concept of barrenness. However, God, through Jesus, offered redemption from the curses of the law. As a result, those who are born again can take solace in the assurance that they are no longer bound by the burden of infertility. Hence, any sorrow or frustration associated with childlessness can be alleviated. Merely having children is not the sole indicator of divine approval; what truly matters is raising children with strong Christian values. In today's challenging world, children are often exposed to various negative influences, including peer pressure, substance abuse, sexual orientation issues, and premarital relationships. Nevertheless, when they are nurtured within a steadfast Christian family, they gain the fortitude to withstand these temptations and to walk a godly path.

Keys to "marriage Paradise"

For any husband who may be reading this, if you are facing challenges in your marriage, the first area to examine is yourself. Ask yourself, "Am I fulfilling my role as a righteous and spiritual guide? Am I leading my wife and children spiritually as I should?" If you find that you are not living up to the spiritual leadership that God expects from you, it is likely the primary source of issues in your marriage. Other problems may manifest as symptoms, but this failure in spiritual leadership is the root cause. God has ordained you to be the leader.

Leading doesn't always involve giving orders or dictating what your family should do. Let me give you an example of how Jesus provided leadership. On one occasion, as Jesus and his disciples gathered at the supper table, He noticed that their feet were soiled. Dining with dirty feet was a significant breach of social etiquette back then. Instead of asking, "Who will clean my feet?" Jesus humbly removed his robe, wrapped a towel around his waist, and proceeded to wash the feet of each of his disciples. This is the epitome of leadership. Leadership involves serving. Being the head of the family doesn't involve bossing everyone around, giving orders like, "Sit here, go there, do this."

Husbands, to lead your wife effectively, sometimes you need to humble yourself and serve. If her feet are dirty, clean them, or offer to massage her feet, which she'll appreciate. It means pitching in with household chores, like helping with the dishes or taking care of the vacuuming duties. This is the essence of being a servant leader as a husband. God has designed husbands not only to lead but also to serve their families.

Love (Jesus is a steady lover who sacrifices)

One major requirement for making your marriage work is love. Love is not optional but mandatory. This love does not have its origin in the world, but in God; as God's Word declares, "God is love" (1 John 4:8).

"Husbands, love your wives, even as Christ also loved the church, and gave himself for it." (Ephesians 5:25)

God entrusted Eve to Adam, instructing him to "love this woman." Ephesians 5 also teaches us to love our wives as Christ loved the church. If I were to ask, "Do you love your wife?" your response might be, "Of course." But the more crucial question is, "Do you love her in the same way that Jesus loves the church?" Jesus exemplifies unwavering, sacrificial love.

According to the Bible, the love we should have for our spouses is described as "agape," an unselfish form of love. As outlined in 1 Corinthians 13, agape is patient, kind, not arrogant, not rude, and it does not keep a record of wrongs. It bears all things, believes all things, hopes all things, and endures all things. This kind of love is enduring and does not fade away. So when a husband says, "I no longer love her," the response should be, "Choose to love her again," because love is not just a feeling; it's a conscious decision. Love is an act of the will. Sometimes we may not feel particularly affectionate toward our spouses, but we can still make the choice to love them. Start loving them in your thoughts. Love is essentially a matter of the heart that eventually finds expression through the mouth and by actions. Husbands must learn, beginning from the thoughts of their hearts to love their wives. Out of the abundance of the heart, the mouth speaks (Matthew 12:34).

When your heart is overflowing with loving thoughts, your words will simply reflect that. For instance, if a man verbally abuses his wife, he is speaking from his heart. He is unable to speak otherwise until he is able to see the intensity of his thoughts. Women react to male initiatives while males take the lead. If you, the husband, start a loving relationship with your wife, she will respond. Your wife will submit to you effortlessly if you love her. Love isn't something you stumble into or out of; it's not a fleeting emotion. It's a choice, an act of the will. You choose to love that person. This is how husbands are meant to love their wives. God has designed husbands to lead and to love.

"Love is very patient and kind, never jealous or envious, never boastful or proud, never haughty or selfish or rude. Love does not demand its own way. It is not irritable or touchy. It does not hold grudges and will hardly even notice when others do it wrong." (1 Corinthians 13:4-5) (TLB)

Do Not Be Selfish, Haughty, or Rude!

So many homes have been ruined by "Me, Myself, and I," which goes by the label of selfishness as well. Respect and selflessness are the foundation of marriage. If a husband wants to have a happy marriage, he must pay the price of selflessness. Love is not rudeness. Men who treat their wives disrespectfully and vice versa to assert their dominance are missing it. Serious insults and sarcasm are not acceptable to God. It is expected of husbands to love their spouses, which entails treating them with decency and respect. If you treat your wife disrespectfully as a husband, your domestic staff, family members, and kids will do the same. It is just incorrect!

An unforgiving attitude is the result of holding a grudge against someone for what they did in the past. Love overlooks and forgives. It does not keep track of transgressions. Knowing that a tiny book exists in which all of your transgressions are documented for future reference is the most annoying thing in the world. We must forgive one another like Christ does because God forgives us and forgets our transgressions (Ephesians 4:32).

For ye know the grace of our Lord Jesus Christ, that, though he was rich, yet for your sakes he became poor, that ye through his poverty might be rich. (2 Corinthians 8:9)

Love doesn't always say "yes." Love sometimes has to refuse something. You can't ignore the times, husband when your wife needs to be corrected. When necessary, practice saying "no" without making them feel bad. At one point, Jesus turned to Peter and commanded him to "get thee behind me, Satan" (Matthew 16:23). Even though Peter needed to be corrected at the time, Jesus did not spare him because if He had, His destiny might have been derailed. He did not detest Peter.

All scripture is given by inspiration of God, and is profitable for doctrine, for reproof, for correction, for instruction in righteousness. (2 Timothy 3:16)

Expecting and Dealing with Change

One of life's certainties is change. The person you marry will undergo transformations over time. It's not uncommon for someone to say, "I need a divorce because this isn't the same person I married." This statement holds wisdom. People naturally evolve, and there's nothing wrong with that. When you exchange vows on your wedding day, you're not just committing to the person they are at that moment but also to whoever they may become in the years ahead. Every married individual has, at some point, made a commitment before a church minister or officiant, promising something along the lines of, "I give myself to you for better or for worse, for richer or for poorer, in sickness and in health, till death do us part."

People often say, "I have issues in my marriage, and it's all their fault," or "I have problems in this marriage, and it's entirely their fault. If only they would change, things would have become better." It's crucial to understand that we cannot change our spouse. This is a fundamental truth to remember. The only behavior we have control over is our own.

However, we do have the ability to change our attitude toward our spouse's behavior. Our attitude is the one thing we can manage.

Allow me to share a humorous story about a nervous bride standing at the back of the church before her wedding. She said, "I've forgotten what I'm supposed to do at the wedding." The wedding director offered a simple reminder: "Just remember three things: Walk down the aisle, walk toward the altar, and turn to walk toward the groom." The guests laughed as the bride, while walking down the aisle, repeated to herself, "Aisle, altar, him: I'll alter, him." The lesson here is that you can't change your partner. Ladies, you can't alter him, and guys, you can't change her. The only aspect we have the power to change is our own behavior and our response to their behavior.

Constantly Praise Each Other

A few things can enhance your marriage quite like regularly complimenting each other. Here's a little insight for men: women can easily find out the difference between insincere flattery and genuine compliments. Many women struggle with self-esteem issues, to the extent that they only accept about half of the heartfelt compliments they receive. So, if you genuinely want to compliment your wife, you may need to do it twice as often as you think.

Husbands, if I had the means to make this happen, I would challenge you with this: "I promise to give you one million dollars, tax-free, after twelve months if you say something genuinely nice about your wife every single day. Find something positive about her and pay her a compliment. You just need to do this for 365 days." I believe many men would take up this challenge without hesitation. However, here's the truth, the rewards in your marriage are worth far more than a million dollars. Do yourself a favor and start appreciating and complimenting each other. Sometimes, guys might struggle to express themselves, but we need to make the effort to say it. It's like the story of an old farmer who said, "I love Ruth so much that sometimes it's all I can do to stop myself from telling her."

Allow God to Rule over Your marriage

Jesus said: "What God has joined together, let no one separate." If you're contemplating divorce and want to know God's will for your marriage, I'll be straightforward with you. Here's God's will for your marriage, clear and absolute, with no room for debate: "What God has joined together, let no one put asunder." That's it. That's God's will for your marriage.

We may not always follow God's will, but that is His unwavering intention for your marriage. Remember the first miracle Jesus performed at the wedding in Cana? He was an honored guest, and when the hosts ran out of wine, Jesus turned water into wine. In your marriage, you should invite Jesus. He can transform bitterness into sweetness and emptiness into fullness. A child in Sunday school once heard the story of Jesus turning water into wine and was asked about the lesson of the story. The child replied, "When you have a wedding, it's a good idea to invite Jesus." Likewise, in your marriage, it's a wise decision to invite Jesus to be the guiding force.

Sometimes all it takes is unwavering persistence, sticking with your partner through the good and bad times. I'll conclude with a story about an old mule that fell into a well. The fall didn't kill the mule, but it caused a commotion. The farmer, after assessing the situation, contemplated the effort it would take to rescue the mule and concluded it wasn't worth it. He decided to bury the mule in the well and gathered his neighbors to fill it with dirt, declaring that the mule wasn't worth saving.

Things That Defile the marriage Bed

Marriage is honorable in all, and the bed undefiled: but whoremongers and adulterers God will judge. (Hebrews 13:4)

The prohibition on having sex after a marriage is solemnized is no longer applicable; in fact, it now becomes a crucial component of marriage. However, the wedded can still defile the marriage bed. If a man or woman is married and engages in sexual activity with someone other than their spouse, they have committed adultery and are now susceptible to God's wrath.

Second, trust—a very delicate material—is the foundation of marriage. One cannot afford to fall victim to adultery because once confidence is lost, mistrust grows and could lead to the dissolution of the marriage. The respect your spouse had for you is also damaged as a result of adultery. Therefore, when you commit adultery, you figuratively take the honor that God bestows upon you and cast it before swine. The Bible also states:

"Give not that which is holy unto the dogs, neither cast ye your pearls before swine, lest they trample them under their feet and turn again and rend you." (Matthew 7:6)

If you commit adultery, the protective hedge that surrounds you when you are married is destroyed, and anything bad can now happen as a result. Ecclesiastes 10:8 says, "Whoso breaketh a hedge, a serpent shall bite him." Because the fence has been breached by infidelity, the serpents of life are biting severely in numerous marriages and families today. Because they ruined the marriage bed, they lack respect and fulfillment. God is not messing around with language, so heed this warning. The serpents will attack your home if you commit adultery.

Finding Strength in God Amid Life's Battles!!!

Life is like a battle, and perhaps no aspect exemplifies life's challenges more vividly than the institution of marriage. Marriage is a serious commitment that demands substantial effort. While success may come more easily in other aspects of life, achieving a thriving marriage requires a significant and deliberate investment of time and effort.

The kind of marriage you will experience is closely tied to the choices you make. Your attitude towards marriage significantly influences the nature of the marriage you will have. When you give substantial time and effort in establishing a strong foundation for your future in the realm of marriage, you will reap substantial rewards in the years to come.

Conversely, a lack of care or negligence will also result in insignificant outcomes.

The trials and tribulations that come with marriage, despite their abundance, become manageable when you welcome God into the journey of your union. There is no challenge that is beyond God's capacity to resolve; there is no marital situation that exceeds the strength and wisdom of the Almighty. When you align yourself with God, you establish an indomitable partnership, making it possible to confront and conquer the battles that marriage may present.

The uncertainties and challenges in your marriage will find effective solutions through divine wisdom. God has the power to turn your home into a haven of peace and joy, and with His guidance, you won't experience failure or casualties. In times of need and when divine intervention is required, God will be by your side. The first essential step is to begin with a foundation of prayer. The path of marriage often involves enduring numerous battles, for there is hardly any marriage untouched by these trials.

Be soaked in the Word

We are commanded in Colossians 3:16 to allow the "message of Christ to dwell among [us] richly." According to Psalm 1:1–2, God's blessing is reserved for those who "delight" in and "meditate on His Law day and night." For this reason, we must regularly spend ample time in the Scriptures. If we want to establish God-honoring marriages, we must continuously hear from God to counteract the voices of the world, the devil, and the flesh. A good marriage also requires regular reflection on verses like 1 Corinthians 13 and Ephesians 5:21–33.

Serve the Lord Together

Towards the end of his life, after years of serving the Lord, Joshua never lost his zeal to serve the Lord. In Joshua 24:15, we read of his holy resolve: "But if serving the Lord seems undesirable to you, then choose for yourselves this day whom you will serve, whether the gods your ancestors served beyond the Euphrates, or the gods of the Amorites, in whose land you are living. But as for me and my household, we will serve the LORD." Regardless of what others around him were pursuing, Joshua resolved to pursue the noble goal of serving the Lord.

Be Humble

Proverbs 16:5 says, "The Lord detests all the proud of heart. Be sure of this: They will not go unpunished." Where there is pride in the marriage, there will never be peace. That's why pursuing humility must be a daily and ongoing priority for both husband and wife. Indeed, while "God opposes the proud," He also promises to "show favor to the humble" [James 4:6].

Want a happy marriage? The answer is found in the daily pursuit of humility! God always blesses the humble because humility is the path Christ walked, and that's the path we are called to walk as well! Dedicate time to pray for your marriage and seek God's guidance in making it strong and enduring.

Guard Your Heart

Proverbs 4:23 says, "Above all else, guard your heart, for everything you do flows from it." That's why the heart must eliminate all kinds of negative thoughts at their inception rather than allowing them to grow, making it much harder to deal with later. James 1:14-15 teaches this principle clearly: "Each person is tempted when they are dragged away by their own evil desire and enticed. Then, after desire has conceived, it gives birth to sin; and sin, when it is full-grown, gives birth to death."

Philippians 4:8 is an excellent verse to meditate on and even memorize for couples to practice regularly when it comes to cultivating positive thoughts instead of negative ones: "Finally, brothers and sisters, whatever is true, whatever is noble, whatever is right, whatever is pure, whatever is lovely, whatever is admirable—if anything is excellent or praiseworthy—think about such things.

The Lord is with You!

Challenges can arise on the wedding day itself. As newlyweds begin to build their new family, they will face numerous hurdles and trials. The phases of child-bearing and child-rearing also bring their own intense difficulties. From nurturing infants to guiding them into adulthood, there are issues that you will encounter along the way. For anyone about to get married, don't walk down the path of marriage without being fully prepared for the ups and downs. It's never too late to start fresh. In a world where Christians are constantly bombarded by temptations, God has promised to shower His grace on those willing to faithfully follow Him. It's easy and tempting to give up prematurely, but this often happens when a person does not adhere to the teachings of Scripture.

I believe in marriages made in heaven! Go for it! And if you have one, thank God for His great gift! If you are a Christian, I want you to know that there are blessed days ahead for you. If you are lost, I want you to know that you need to get ready to meet the Lord. He is coming, and He is coming for His people. "Trust in the LORD with all your heart, and lean not on your understanding. In all your ways acknowledge Him, and He shall direct your paths" (Proverbs 3:5, 6). "...and as your days, so shall your strength be" (Deuteronomy 33:25).

In Jeremiah 32:27, we read God saying, "I am the Lord, the God of all mankind. Is anything too hard for me?" He can deliver you right this hour if He chooses to. However, if it is God's will that you endure through this for some more time, do not resist Him. Yield to His plans and trust in His grace to carry you through this situation [2 Cor 12:9]. Continue to love your spouse, and that will gradually make you realize that you made the right choice.

Chapter 25

Navigating Conflict with Grace and Truth

In the intricate tapestry of human relationships, conflict is a natural thread. Whether it's a clash of opinions, a difference in values, or a simple misunderstanding, conflict is inevitable. However, what truly matters is how one handles these conflicts without losing their voice, their essence, or their connection to others.

The Nature of Conflict

Conflict is a multifaceted and often emotionally charged experience that stems from differences in perspectives, values, and expectations. These differences can arise due to diverse backgrounds, experiences, and even distinct personality traits. In the intricate tapestry of humanity, it's not a question of if conflict will arise but when and how it will be managed.

At its core, conflict signifies a clash of ideas, emotions, and interests. When individuals engage in conflict, it is rarely their intention to harm one another but rather to assert their point of view or protect their interests. It is vital to recognize that conflicts are not inherently negative; they are natural expressions of human diversity and individuality.

The Universal Nature of Conflict

The Apostle Paul's words in Romans 12:18 (NKJV) echo across the ages, offering a profound insight into the universal nature of conflict.

"If it is possible, as much as depends on you, live peaceably with all men."

Underscores the idea that, while conflict may be inevitable, the pursuit of peace should always be a priority.

This biblical verse encourages individuals to strive for peaceful resolutions whenever possible. It acknowledges the complexity of interpersonal relations and the reality that, due to our unique life experiences and values, we will inevitably find ourselves at odds with others. But it also emphasizes that even amid these conflicts, the aim should be to maintain peace and harmony, with the understanding that conflict doesn't have to lead to the loss of one's voice or the disintegration of relationships.

Conflict as an Opportunity for Growth

Understanding conflict as an opportunity for personal growth and relational strengthening is a vital perspective. In the crucible of conflict, individuals have the chance to refine their communication skills, develop empathy, and strengthen their emotional intelligence. When approached with the right mindset, conflicts can serve as catalysts for personal and interpersonal development.

Paul's message in Romans 12:18 challenges individuals to become peacemakers and exhaust every reasonable effort to maintain harmonious relationships. This involves a commitment to effective conflict resolution, which seeks not only to resolve the immediate issue but also to preserve the essence of each individual's voice within the relationship.

Effective Conflict Resolution

To resolve conflicts effectively without sacrificing one's voice, it's essential to adopt a holistic approach that combines empathy, active listening, and a commitment to grace and truth.

1. **Empathy**: Recognize that the other party may have valid reasons for their perspective and emotions. Empathy allows you to see the situation from their point of view, which can foster understanding and compassion.

2. **Active Listening**: Active listening involves not only hearing the words being spoken but also understanding the emotions and needs behind them. It shows respect for the other person's voice and feelings.

3. **Grace and Truth**: Balance grace, which includes forgiveness, compassion, and understanding, with truth, which involves honesty, transparency, and asserting your perspective and values. Striking this balance ensures that you respect both your voice and the other person's.

4. **Resolution-Oriented Approach**: Conflict resolution should aim not just to end the disagreement but also to improve the relationship. Seek common ground, compromise when possible, and work together to find solutions that honor both parties' voices.

5. **Personal Growth**: View conflict as an opportunity for personal growth and self-reflection. Ask yourself what you can learn from the conflict and how you can become a better communicator and relationally stronger individual.

The Balance of Grace and Truth

In navigating conflict, it's crucial to strike a balance between grace and truth. The Bible presents this beautifully in the Gospel of John 1:14, which says,

"And the Word became flesh and dwelt among us, and we beheld His glory, the glory as of the only begotten of the Father, full of grace and truth."

Just as Jesus embodied both grace and truth, so should individuals aspire to do the same in their relationships.

1. **Grace**: When it comes to conflict, grace involves extending forgiveness, compassion, and understanding. It's the ability to empathize with the other person's perspective and feelings. In Matthew 5:7 (NKJV), Jesus teaches,

"Blessed are the merciful, for they shall obtain mercy."

This verse underscores the significance of showing mercy and grace, even in the heat of a dispute. By doing so, you can avoid losing your voice by preserving the quality of your character, which is rooted in grace.

2. **Truth**: Truth, on the other hand, represents honesty, transparency, and standing firm in your convictions. Proverbs 12:22 (NKJV) reinforces the importance of truth when it says,

"Lying lips are an abomination to the Lord, but those who deal truthfully are His delight."

While extending grace, one must not compromise their values or principles. Truth, in this context, safeguards your voice, ensuring you remain true to yourself.

Maintaining Your Voice in Conflict

Conflicts can be testing grounds for the authenticity of our voice. When navigating disagreements, it's essential to employ strategies that allow you to stand your ground while promoting understanding and reconciliation. Here are some practical steps to maintain your voice in conflict:

1. **Active Listening**: James 1:19 (NKJV) advises,

"So then, my beloved brethren, let every man be swift to hear, slow to speak, slow to wrath."

Active listening is crucial in conflict resolution. It involves not just hearing but genuinely understanding the other person's perspective. By doing so, you can communicate that you respect their voice while also ensuring they respect yours.

2. **Choose Your Battles**: Not every conflict warrants a full-scale confrontation. Proverbs 19:11 (NKJV) emphasizes,

   "The discretion of a man makes him slow to anger, and his glory is to overlook a transgression."

   Sometimes, choosing to overlook minor disagreements can preserve your voice for more significant matters.

3. **I-Statements**: Instead of accusatory "you" statements, use "I" statements. For instance, say, "I feel hurt when..." rather than "You always make me feel..." This shift in communication helps you express your feelings without attacking the other person, preserving your voice and maintaining respect.

4. **Seek Mediation**: In some cases, seeking a neutral third party, like a trusted friend or therapist, can help facilitate a constructive conversation. This demonstrates your commitment to resolving the conflict while maintaining your voice.

The Bible is replete with examples of conflict and its resolution. One such example is found in Acts 15, where early Christians faced a significant conflict concerning the inclusion of Gentiles in the Christian community. The Apostles and elders came together to discuss the matter, employing active listening, grace, and truth. In Acts 15:7 (NKJV), Peter says,

"Men and brethren, you know that a good while ago God chose among us, that by my mouth the Gentiles should hear the word of the gospel and believe."

This conflict was resolved with grace and truth, leading to a unified decision.

Another remarkable example can be found in the book of Genesis. In Genesis 13, we see a conflict between Abraham and his nephew Lot over land and resources. In this situation, Abraham displayed grace by allowing Lot to choose the land he desired. Abraham also upheld the truth of their familial relationship and maintained his voice as a leader.

These biblical examples illustrate how individuals can navigate conflicts with grace and truth, thereby preserving their voice while seeking resolution.

The Role of Forgiveness

Forgiveness is a powerful tool in preserving your voice in conflict. Jesus, in His teaching on prayer, said in Matthew 6:14 (NKJV),

"For if you forgive men their trespasses, your heavenly Father will also forgive you."

This verse underscores the importance of forgiveness in maintaining our spiritual and emotional well-being. When we choose to forgive, we free ourselves from the burden of anger and resentment, enabling us to maintain our voice and continue fostering healthy relationships.

Nurturing Healthy Boundaries

Ephesians 4:26 (NKJV) offers wisdom in conflict resolution by saying,

"Be angry, and do not sin: do not let the sun go down on your wrath."

While conflicts may stir emotions, it's essential to set and maintain healthy boundaries for the sake of your voice and the relationship. This verse suggests addressing conflicts promptly so they don't fester and grow.

Conflict is an inescapable facet of human relationships. However, it is also an opportunity for growth, understanding, and strengthening bonds. The New King James Version of the Bible offers invaluable guidance on preserving your voice amid conflict through grace and truth, active listening, forgiveness, and nurturing healthy boundaries.

Remember that in maintaining your voice in conflict, you not only honor yourself but also demonstrate love, grace, and truth in your relationships, just as Jesus did during His time on Earth. As you strive for effective conflict resolution, may you find the balance between grace and truth, allowing your voice to be heard without losing the essence of who you are. In doing so, you honor the biblical call to

"live peaceably with all men."

(Romans 12:18, NKJV), even in the face of conflict.

Chapter 26

Getting in Sync Emotionally and Sexually: Talk, Tease, Touch, and Transformation

In the intricate dance of human relationships, emotional and sexual intimacy holds a special place. It's common for longtime partners to fall into romantic immobility. There are times when romance and sex get routine and less exciting within the relationship. What can you do when you and your life partner are emotionally and sexually out of sync? As with most things in life, if you want to change, then you must be willing to change, and that change first starts with you. This means giving your relationship the attention it needs to get it UNSTUCK. It's time to correct your out-of-sync emotional and sexual relationship with your life partner that has been on autopilot for too long.

The Power of Words: Proverbs 15:1 from the New King James Version of the Bible aptly encapsulates the profound influence of words on human interactions: "A soft answer turns away wrath, but a harsh word stirs up anger." This verse emphasizes the potential of words to either fortify or undermine the foundation of a relationship. In the context of emotional and sexual intimacy, this verse holds several key insights:

1. Soft Answers and Emotional Safety: Responding with a "soft answer" implies using gentle, kind, and empathetic words when addressing your partner's concerns, desires, or vulnerabilities. Doing so creates an emotionally safe space within the relationship where both partners feel comfortable expressing themselves without fear of harsh criticism or judgment.

2. Harsh Words and Emotional Distance: Conversely, "harsh words" can escalate conflicts and create emotional distance. Such words can provoke anger and defensiveness, making it difficult to communicate openly and honestly. The emotional walls that result from harsh communication hinder the development of intimacy.

Open and Honest Communication

Openness and honesty are vital in fostering emotional and sexual intimacy. Here's why:

1. **Vulnerability and Trust**: Being open and honest involves sharing your thoughts, desires, fears, and vulnerabilities with your partner. This vulnerability builds trust because it demonstrates your willingness to expose your true self, moles and all, to your partner. When trust is established, emotional intimacy can flourish.

2. **Building a Deeper Connection**: Open and honest communication allows you to create a deeper connection with your partner. When you share your innermost thoughts and feelings, it creates an emotional bond that is fundamental to intimacy. Your partner gets

to know you on a profound level, which in turn can enhance your sexual connection.

3. **Resolving Issues**: Open and honest communication is essential for resolving conflicts and addressing relationship challenges. When both partners are candid about their concerns and needs, they can work together to find solutions and compromises that strengthen the relationship.

Active Listening

Active listening is a skill that goes hand-in-hand with effective communication. It involves more than just hearing; it's about truly understanding what your partner is saying. Here's why it's crucial:

1. **Empathy**: Active listening requires empathy—the ability to put yourself in your partner's shoes and understand their perspective. When you actively listen, you convey that you genuinely care about your partner's thoughts and feelings, fostering emotional intimacy.

2. **Validation**: Listening actively involves validating your partner's emotions. Even if you don't agree with their viewpoint, acknowledging their feelings as valid helps them feel heard and respected. This validation is key to building an emotional connection.

3. **Preventing Misunderstandings**: Active listening reduces the likelihood of misunderstandings. When you make an effort to comprehend your partner's viewpoint, you're less likely to

misinterpret their words, which can lead to unnecessary conflicts or hurt feelings.

Respectful Disagreements

Disagreements are a natural part of any relationship, but how they are handled can make a significant difference. It's essential to approach disagreements with respect and care:

1. **Respect for Differences**: Every individual is unique, and differences in opinions and desires are normal. It's crucial to respect these differences and approach disagreements as opportunities for growth and understanding.

2. **Caring Expressions**: Expressing disagreements with care and respect helps prevent conflicts from escalating into destructive arguments. Use "I" statements to convey your perspective, and avoid attacking or blaming your partner.

3. **Conflict Resolution**: A respectful approach to disagreements paves the way for constructive conflict resolution. Instead of viewing disagreements as threats to the relationship, see them as opportunities to find common ground and strengthen your emotional connection.

Fostering Emotional Connection

Conversations that are deep, meaningful, and geared toward building intimacy are essential for fostering emotional connection. In these moments, you come to understand your partner's heart on a profound level. Here are some additional insights:

1. **Shared Dreams and Goals**: Discussing shared dreams and goals helps you build a vision for your future together. These conversations foster emotional intimacy as you envision your lives entwined.

2. **Emotional Support**: Opening up about personal struggles, fears, and insecurities allows your partner to provide emotional support. This support builds trust and intimacy, as you know you can rely on each other in times of need.

3. **Appreciation and Affection**: Regularly express appreciation and affection for your partner. These affirmations of love and care nurture your emotional connection.

4. **Quality Time**: Spending quality time together without distractions allows for deeper, more meaningful conversations. It's in these moments that you truly come to know each other's hearts.

The Healing Power of Laughter

Proverbs 17:22 in the Bible wisely reminds us that

"A merry heart does good, like medicine, but a broken spirit dries the bones."

This verse highlights the therapeutic effect of a joyful heart, underlining the importance of laughter and playfulness in sustaining a healthy emotional connection.

1. **Shared Laughter as Bonding**: Laughter is a universal language that transcends cultural and language barriers. When couples share moments of laughter, it creates a bond that reinforces their emotional connection. Inside jokes and playful teasing are ways to tap into this shared humor, reminding partners of the joy they find in each other.

2. **Stress Relief**: Laughter and playfulness serve as natural stress relievers. Amid life's challenges, moments of shared laughter can ease tension, promote relaxation, and remind couples of the strength they draw from each other's company.

3. **Enhancing Emotional Connection**: The act of laughing together brings about positive emotions and creates fond memories. These shared experiences enhance emotional intimacy by providing couples with a sense of togetherness and unity.

Flirting and Anticipation

Flirting is an artful expression of playfulness and desire that adds an exciting dimension to a relationship. When conducted with mutual consent and respect, flirting can kindle the flames of desire and enhance emotional and sexual intimacy. It is important to understand that women are very particular in the area of and that for women, unlike most men, sex does not start in the physical realm; it ends in the physical realm. For a woman, sex starts in the psychological realm and then moves outward from there. Most men need to learn to make love to a woman's mind before they can make love to her body.

Most women will never allow their body to take them where their mind hasn't gone first. She must feel her man before she will allow him to fill her. When a woman thinks of sex, she thinks of intimacy, which involves communication, caressing, and compassion, not just penetration. Nothing can be so annoying to a woman as to discover that her man doesn't have a dawggone clue as to what it takes to fulfill her sexual needs. If you healthily talk to your partner, tease them throughout the day with text messages and post notes left throughout the house before you go to work, and touch them when they come home; this will lead to having them transform their body to desire mode and be ready for some bedroom action.

1. **A Light-Hearted Exchange**: Flirting is a light-hearted and fun way to express attraction and affection for your partner. It allows couples to keep the romance alive and maintain the excitement they felt during the early stages of their relationship.

2. **Expressing Desire**: Flirting communicates that you desire your partner both emotionally and sexually. This verbal and non-verbal expression of desire reinforces the emotional connection by making your partner feel wanted and appreciated.

3. **Rekindling Passion**: The anticipation created by flirting can reignite the passion within a relationship. The teasing and

playful banter evoke excitement and longing, making couples feel like they're experiencing a new phase in their romance.

Building Anticipation

The process of building anticipation through teasing and playfulness contributes significantly to the emotional and sexual aspects of a relationship. It is important to understand that women are very particular in the area of se and that for women, unlike most men, sex does not start in the physical realm; it ends in the physical realm.

1. **Stoking Desire**: Teasing and playful banter can ignite desire by creating an atmosphere of anticipation and excitement. Couples begin to long for the moments that follow, deepening the emotional and sexual connection.

2. **Heightening Sensual Connection**: The anticipation generated by teasing and playfulness intensifies the sensual connection between partners. It enhances the experience of intimacy, making it more fulfilling and satisfying.

3. **Exploration and Experimentation**: As the anticipation builds, couples become more open to experimentation and exploration in their intimate moments. This sense of anticipation encourages partners to step out of their comfort zones, further enhancing the depth of their connection.

The Language of Touch

The Bible offers several verses that highlight the significance of touch in fostering emotional and sexual intimacy. For example, in Song of Solomon 2:6 (NKJV), it is written,

"His left hand is under my head, and his right hand embraces me."

This intimate image reflects the power of touch in conveying love, tenderness, and connection.

1. **Physical Affection**: Physical affection, from holding hands to cuddling, provides a tangible expression of love and connection. It reassures your partner of your desire to be close.

2. **Intimate Touch**: Intimate touch, such as kissing and caressing, is a vital component of sexual intimacy. It allows partners to express desire and build anticipation.

3. **Comforting Touch**: In moments of emotional vulnerability, a comforting touch can speak volumes. A gentle stroke or hug can offer solace and reassurance in times of need.

4. **Exploration and Sensuality**: The power of touch extends to sexual exploration. The act of exploring your partner's body and experiencing the same in return builds a profound sense of intimacy.

Transformation through Intimacy

The transformative potential of emotional and sexual

intimacy is a recurring theme in the Bible. In Ephesians 5:31-32 (NKJV) states:

"For this reason, a man shall leave his father and mother and be joined to his wife, and the two shall become one flesh. This is a great mystery, but I speak concerning Christ and the church."

This verse alludes to the concept of transformation through a spiritual connection, but it can also be applied to the transformation that occurs within a relationship through deep emotional and sexual intimacy.

1. **Emotional Transformation**: The emotional connection created through effective communication, playfulness, and touch can transform both partners. It deepens their understanding of each other, fosters empathy, and enhances their overall emotional well-being.

2. **Sexual Transformation**: Sexual intimacy is not just a physical act but also a profound expression of emotional connection. When couples are in sync emotionally, their sexual encounters become more fulfilling and transformative, leading to greater satisfaction and personal growth.

3. **Strengthening the Relationship**: Transformation through intimacy strengthens the foundation of the relationship. Couples who are deeply connected emotionally and sexually are better

equipped to face challenges, work through difficulties, and grow together.

Practical Steps for Getting in Sync

To foster emotional and sexual intimacy, it's crucial to take practical steps that align with the principles of effective communication, playfulness, and touch.

1. **Schedule Quality Time**: Set aside regular, uninterrupted quality time for open and honest conversations. This could be a weekly date night or simply dedicated moments of connection.

2. **Express Appreciation**: Regularly express your love and appreciation for your partner. Small gestures of love and kindness can go a long way in building emotional intimacy.

3. **Prioritize Physical Affection**: Make physical affection a part of your daily routine. Hold hands, hug, and kiss your partner to maintain a strong sense of closeness.

4. **Create an Intimate Environment**: Set the mood for emotional and sexual intimacy by creating a comfortable and inviting space. This could be as simple as lighting candles, playing soft music, or ensuring privacy.

5. **Mutual Exploration**: Take time to explore each other's bodies and desires. Open communication about desires and boundaries is essential for sexual intimacy.

Getting in sync emotionally and sexually is a journey that requires effort, commitment, and a deep understanding of your partner. By following the principles of effective communication, playfulness, and touch, you can build a strong emotional connection that lays the foundation for a fulfilling sexual relationship. This transformation through intimacy not only enhances your personal growth but also strengthens your relationship, aligning with the biblical idea of becoming a new creation through the power of love and connection.

About The Author

Jonathan Devon Bryant, Sr. is the founder, Pastor and a teacher of Faith Outreach Church-FL, a vibrant, non-denominational Spirit-filled Church. He has impacted church leaders worldwide by preaching the unadulterated gospel of Jesus with boldness. He is known for teaching God's Word in a fresh, practical, and revelatory way that always unveils Jesus. His humorous, dynamic and engaging style of preaching and teaching has also endeared him to a wide spectrum of viewers who tune in to watch him online.

Jonathan believes that what can make a relationship is remarkably simple. Couples who have successful relationship aren't' richer, smarter, or more psychologically intelligent. They have made a deliberate decision to keep their negative thoughts and feelings about each other (which all couples have) from consuming the positive ones. Rather than create a climate of conflict and confrontation, they embrace each other's needs. Too often a great relationship is taken for granted than given the supporting and honor it deserves and desperately needs.

Pastor Jonathan is devotedly married to Stephanie Bryant, with whom he pastors Faith Outreach Church-FL. They have three beautiful children: Jaleesha (Alonso), Jonathan II, JaRhonda and two grandchild Amari and Amiyah Bradley.

A retired Chief Warrant Officer Three (CW3) with over 20

years of service to the United States Army, Pastor Jonathan has traveled extensively and been given the opportunity to sit under some great men and women of God. He is fondly referred to as "The Original Facebook Pastor" and is a Spiritual Father and mentor to many.

A believer in education, Pastor Jonathan holds an Associates of Arts Degree, Bachelors in Biblical Studies, a Bachelors of Science in (Business and Psychology) from Liberty University and a Masters of Arts in Religion with a prominence in Church Ministries from Liberty Theological Seminary. His studies included dynamic leadership theories, exegetical teaching, methodologies and concepts that seek to create, develop, and sustain believers without compromising the scriptures, as he holds expository preaching in the highest regard.

48000CB00001B/5